ᵉds metropolitan university

date

HANS KELLER AND THE BBC

Lithograph of Hans Keller by Milein Cosman

Hans Keller and the BBC

The musical conscience of British broadcasting, 1959–79

A.M. GARNHAM

ASHGATE

© A.M. Garnham, 2003

All rights reserved. No part of this publication may be reproduced, stored in a retrieval system, or transmitted in any form or by any means, electronic, mechanical, photocopying, recording or otherwise without the prior permission of the publisher.

The author has asserted her moral right under the Copyright, Designs and Patents Act, 1988, to be identified as the author of this work.

Published by
Ashgate Publishing Limited
Gower House
Croft Road
Aldershot
Hants GU11 3HR
England

Ashgate Publishing Company
Suite 420, 101 Cherry Street
Burlington, VT 05401-4405 USA

LEEDS METROPOLITAN
UNIVERSITY
LIBRARY
1704848421
KV-B
CC-86499
15/06/07
780.92 GAR

British Library Cataloguing in Publication Data
Garnham, A.M.
Hans Keller and the BBC : the musical conscience of British broadcasting, 1959-79
1. Keller, Hans, 1919-1985 2. British Broadcasting Corporation 3. Radio Three (London, England) 4. Musicians - England - Biography 5. Musicians - Austria - Biography 6. Radio broadcasters - England - Biography 7. Radio broadcasters - Austria - Biography 8. Music radio stations - Great Britain - History
I. Title
780.92'2

Library of Congress Cataloging-in-Publication Data
Hans Keller and the BBC : the musical conscience of British broadcasting, 1959-79 / A.M. Garnham.
p. cm.
Includes bibliographical references (p.).
ISBN 0-7546-0897-2
1. Keller, Hans, 1919- - -Influence. 2. British Broadcasting Corporation- -History- -20th century. 3. Radio broadcasting- -Great Britain- -History- -20th century. I. Garnham, A.M.

ML423.K45 H36 2002
780'.92- -dc21

2002018203

ISBN 0 7546 0897 2

Printed and bound in Great Britain by MPG Books Ltd, Bodmin, Cornwall

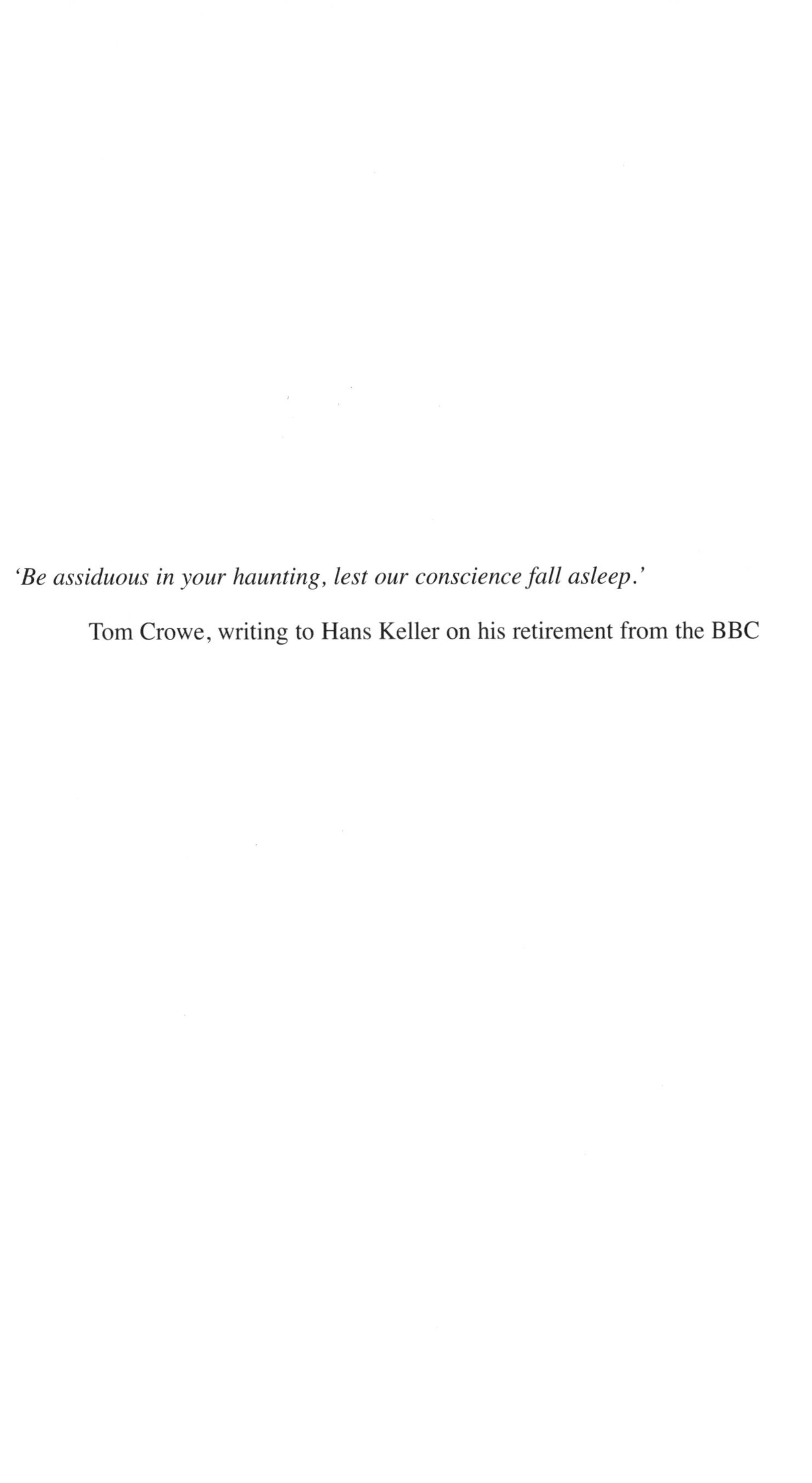

'Be assiduous in your haunting, lest our conscience fall asleep.'

Tom Crowe, writing to Hans Keller on his retirement from the BBC

For Milein

Contents

Illustrations

Note

Every effort has been made to trace all the copyright holders, but if any have been inadvertently overlooked the publishers will be pleased to make the necessary arrangements at the first opportunity.

Acknowledgements

This book has been long in coming and, during the lengthy period of its composition, I have incurred more debts than I can possibly acknowledge here. First and foremost I thank Christopher Wintle, who originally suggested to me, not long after Keller's death, that I should study his work for the BBC, and who supervised the thesis on which this book is based. I am very grateful for his wisdom, patience and inspiring teaching – not to mention his generous sharing of his unrivalled knowledge of Keller's writings. I also thank the Music Department of Goldsmiths' College, University of London, for their patient support (in particular, the encouragement of Simon McVeigh, Craig Ayrey and Anthony Pryer), and the University's Central Research Fund for financial assistance when this project was in its early stages.

Many thanks are due to the staff of Cambridge University Library, the BBC's Written and Sound Archives, and the National Sound Archive for all their help with my research, and for permission to publish material from their holdings, as well as to the Britten–Pears Foundation for permission to quote from the letters of Benjamin Britten. I should like to mention in particular Neil Somerville of the BBC Written Archive Centre in Caversham, who patiently answered my many questions and guided me through the BBC's idiosyncratic filing system; Timothy Day of the National Sound Archive, who enabled me to hear so much of Keller's voice; and Richard Andrewes and Patrick Zutshi of Cambridge University Library for entrusting to me the cataloguing of the Hans Keller Archive. I am also extremely grateful to Julian Hogg, Keller's amanuensis and literary executor, who was very helpful in facilitating introductions to the various sections of the BBC.

Indeed, many of Keller's friends and colleagues have most kindly assisted my research in a variety of ways, and I am grateful to all those who gave lengthy interviews, discussed Keller over the telephone, lent their own papers and recordings, answered queries and corrected my ideas: Pauline Beesley, Leo Black, Susan Bradshaw, David Cox, Misha Donat, Alexander Goehr, Paul Hamburger, Stephen Hearst, Robert Layton, Keith Lovell, Ian McIntyre, Donald Mitchell, Christopher Nupen, Stephen Plaistow, Robert Ponsonby, Lionel Salter, Graham Sheffield, Gordon Stewart, Alan Walker, Eleanor Warren and Hugh Wood. The interviews, in particular, were among the most fascinating and pleasurable aspects of my research, and brought home to me the wealth of talent the BBC has been fortunate enough to employ. Most of all, I am eternally grateful to Hans Keller's widow, Milein Cosman, who, as well as allowing unrestricted access to her husband's manuscripts and welcoming me into her home most hospitably on countless occasions, has been a source of much support. Her kindness and generosity have been unfailing.

Milein Cosman was also one of those who have read this book in manuscript and made various helpful suggestions; others include Leo Black, Asa Briggs, Julian Hogg, Donald Mitchell and Hugh Wood. I have very much appreciated all their comments (although I take full responsibility for any errors which remain) and in particular their confirmation that the Hans Keller they knew is recognizable in this portrait.

Finally, my most heartfelt thanks go to my husband Chris, my family and my friends, without whose cheerful encouragement, discussion and practical help, this book would never have seen the light of day. I suspect their relief that I have finally finished it exceeds even mine.

Introduction

This is the story of one remarkable individual's involvement with twentieth-century Britain's most powerful musical institution. It was to many eyes an unlikely relationship – certainly it was never an easy one – but it left the cultural life of this country significantly affected and immeasurably widened the influence of a brilliant and original musical mind. Broadcasting was only a part of Hans Keller's musical life, however; as a critic, teacher, analyst, psychologist, sociologist and polemicist, he was already an important figure in musical London before he joined the BBC and, partly through his association with the Corporation, he became a profound influence on a whole generation of musicians. Nevertheless, as he wrote shortly after his retirement, 'I gave 20 years of my life and its central loves to the BBC',[1] serving a medium which he believed was of crucial importance to the future of music.

Born in 1919 in Vienna, into an affluent and music-loving family, Hans Keller saw his life change dramatically on 11 March 1938, his nineteenth birthday, when the Austrian Chancellor resigned and Hitler entered Vienna the following day. What happened afterwards – *Kristallnacht*, his own consequent arrest by the Gestapo, the death of his father, and finally his escape to England – Keller later made the subject of an unforgettable BBC broadcast in the Radio 4 series *The Time of My Life*.[2] On arrival in London, he joined his mother and sister (who was married to an Englishman) in Herne Hill, South London, where he lived until he was interned on the Isle of Man in 1940. After his release nine months later (apparently at the intervention of Ralph Vaughan Williams), he lived the life of a freelance orchestral and chamber music player in London and in Cumbria, where he travelled to give concerts with Dr Oskar Adler, with whom he had previously played quartets in Vienna. Adler had been a close friend of the young Schoenberg – and effectively his first teacher, as Schoenberg describes in his 1949 essay 'My Evolution':

> Only after I had met three young men of about my own age and had won their friendship did my musical and literary education start. The first was Oscar Adler, whose talent as a musician was as great as his capabilities in science. Through him I learned of the existence of a theory of music, and he directed my first steps therein ... All my acquaintance with classical music

1 Letter to *The Times*, 15 August 1980.

2 'Vienna 1938' was first broadcast on 3 February 1974 and repeated on 24 August the same year. It was reprinted in *The Listener* (28 March 1974) and later as the first chapter of Keller's book *1975 (1984 minus 9)*, (1977).

derived from playing quartets with him, for even then he was an excellent first violinist.[3]

Keller similarly credited Adler with having shaped his whole future approach to musical analysis:

> From my early childhood I lived in his chamber-musical world, first passively, later actively. He did not care two hoots about analysis, but his uniquely organic and motif-conscious way of playing taught me more about the essentials of chamber-musical forms and textures than any analytical teacher could possibly have done.[4]

Keller was also a prolific writer during these years, but not yet on music. His principal writings during the war were on psychological and sociological subjects, and he was deeply immersed in Freudian psychoanalysis. Although he published little of his work from this time, his 'overriding'[5] psychological interests were to colour his musical writings for the rest of his life. The central plank of his approach to musical analysis – the uncovering of the latent unity behind manifestly contrasting themes – is clearly Freudian, and so, on occasion, was his methodology, as in his explication of a Mozartian parapraxis in his 1956 article, 'A Slip of Mozart's: Its Analytical Significance'.[6]

He was concerned not only with the unconscious and preconscious motivation of composers, but also of their critics. Particularly striking is his brilliant 'Resistances to Britten's Music: Their Psychology'[7] in which he applied J.C. Flügel's 'Polycrates complex' to Britten's audience, as well as his own ideas on British musical 'group self-contempt'. This article, together with 'Schoenberg and the Men of the Press',[8] which followed it the next year, both appeared in *Music Survey*, the journal of which Keller became co-editor (with Donald Mitchell) in 1949. Short-lived (it succumbed to financial pressure in 1952), but disproportionately notorious, *Music Survey* plunged into a spirited attack on the musical received opinion of the day. 'The aims I had in mind,' Keller later explained, 'were, simply, the defence of great or substantial composers whom our musical world neglected. Such defence, of course, inevitably took polemical shape, since one fought people who said

---

3 'My Evolution' was first published in English (in which it was originally written) in the *Musical Quarterly* in October 1952; it was reprinted in Arnold Schoenberg, *Style and Idea*, London (Faber and Faber) 1975, pp. 79–92. The other two young friends whom Schoenberg credits with his education were David Bach and Alexander von Zemlinsky.

4 'The Chamber Music', in H.C. Robbins Landon and Donald Mitchell (eds) (1956), *The Mozart Companion*, p. 93.

5 See *1975* (1977), p. 81.

6 Written at the end of what Keller called the 'Mozart/Freud year' – the centenary of Freud's birth and the bicentenary of Mozart's – this article appeared in the Winter 1956–57 issue of *Tempo*.

7 *Music Survey*, Spring 1950.

8 *Music Survey*, Spring 1951.

that those composers were no good or were not composers at all.'[9] The quotation from Isaacs which Keller placed at the top of his 1951 Schoenberg article accurately summarizes his attitude to music critics – 'The critic stumbles along behind the artist' – an attitude which he always retained. The BBC was not exempt from assault during this period: one example is the blistering attack Keller and Mitchell launched on the Third Programme's Schoenberg series in 1952, in an article which could not have opened more dramatically: 'Schoenberg dies. The horde, true to primordial savage precedent, falls upon the father and devours him.'[10]

All this meant that Keller was no stranger to controversy, but there were many who admired his honest and perceptive writing, not least the composers whom he defended. These included Schoenberg himself, who wrote to Keller in 1951 to enlist his support against 'a very unpleasant review, written by one of these non-musicians, who look in my music only for the twelve notes – not realizing in the least its musical contents, expression and merits. He is very stupid and insolent and would deserve a treatment like that you can give him. I hope you are interested! Now sharpen your pen.'[11] Nevertheless, it can not have been easy for the BBC to appoint him, as William Glock later acknowledged: 'No doubt the most controversial decision was to invite Hans Keller on to the staff.'[12] However, the BBC was changing rapidly at that time, and the appointment of Glock himself, then Chairman of the Music Committee of the Institute of Contemporary Arts, constituted a significant move away from the Corporation's earlier rather cautious attitude to contemporary music, particularly Continental composers. (This attitude is well exemplified by an internal discussion from 1956 about the merits of Henze and Boulez: 'On balance, it was felt that to broadcast a few of their better works would not blunt our reputation for acute critical assessment'.[13])

Such 'narrow horizons', as Glock called them,[14] had not always been a feature of the BBC's music policy. Edward Clark, pupil of Schoenberg and husband of Elizabeth Lutyens, had been a BBC programme-builder of extraordinary imagination and enterprise in the inter-war years. The rather more insular atmosphere of the 1950s could be seen as an inevitable result of the war, although the early days of the Third Programme (founded in 1946) were determinedly international in nature. Indeed, Glock himself was sent by the Third's first Controller, George Barnes, on a tour of occupied Europe in 1947, to bring back news of what, musically speaking, had been happening there during the war. The trouble, as Glock saw it, was that while 'the horizons of the programme planners of the Third were European', those of

9 Preface to the collected edition of the journal published in 1981.
10 'The BBC's Victory over Schoenberg', *The Music Review*, May 1952.
11 See 'Unpublished Schoenberg Letters', *Music Survey*, Summer 1952.
12 W. Glock (1991), *Notes in Advance*, p. 103.
13 Quoted in N. Kenyon (1981), p. 278.
14 Glock (1991), p. 100.

the rest of the BBC were not, 'which brought the most violent opposition from many provincial factions both outside and inside the BBC'.[15]

The Third Programme, 'conceived in war as an act of faith', as one BBC staff member put it,[16] was a most extraordinary (and probably rather un-English) creation, about which the BBC seems to have started having second thoughts almost immediately. By the time Keller began broadcasting in 1956, it was approaching a crisis. Despite the palpable success of the Third – its tenth anniversary celebrations that year only emphasized the extent to which it had become an international byword for excellence in broadcasting – the atmosphere in Broadcasting House was then one of anxiety and retrenchment, with widespread uneasiness about the rather patrician and didactic features of Sir William Haley's original vision. Television had swiftly overtaken radio as the prime medium and, in 1955, commercial television had broken the BBC's broadcasting monopoly. The spectre of commercial radio had long haunted the BBC, and although it was not to gain substance for many years to come, it was a growing factor in the Corporation's policy-making. The BBC followed the tenth-anniversary celebrations with a major review of sound broadcasting which culminated in a drastic cut in the airtime allotted to the Third Programme. Many of the public and private arguments over that decision mirrored those which took place during the BBC's next big review of its radio policy, *Broadcasting in the Seventies* (1969), when the Third finally disappeared altogether, and Keller's life as a BBC rebel began.

To Hans Keller, *Broadcasting in the Seventies*, which was published half-way through his BBC years, was a disastrous turning point, and marked 'an abrupt change of corporate personality'[17] on the part of the BBC. It caused profound changes to his relationship with the Corporation, as well as bringing him to consider, for the first time in such depth, issues of broadcasting beyond the musical. Yet, as will be seen, most of the ideas contained in this document were not new; indeed it could almost be said that the battle which preoccupied Keller during his second decade on the BBC's staff was already lost before he arrived at the Corporation in 1959.

Even so, it was not in Keller's nature to give up. 'He was,' says Susan Bradshaw, 'the only person I ever met to whom everything (particularly, of course, musical things) really *mattered*.'[18] The BBC was abandoning principles of fundamental significance and, given Keller's conviction that radio was vital to the very survival of music as a living art, political and pragmatic arguments could do nothing to dissuade him from struggling

15 Ibid., p. 45.

16 Unsigned undated memorandum to the Director of Sound Broadcasting (BBC Written Archive Centre, henceforth WAC, R34/1022/3, The Future of Sound Broadcasting in the Domestic Services: Working Party, 1956–57).

17 'Fare Better, BBC', *The Spectator*, June 1979.

18 Susan Bradshaw, in Wintle (1986), p. 377.

against reforms which he thought would guarantee the demise of radio as a major cultural force.

One of the most important characteristics of Keller's life and thought is its unity. Thought *is* life, and it cannot be divided or compartmentalized. He even disliked categorizing music as an art: 'I should prefer to call it a mode of thought, and hence of life,' he wrote in 1970.[19] His conviction (formed partly as a result of his early psychoanalytical work) of the unique and separate nature of musical thought had, therefore, for him an inevitable practical application. If music does indeed convey truths which are incommunicable by any other means, the BBC's duty as a powerful musical patron was clear. Particularly at a late cultural stage, when a long-standing and rich musical tradition was breaking up, it was insupportable to Keller that the BBC should seem to want to hasten its decline.

Keller never gave up on the BBC. Even after his retirement, he continued to encourage and admonish his former colleagues. Having promised Glock on the very day of his arrival 'I shall put my whole mind and heart into the BBC job,'[20] he continued to do this, without reservation, for the next 20 years and beyond.

---

19 'Towards a Theory of Music', *The Listener*, 11 June 1970.

20 Letter from Keller to Glock, 1 September 1959 (Cambridge University Library, henceforth CUL, Keller Archive).

Chapter 1

In the Beginning

In February 1946, Hans Keller made his first approach to the BBC, offering a talk on Freud. Freud's ninetieth birthday would have fallen on 6 May that year and, taking advantage of the perennial interest in anniversaries, Keller suggested that the occasion might be marked by a talk 'on, say, Freud's position in the development of our culture'.[1] Although this idea came to nothing and it was to be another ten years before he actually began broadcasting, the story of Keller's association with the BBC does nevertheless begin in 1946, and their later relationship is much illuminated by the events of the decade before they came together.

It was a momentous year for both Keller and the Corporation. For the BBC, 1946 was the year in which its unprecedented experiment in cultural broadcasting, the Third Programme, with which Keller was later to be so passionately allied, first went on the air. For Keller, it was the point at which he fundamentally redefined himself as a writer and musician, switching both from playing to writing as his main source of income and, in his writing, from psychoanalytical to musical subjects. This was also the year in which he first heard *Peter Grimes*, an event which appears to have affected him so profoundly that it might actually have been the catalyst of his change of direction.

Keller's suggestion to the BBC of a talk on Freud is indicative of his predominant intellectual preoccupations up to that time. Throughout the early 1940s, he had read widely in psychoanalytical literature, corresponded and collaborated with professionals in the field, and even undertaken an extended self-analysis. He took Freud's own self-analysis as a model, although his original motivation had been his discovery that 'it was impossible to obtain a training analysis without paying for it – what to me, then, were unfathomable sums of money'.[2] The self-analysis took the form of an hour's writing down free associations, and then analysing them, every day for five years. It is not clear exactly when he began and ended this process, but the five years certainly included 1943 and 1944, during which time he was apparently considering a career as a psychoanalyst.[3]

---

1 Letter from Keller to the Director of Talks, 14 February 1946 (BBC WAC Talks Contributor File: Hans Keller, File 1, 1946–62).

2 *1975* (1977), p. 87.

3 See Keller's correspondence with Margaret Phillips (CUL Keller Archive). Keller later recalled that his interest in psychology had dated back to his schooldays, remembering that, for part of his school matriculation examination, he had written an extended essay on

Keller wrote a number of essays on psychological subjects during this period, but most of them remained unpublished. Their subjects are varied and include 'War, Peace and Psychology', 'The Psychology of Leadership', 'Peace and Pessimism', 'Apropos of Beauty and Reflection', 'A Sixteen Months Old Boy and his Mother Substitutes', 'Self-Knowledge', 'Religion' and 'The Need for Pets'.[4] The issue which engaged his interest above all others, however, and which he made the subject of prolonged and detailed study, was the psychology of different social groups – and in particular a phenomenon which he identified as 'group self-contempt', or, more technically, 'nemesistic displacement'. In a letter written after he had been considering this idea for some time, he defined it as follows:

> As a result of studying the psychology of certain Jewish attitudes (I'm a Jew), of certain common traits in prostitutes, and in women, I have come to feel justified in assuming the existence of a phenomenon which could be called group self-contempt, or, in more exact language, nemesistic displacement. (In adopting the term nemesism as designating inturned aggression I follow the suggestions of Rosenzweig and Flügel.) It seems to me that this phenomenon always appears in groups whose members are, or regard themselves as being, in some way persecuted by members of other groups which occupy an authoritative position. Margaret Phillips (*The Education of the Emotions*), with whom I am working on group research, has drawn my attention to the appearance of 'group self-contempt' in teaching groups, and Meerlo's 'Psychopathic Reactions in Liberated Countries' (7.4.45, *Lancet*) seems to confirm my assumption.[5]

Keller's work and correspondence with the educational psychologist Margaret Phillips was very significant in the development of his psychological interests. They met in August 1943, but had been corresponding for a year before that, ever since Keller had sent her a lengthy reply to the research questionnaire on social groups which she had been circulating the previous summer.[6] They corresponded frequently and at length, discussing their current studies and wider ideas, with the result that Keller abandoned the work on shame with which he had been previously involved (fragmentary drafts for 'The Psychology of Pudency' dating from

'*The Brothers Karamazov*: A Contribution to Dostoevsky's Depth Psychology'. He later described the title as 'pretentious', adding that 'nowadays … I'm not interested in my contribution to Dostoevsky's depth psychology, but in his to ours.' (Letter from Keller to Mrs G. Learner, Librarian of the British-USSR Association, 24 March 1981, CUL Keller Archive). Keller appears not to have begun his serious study of psychology, however, until after his release from internment.

4 The last three of these pieces have been published posthumously as an appendix to Keller (1995) *Three Psychoanalytic Notes on Peter Grimes*.

5 Letter to Dr Rickman, editor of *The British Journal of Medical Psychology*, 3 April 1947 (CUL Keller Archive).

6 The social groups which Keller took as his subject on this occasion were the string quartet and the internment camp.

1942–43 are still extant in CUL Keller Archive) and joined Phillips in a long study of small social groups in wartime Britain.[7] The study of teaching groups to which Keller refers in the letter quoted above was a joint project which resulted in a 96-page report, drafted by Keller, on the 'Psychology and Ethics of School Staff Groups'.[8] As he explains in the Preface to this report, central to their method of collaboration was the contrast between their two approaches to the task: Margaret Phillips embarked on it 'without being attached to any particular psychological school', while Keller, who was deeply immersed in Freudian literature (to the extent that the psychoanalyst Willi Hoffer considered his knowledge to be 'unequalled'[9]) provided an alternative psychoanalytical view. Working in this way, Keller hoped, would mean that 'the resulting treatment of evidence will perhaps be marked by a greater degree of realism than would be possible without that kind of collaboration. The occasions on which conclusions compatible with each other were arrived at by the investigators were numerous.'[10] To increase this 'realism', Keller concluded the report by presenting the reactions of other psychologists who had read it in draft.

As well as their observation of school groups, Keller and Phillips also looked at the dynamics of such groups as fire brigade staff,[11] youth clubs, evening classes and bridge parties (Keller defined the latter as 'sadism on a sublimated level'). On a more theoretical level, on 29 September 1945, they presented to the British Psychological Society a joint paper on 'The Psychological Significance of some Sociological Conceptions of the Group' in which, during alternate presentations, they outlined the different ways in which 'associative' and 'community' groups are related to the family pattern, with Keller concluding that the development of 'community' groups into 'associations' is a natural transition, paralleling the development of the individual from childhood to maturity.[12] Keller later presented to the Society

7 Their work together took place principally in 1944–47, during which time their main project was a joint book, 'The Psychology of Social Unity', of which a large proportion survives (CUL Keller Archive). Their collaboration became more sporadic after 1947, by which time Keller was turning his attention increasingly to musical subjects, but it was still intended that he should make a contribution to the book as late as 1960. Eventually, however, Phillips published her research alone, as *Small Social Groups in England* (1965).

8 The unpublished report is undated, but was probably written early in 1946, as a footnote on page 80 refers to Keller's 1946 article 'Male Psychology' as 'going to press as I write'. It contains a chapter on 'group self-contempt' as observed in teachers (CUL Keller Archive).

9 See *1975* (1977), p. 87.

10 From the Preface to the report.

11 It was 'in the diary of an Auxiliary Fire Brigade's group life during the war' that Keller says he first encountered group self-contempt. ('Resistances to Britten's Music: Their Psychology', *Music Survey*, Spring 1950.)

12 The definitions of 'community' and 'association' are missing from Keller's copy of the paper, as Margaret Phillips gave the opening section which defined these terms. However, the same terms are used in their report on school staff groups, in which Keller

his theory of group self-contempt as applied to music, in a paper on 'Musical Self-Contempt in Britain' – an idea which he had also applied to Britten's critics, to great effect.[13]

Keller's intense interest in the psychology of social groups is significant, as he was throughout his life a passionate individualist. His individualism was central to his personality and was continually in evidence, but nowhere more so than in his often stormy relations with the BBC, the only organization of which he was a full-time member. His many battles with his employer (particularly during his second decade on the staff, when he felt himself increasingly out of sympathy with prevailing policies) are now legendary: his refusal to participate in the 'depersonalising' annual report system, his railing against 'the myth of management', his opposition to the BBC's staff publishing restrictions, and his refusal to drop the issues behind the *Broadcasting in the Seventies* rebellion. 'Organised, collective life,' he later wrote, is:

> the seamy side of human existence ... The evil, that is to say, is collectivity as we know it and accept it, with effective power on the one hand and the happy abrogation of individual judgement on the other ... I have learnt about one ultimate value without which there are no human beings to speak of, and one ultimate vice with which there are no human beings to speak of. The ultimate value is the independence of individual conscience, while the ultimate vice is its cession, capitulation, loving surrender, arrested development, collective envelopment. There is no collective wisdom; there is only unacknowledged, collective stupidity. Man has lived for quite some time now and still hasn't discovered, once and for all, that a group doesn't think.[14]

Undoubtedly, some of the emotional impetus behind the strength of those views came from the 'indiscriminate, enthusiastic, collective sadism'[15] which he had witnessed – and experienced – in Nazi-occupied Vienna before the war. Be that as it may, he was always concerned to avoid becoming a comfortable insider anywhere, and reserved his most ferocious criticism for those groups which might otherwise claim him as a member: 'I am an experienced traitor: as an anti-critic critic, anti-word writer on music,

defines them as follows: 'There is the "association", a purposive group pursuing a common aim which is not directly or mainly related to the immediate welfare of the group; and there is the "community", the essence of which lies in personal relationships between group members and in attempts at achieving their immediate welfare.'

13 'Musical Self-Contempt in Britain' was prepared for the meeting of the British Psychological Society held on 4 November 1950, and was written in response to J.C. Flügel's enthusiasm for Keller's article 'Resistances to Britten's Music: Their Psychology'. Flügel suggested that Keller should take his ideas on musical group self-contempt further (Letter from Flügel to Keller, 22 June 1950, CUL Keller Archive).

14 From the Preface to *1975* (1977), the publication of which caused another upset at the BBC.

15 Ibid., p. 47.

anti-teacher teacher, and perhaps even anti-radio radio man, I have learnt to help many a struggle by fighting it.'[16]

Writing to a young musician and would-be author many years later, Keller talked of the importance to a developing writer of not rushing into print too soon, recalling that 'when I was your age [23], I was well aware that I had to wait'.[17] He did not publish his own first major article until he was twenty-seven.[18] 'Male Psychology', which was written (though possibly not in its final form) at least two years earlier, first appeared in the *British Journal of Medical Psychology* in 1946 and was reprinted in *World Psychology* the following year. It is a highly ordered and technical piece of writing, of which Keller was evidently proud. Regarding it as 'something of an open letter to all women psychologists',[19] he was anxious to give it 'the widest possible publicity', and so submitted it for republication to a number of different journals, including *The Journal Press*, *Life and Letters Today*, *New Statesman and Nation*, *Pilot Papers* and *Time and Tide*, as well as *World Psychology*. The basic argument of this 'open letter' is that the existence of a mass of psychological literature on the female mind, without there being any comparable study of the male, is the result of our society's regarding the male as a norm from which the female is a deviation. This relegation of women to 'the department of abnormal psychology' could be corrected, Keller suggests, by studies of male psychology by female psychologists 'who investigate not the points in which they differ from men, but those in which men seem different from themselves'. Although the concerns of this essay are not related to his work on social groups, it was nevertheless very much a part of Keller's individualism to suspect any unthinking concept of 'the norm'.[20]

In the years immediately before the appearance of this article, Keller had been experimenting with various forms of writing, including short stories, a play, and even occasional verse (not his natural idiom: he later wrote to a friend, 'as you know, my understanding of poetry is sub-normal'[21]). One form which was evidently immediately appealing to him – for he felt

---

16 'Schoenberg: The Future of Symphonic Thought', *Perspectives of New Music*, Winter 1974.

17 Letter to Robert Turnball, 4 April 1981 (CUL Keller Archive). Keller also told him: 'The first requirements [of a writer] are (a) discovery of as yet unrecognized essentials, and (b) a firm knowledge of one's understanding and one's incomprehension.'

18 At the suggestion of the psychologist J.C. Flügel (at whose recommendation Keller joined the British Psychological Society) Keller sent 'Male Psychology' to an American journal *Character and Personality* (published by Duke University Press) in October 1944. Despite a subsequent letter in March 1945, the editor never responded, and Keller withdrew the article in June 1945, 'having an opportunity to publish the paper elsewhere' – presumably the *British Journal of Medical Psychology*, in which it appeared in the following year.

19 Letter to Dr Rickman, the editor of the *British Journal of Medical Psychology*, 3 April 1947 (CUL Keller Archive).

20 Keller returned to misleading pictures of what is 'normal' in, for example, 'Music and Psychopathology', *History of Medicine*, Summer 1971.

21 Letter to John Greening, 3 December 1980 (CUL Keller Archive).

confident enough to publish in it early – and which was a lasting love of his, was the aphorism. Two early publications which preceded 'Male Psychology' were in the form of sets of aphorisms: an assorted set in the case of 'Schonend, weil in Kuerze',[22] and variations on a theme in the case of 'On Maturity'.[23] Examples from the latter are, 'Intellectual maturity is reached when disbelief is superseded by doubt and conviction by opinion' and 'Artistic maturity is reached when both need for and contempt of applause are superseded by the desire to be understood'.[24] A third early publication which preceded 'Male Psychology', and which was the only attempt at fiction which the adult Keller ever published[25] (although several unpublished stories still survive), was a psychological short story entitled 'Don Juan Again', which was published in the magazine *Kite* in December 1945.[26]

In the early 1940s, while Keller pursued his psychological researches, he was earning his living as a freelance chamber and orchestral musician, including playing second violin in the string quartet formed by Oskar Adler when he also fled Vienna for London. In addition, Keller took an LRAM teaching diploma in 1942. It is striking that, during a period when he was more active as a practising musician than at any subsequent time, music should be almost completely absent from his writing, as represented by those of his early notes and unpublished essays which survive, as well as the publications cited above. It illustrates, perhaps, that his later assertion of the incompatibility of words and music, of their being two completely different modes of thought, found its roots in his own early experience. Moreover, when he did begin writing about music, around the time of the publication of 'Male Psychology', he began away from what might be thought to be his natural repertoire. It is not the string quartets of Haydn, Mozart and Beethoven which are the subject of his early publications, but film scores

22 *Zeitspiegel*, 25 October 1941.

23 *The Psychologist*, July 1945. *The Psychologist* published four further sets of Keller's aphorisms on this subject: 'What IS Maturity', August 1947; 'On Maturity ...', September 1947; 'Maturity', October 1947; 'On Maturity', November 1947. The Zurich journal *Die Weltwoche* published Keller's own translation of the 1945 set under the title 'Reife' on 27 December 1946, but turned down the next set.

24 A memorable description of the role of an aphorism, aphoristically expressed, can be found in 'Mental Shorthand', one of Keller's many sets of unpublished aphorisms: 'Aphorisms are not valuable on account of their substance, but on account of their function. They transmit little truth, but they provoke the desire for it' (CUL Keller Archive).

25 He did publish one story when he was a child: 'The first thing I ever published, as a little boy and in a children's newspaper, was called 'Inge's Cloud Journey' – Inge being my little cousin.' 'Truth and Music', *Music and Musicians*, April 1970.

26 *Kite*, subtitled 'A Factory Journal', was a publication whose policy was 'presenting the best which the writer in industry has to offer'. According to the editorial in the issue in which Keller's story appeared (the fourth), its contributors were 'all factory workers', and it is unclear from Keller's correspondence with the magazine why they decided to depart from this policy in his case. Certainly his contributor's biography looks unusual among those of the metal turners and electricians who appeared alongside him.

and the music of Benjamin Britten. After 1946, music very quickly replaced psychology as Keller's prime subject, but his psychological knowledge continued to inform his writing for the rest of his life and remained one of his style's most characteristic elements.

Keller's earliest musical publications took him initially in three main directions: general musical journalism, film music, and the music of Benjamin Britten. The first of these was largely stimulated initially by the need to earn money. Keller later recalled that, during the late 1940s, 'my chief living came from contributions to *National Entertainment Monthly*, *The Stage* – to twenty-odd awful publications'.[27] It was evident that his psychological writings would never be very remunerative, so he made a concerted effort during 1946 and 1947 to establish himself as a music critic, offering his services as a pre- and reviewer to a huge number of newspapers, magazines and journals all over the country. Whenever he planned visits to important musical events and festivals, he trawled the press in an effort to place reviews in as many publications as possible. His interest in film music he also turned to good financial effect, reviewing regularly for film magazines like *Contemporary Cinema* and *Sight and Sound*, as well as suggesting to sundry other publications that they might consider starting a film music column. All this was so successful that within two years he could write 'I am depending entirely on my writing for my living'.[28]

Keller's involvement with film music stemmed partly from his increasingly broad application of psychoanalytical ideas and partly from an intense interest in contemporary mass media. Although it eventually took him to the BBC, this interest was not without its internal complications. The power of the mass media was naturally exciting to such a born communicator as Keller, but brought with it, to his mind, enormous moral responsibilities. His standards were high and his individualistic character was revolted by commercial populism. At the same time, he would not dismiss an art form simply because it was popular, and during his BBC years he rather enjoyed surprising his colleagues by, for example, trying to get the Beatles on to the Third Programme, or suggesting a functional analysis of Gershwin. He was opposed to what he saw as the false esotericism with which art is sometimes surrounded, preventing its wider understanding. In his own writings and broadcasts, he became increasingly careful to avoid technical jargon, and was eloquent about the unjustifiable barriers which over-complicated academic language sets up before the ordinary man: 'it distorts or obscures the truth and so creates a superfluously professional world of thought, a cast to which the pariah, try as he may, finds no access.'[29] Looking back at the

---

27 From the (unpaginated) Preface to the collected edition of *Music Survey* which was published in 1981.

28 Letter to George Taylor, editor of *Radio Affairs*, 13 January 1948 (CUL Keller Archive).

29 'Schoenberg: The Future of Symphonic Thought', *Perspectives of New Music*, Autumn–Winter 1974.

Third Programme in later years, his own criticism of it was that it sometimes succumbed to the temptations of cultural snobbery.[30] Nevertheless, he himself was also accused of being part of the problem – on one occasion by the BBC's Director-General, whose comment that 'Hans is following his usual elitist line'[31] elicited an interesting response from Keller: 'Elitism is a concept which was invented as recently as a decade or two ago, an emotive, derogatory, pseudo-democratic, almost psychotic denial of the fact that all men are not equal.'[32] Indeed, he was not remotely interested in any kind of cultural democracy (and was not above describing the ordinary cinema-goer, in one instance, as '*sus domesticus*'[33]).

In October 1947, Keller set out some of his concerns about film music in a pamphlet published by the British Film Institute: *The Need for Competent Film Music Criticism*. While recognizing that the cinema was bringing classical music to many people who would never normally go to a concert, Keller considered the quality of film scores to be a matter of serious concern: 'film music is capable of becoming a weapon of musical mass destruction.' He therefore argued for 'continuous, generally accessible, and competent film music criticism' to combat the tendency towards solely commercial film music. Keller's assigning such an important role to the critic, and his opening statement that there is an aesthetic need for such criticism, is interesting in view of the poor opinion which he held of many of his critical contemporaries, and his later view that criticism is the product of sociological and psychological – not artistic – needs.[34]

One of Keller's anxieties about film music, which prefigures some of his later arguments about broadcasting, was the problem of 'background music':

> I have often asked people how they liked the music in a particular film. 'Was there any?' Nor is this reaction to be wondered at, since a good deal of film music is offered for the express purpose of its not being listened to: incidental film music, we are told, has to be 'unobtrusive.' Its habit, however, of hitting the audience below the belt of full consciousness is not without danger; trash must be perceived before it is recognised. And why should good film music, if it is unobjectionable by intra-musical standards and well suited for the emotional or

30 See, for example, 'Broadcasting: In the 'Eighties', *The Spectator*, 10 July 1976, and 'Fare Better, BBC', *Spectator*, 30 June 1979.

31 Charles Curran, letter to *Ariel*, 17 November 1976.

32 'Description, Analysis and Criticism: A Differential Diagnosis', *Soundings*, 6 (1977), pp. 108–20.

33 'Film Music – The Question of Quotation', *Music Survey*, 1949. This article opens with one of Keller's most telling aphorisms: 'Art arises where the arbitrary and the predictable are superseded by unpredictable inevitability.'

34 'While criticism is not really necessary artistically, it is sociologically inevitable' ('Problems in Writing about Music', *Times Literary Supplement*, 10 September 1969); 'The need to criticize, and/or to have and see things criticized, is so elemental, so inescapable psychologically, that the musician has to forgive the critic the way religious people forgive original sin' (*Criticism*, 1987, p. 2).

> spiritual underlining of the film, be afraid of the audience's intelligent musical perception?[35]

Although he designated film music as 'applied' rather than 'pure', this did not make it more acceptable as a background nor in any way diminish its importance as music. Indeed, in an interesting article on 'The Psychology of Film Music', published in *World Psychology* in 1948,[36] Keller warns that 'it would be disastrous for the musico-psychologist to assume, however silently, that as soon as he has explained the relation between applied music and the ideas to which it is applied, he may proceed to explain away music-as-such merely in terms of its extra-musical relations.' Keller considered film music to be particularly interesting to psychologists, first because it is 'born into, and also out of, a psychological age', and also because it has 'a well-definable psychological function … film music aims to an unusual extent, indeed often primarily, at suggesting psychological truth.'[37] He goes on to say, however, that film music is not the only manifestation of the psychological aspect of music, merely the youngest: Keller cites Mozart as 'a unique figure in this as in many another respect, in that he succeeded in uniting, to the highest degree, an unsurpassed artistico-psychological insight with an unsurpassable aesthetic sense'.

It would seem from this article, as well as from parts of *The Need for Competent Film Music Criticism*, that Keller regarded opera as another form of 'applied music'.[38] Furthermore, he thought that 'applied music' offered an

---

35 'A Note on Film Music', *Tribune*, 13 June 1947.

36 *World Psychology*, March 1948.

37 To support this theory, Keller gives an analysis of two films, one of which is *Master of Bankdam* (1947), in which the music is by Arthur Benjamin. Keller describes how the theme song 'The Fire of Your Love', which originally appears (in A major) as the love song of Annie and Joshua, returns (in E major) at the end of the film, as Annie, after Joshua's death, sees her son Simeon's accession to the mastership of Bankdam. Quoting Flügel's observation that 'widowers, widows and those who are unhappily married frequently display a more than normal degree of attachment to their children, the latter receiving, in addition to the love that would ordinarily fall to their share, the displaced affection which would otherwise find its outlet in the love of wife and husband', Keller concludes that 'the final appearance of the theme song, then, imparts this piece of exact psychological information: Annie has eventually overcome her grief by displacing her cathexis of the (internal) object-imago of her husband on to an actual (external) object, i.e., her son. The fact that this final version of the theme song is in E major, i.e. the dominant of the key in which it is originally sung … adds a subtle finishing touch to the music's psychological significance. For the dominant, which appears of course after the tonic in the harmonic series, is the tonic's off-spring, its 'child'.

38 Keller does not specifically state this, but it is presumably in Mozart's operas that his 'artistico-psychological insight' is particularly in evidence. In *The Need for Competent Film Music Criticism* Keller speculates on the 'impending re-birth of opera into film' as well as 'another semi-musical art-form which, I think, will be drawn into the sphere of the cinema' – ballet. Keller's attitude to opera as a musical form was equivocal: 'I never was an opera fan – about twenty-five musically supreme masterpieces in this curious medium apart' (*Criticism*, 1987, p. 5).

entry into the difficult subject of musical psychology, as he explains at the beginning of the *World Psychology* article:

> The psychology of music is the most difficult branch of applied psychology, but the psychology of what we might call applied (as distinct from absolute or pure) music offers a comparatively easy approach ... Whereas in pure music we encounter processes which, at any rate on the surface, bear little relation to such mental phenomena as have already been elucidated by psychological analysis, the processes that make up applied music, though in themselves as mysterious psychologically as those of pure music, are at least definitely related to extra-musical mental processes which have already been successfully subjected to scientific research.

It is therefore not surprising that among his own first attempts to apply psychology to music should be the three essays which he wrote on the psychology of *Peter Grimes*.

The *Three Psychoanalytic Notes on Peter Grimes*, which remained unpublished during Keller's lifetime, were probably written soon after the opera's first performance in 1945.[39] Apparently, Keller originally heard *Peter Grimes* only by accident: 'After the war he used to attend almost every performance of *Cosí fan tutte* given by Sadler's Wells Opera. One evening, instead of the overture to Mozart's opera, he found himself listening to something quite strange – it was *Peter Grimes*. He immediately regarded it as a masterpiece. From then on he determined that he would acquaint himself with as much of Britten's music as he could.'[40] That *Peter Grimes* made a profound impression on him the 'Open Letter to the Authors' which accompanies the *Three Notes* attests: 'I don't think you'll find a great many people who are more lastingly grateful to you for this work than I am.' In the *Three Notes*, which examine in turn 'Grimes' Character', 'Grimes and His Mother' and 'Grimes and His Father', Keller was really addressing the libretto rather than the music, but he had become deeply interested in Britten's music, which he made the subject of a large proportion of his early writings, including his first three substantial essays on music.[41] We have already noted that when Keller started writing about music he began away from his natural repertoire, with Benjamin Britten and film composers, rather than the central works of the Austro-German tradition (a repertoire which he used famously to say that he had known in full by the age of ten). Many of his writings on Britten take psychological rather than musical issues as their starting point, in particular the psychology of Britten's critics and

39 The notes were published in 1985, together with Keller's 'Open Letter to the Authors of *Peter Grimes*' and three other contemporaneous essays on psychological subjects as *Three Psychoanalytic Notes on Peter Grimes*, edited by Christopher Wintle.

40 See Alan Blyth's collection of Britten memoirs, *Remembering Britten* (1981), p. 87.

41 'Britten and Mozart', written in 1946, 'Benjamin Britten's Second Quartet', written in January–February 1947, and 'A Great English Composer', an unpublished essay written early the same year (CUL Keller Archive).

issues of musical 'nationality'. Keller was undoubtedly attracted by the paradox of a composer who was both unusually popular – he himself felt that 'Britten's popularity needs a special explanation'[42] – and the object of what he considered unjustly harsh criticism. Britten's nationality provided a reason for both: while England was glad to acclaim him after centuries of subordinate musical status, its group self-contempt simultaneously unleashed bitter attacks. This extra-musical motivation was probably responsible for the fact that Britten's critics continually singled out what were to Keller 'the most immediately striking of [Britten's] musical endowments and attainments'[43] for special denigration.

The most provocative of these early articles on Britten was the first to be written, and it offers another insight into what attracted Keller to Britten.[44] 'Britten and Mozart' took two years to see the light of day,[45] having been initially rejected by several journals,[46] including *The Music Review*, whose editor, though otherwise interested in Keller's writings, found this comparison unacceptable. Despite Keller's insistence that he was comparing musical characters, not merits, and that 'this is not the time, and I am not the man, to decide about the relative greatness of Mozart and Britten', the essay was widely read as making ludicrously high claims for a composer who was, after all, still very young. The parallels which Keller draws – their classical restraint (*not* inhibition), their impeccable sense of form, their versatility, eclecticism and precocious talent, and their common love of virtuosity and the dramatic – are convincingly presented, and several times Keller uses to striking effect the device of quoting passages from some of Mozart's contemporary critics echoing current reviews of Britten. Keller also compares the popularity of both composers, observing memorably that 'Mozart and Britten are the only two composers I know who strongly and widely attract people who do not understand them'.

'Britten and Mozart' was reprinted four years later in the symposium on Britten's music which Keller edited with Donald Mitchell and which was published amid a storm of contentious comment at the end of 1952.[47] Here, 'Britten and Mozart' appears as the first half of an extended essay on 'The Musical Character', in which Keller casts a musico-psychoanalytical

42 From the draft of 'A Great English Composer' (CUL Keller Archive).

43 'Resistances to Britten's Music: Their Psychology', *Music Survey*, Spring 1950.

44 Its central thesis is echoed many times in Keller's other Britten writings of this period, for example early drafts of the Second Quartet article and in 'A Great English Composer': 'Spending a considerable part of my professional and my private life with the works of both Mozart and Britten, I realise more and more that there is an astounding number of strong similarities between these two composers who are both so widely – rather than sufficiently deeply – appreciated, and who are both classical composers in the artistic sense of the word.'

45 First published in *Music and Letters*, January 1948.

46 *The Musical Times* (February 1946), *Polemic* (November 1946) and *Horizon* (December 1946).

47 *Benjamin Britten: a Commentary on his works from a Group of Specialists*, 1952.

eye over the twentieth century's 'crisis of beauty and melody' and its psychologically inevitable 'development from beauty to truth'. Beside the Britten–Mozart character-comparison Keller places the pairing of Schoenberg and Beethoven: 'the relation between Britten and Schoenberg shows many striking parallels with that between Mozart and Beethoven.' Again, Keller brings in Britten's 'Englishry' and his 're-created modality' which both mediates between English and continental thematicism and 'serves as a strong bridge between the diatonicism of the past and the anti-diatonicism of the present'. The whole piece is full of stimulating ideas, but it was probably Keller's incidental psychological characterizations of various twentieth-century composers which particularly irritated his critics, when he diagnosed 'sadism' in Bartók, 'sado-masochism' in Stravinsky, 'aggressive narcissism' in Boulez, 'asceticism' in Webern and a 'violent repressive counter-force against his sadism' in Britten himself.[48]

This 'orgy of psycho-analysis in which Mr Keller indulges'[49] brought an almost apoplectic reaction from some reviewers:

> The final chapter, by Hans Keller, on Britten's musical character should be avoided by anyone suffering from high blood pressure. One is strongly tempted on first reading it to throw the book into the nearest convenient receptacle; but the thing has an odd fascination, and on re-reading it a lot of wheat appears among the tares. One certainly cannot ignore Mr Keller, a fact of which he is probably well aware.[50]

The whole symposium, moreover, was widely thought to be unnecessarily laudatory, either because Britten's music did not deserve such attention, or because it was good enough to stand alone: 'Britten is too potent a figure to require a bodyguard', as one critic observed.[51] When Donald Mitchell was asked about this 40 years later, he described the book as 'a necessary corrective to critical attitudes to Britten at that time. These were often

---

48 Imogen Holst's diary (quoted in Carpenter, 1992, p. 317) records on 4 December 1952 that Britten read out from the book 'a terrible sentence about "sado-masochism":– he said they must have noticed in my chapter that his favourite instrument was the whip!' (Keller does indeed make frequent reference in 'The Musical Character' to the other essays contained in the symposium.) Some years later, Britten was asked by an interviewer what he thought of Keller's remarks: 'It is difficult, if not impossible, to comment objectively on what is written about oneself. But I admire Keller's intelligence and courage enormously, and certainly about *others* he is very perceptive!' (Schafer, 1963, p. 117). Keller later wrote to a BBC colleague that this response of Britten's had 'touched me … and showed me a genius's incisive insight into his own psyche, including those aspects of it which he may not find altogether acceptable' (letter to Richard Shead, 20 April 1979, CUL Keller Archive).

49 Unsigned review in 'The Listener's Book Chronicle', *The Listener*, **49**/1252 (26 February 1953), p. 361.

50 Review [probably by Alec Robertson] in *Time and Tide*, **34**/12 (21 March 1953), p. 392.

51 Peter Tranchell, 'Britten and Brittenites', *Music and Letters*, **34**/2 (April 1953) pp. 124–32.

prejudiced or ignorant; and even when they weren't, it seemed to us that the positive comment was almost as ill-informed as the negative.'[52] The extent of Britten's neglect was arguable, however, and some felt that Keller's and Mitchell's picture of critical hostility was exaggerated:

> Britten's extraordinary musical gifts were recognised from the start; he has met with a minimum of misunderstanding; and for many years each new work from his pen has been immediately hailed as a masterpiece of its kind. It is puzzling, therefore, to the ordinary reader to meet in several of the essays included here a note of defensiveness, even a hint of defence by aggression, as though Britten's music were deliberately underestimated or spitefully ignored by critics or public.[53]

However, there was one particularly close associate of Keller's at that time – Geoffrey Sharp, the editor of *The Music Review* – who was strongly prejudiced against Britten (a fact which he was happy to admit) and whose views probably stimulated Keller towards a more aggressive defence of the composer. Despite Sharp's rejection of 'Britten and Mozart', he published shortly afterwards the essay 'Mozart and Boccherini', in which Keller examined Mozart's various uses of a Boccherini theme and speculated persuasively about his underlying psychological motivation.[54] Keller then became a regular reviewer in *The Music Review* (including of film music: it was undoubtedly at his suggestion that film reviews began to appear there) and he and Sharp were good friends. Keller always felt he had 'total freedom'[55] in *The Music Review* (Britten excepted) and, even after his *Music Survey* days, referred to the journal as 'home'.[56] Nevertheless, about Britten he and Sharp were totally opposed, and their exchange of letters after the publication of the symposium makes entertaining reading: 'The Britten book' wrote Sharp to Keller on 4 January 1953,

> is a painstaking effort … but who is Benjamin Britten to merit such detailed investigation of his work?? Now Bartók, Walton, Rubbra or Rawsthorne I could have understood, or Gottfried von Einem, K.A. Hartmann, Roy Harris or Samuel Barber; perhaps even Arthur Somervell whose violin Concerto seems to me incredibly good … I fear that in future years you and Donald may both come to regret this mountain you have built out of a molehill … I have tried to read part two of your final chapter and agree with that part of it that I can understand. It does however seem to me to be over abstruse and, as I have suggested before, I think you would be very well advised to concentrate on trying to express what you have to say in half the verbiage you at present employ … readers can always

---

52 Donald Mitchell interviewed by Humphrey Carpenter (quoted in Carpenter, 1992, p. 315).

53 Martin Cooper, 'Crown for Britten', *The Spectator*, 6499 (16 January 1953), pp. 72–3.

54 'Mozart and Boccherini', *The Music Review*, November 1947.

55 *Music Survey* (1981), preface, n.p.

56 Letter from Keller to Sharp, 30 June 1956 (CUL Keller Archive).

be found for terse and trenchant prose, while even the most assiduous get sick and tired of eternal parentheses and footnotes, the more so when the footnotes refer to obscure extremities of the magnum corpus of meisterwerke of the author himself! … This is candid and to the point. I think highly of your ability or I would not have taken the trouble to write as I have … Faffs of verbosity are likely to infuriate, whereas I am sure that what you want to do is to convince… … But of course in the case of Benjamin Britten you could not hope to do that![57]

Keller and Mitchell replied the following day:

Candid you are; to the point you aren't. We intend to be both. As you said yourself a few days ago, you are unfavourably prejudiced against Britten, so we don't see why we should be interested in an opinion which you yourself would not consider sufficiently objective for general consumption. Including as it does a highly diverting list of candidates for future symposia (we are looking forward to your editing the one on Arthur Somervell), your letter must however be preserved for your biography … As for your fear that we may have built a mountain out of a molehill, we prefer this danger to the opposite risk, of reducing a mountain to a molehill.[58]

It was through *The Music Review* that Keller had first met Donald Mitchell. Mitchell was teaching at Oakfield Preparatory School in Dulwich in the late 1940s, when he read Keller's articles in *The Music Review* and was immediately struck by their distinctive style:

There were two things about his reviews that caught my attention at the time: first of all the combative manner of the criticism, and then the detailed information that backed it up, which often included an array of footnotes. I thought that anybody who could mount a serious critical assault or for that matter a serious critical appraisal on a given work or composer and reinforce it with a bibliography – this was something that I found entirely gripping. Then – a curious coincidence – we found that we were both living in South London, only a mile or two apart. I think it was out of my response to something very special embodied in Hans' critical work that a meeting finally emerged; and out of that meeting developed our partnership as editors of *Music Survey*.[59]

Mitchell had been editing *Music Survey*[60], which he had founded with financial support from the headmaster of the school in which he taught, for a year before he asked Keller to join him as co-editor in 1949. 'Combative criticism' then became very much a hallmark of the journal's style, but it was always – the editors insisted – an entirely positive aggression, dedicated to

57 CUL Keller Archive.

58 Letter from Keller and Mitchell to Sharp, 5 January 1953 (CUL Keller Archive).

59 *Music Survey* (1981), preface, n.p.

60 The original title was *Music Journal*, but this was changed at the request of the Incorporated Society of Musicians, who felt that it was too similar to their own publication *A Music Journal*.

'the defence of great or substantial composers whom our musical world neglected'.[61] One of the composers thus defended was, of course, Britten, to whose music a whole issue of *Music Survey* was dedicated (vol. 2, no. 4, Spring 1950); another was Arnold Schoenberg. In the same issue which celebrated Britten, Keller and Mitchell made the following announcement:

> As long as any great music needs partisanship we shall be found to be partisans. From now on, every issue of this journal will reserve space for the special subject of Schoenberg until, with our help or without, he has ceased to be a special subject. If we are the first who, while not members of the Schoenberg school, decide upon such constant support, this is Schoenberg's merit as well as a reminder of history at which we are ourselves, as it were, surprised.

The Schoenberg column had, in effect, already begun in the previous issue, which had marked the composer's seventy-fifth birthday. The letter which he had sent to friends and well-wishers in response to their birthday greetings was printed, together with three short articles on his music, including a piece on 'Recent Schoenberg Performances' by Edward Clark. Clark, a Schoenberg pupil, had been on the staff of the BBC from 1924 until 1936, and had been responsible for contemporary music programming of an adventurousness which parallels that which William Glock achieved 30 years later. Years earlier, in January 1914, Clark had been instrumental in bringing Schoenberg to London to conduct his music there for the first time. In February 1933, Schoenberg returned to conduct the BBC Symphony Orchestra in a broadcast of his Variations Op.31,[62] a work of which the Orchestra gave the first performance in Schoenberg's native Vienna three years later – again a result of Clark's endeavours.[63]

The BBC of the 1950s, despite the opportunities offered by the Third

---

61 *Music Survey* (1981), preface, n.p. A vivid (unsigned) picture of how this 'positive aggression' was received by critical contemporaries can be found in *The Musical Times* in 1951: 'The tower inhabited by *Music Survey* is also armed with machine guns; and it is a dull number that does not hit twenty targets. One is reminded of a famous description of rough justice: "they all had to suffer, the guilty as well as the innocent". There is little pretence of quarterly style; but the English is vivacious, sinewy and free from waste. Undoubtedly one wants to read *Music Survey* for its *bravura*, its ungoverned cleverness, and (let us, too, be just) the large amount of scholarly and musicianly comment that fills the spaces in between.' ('Notes and News: The Quarterlies', *The Musical Times*, **1295**/92 (January 1951), pp. 38–40).

62 One who did not approve of this broadcast, however, was Sir John Reith, who is reported as saying, during a speech given the following day, 'I am going to a meeting of the Music Advisory Committee … If you have any message to send them concerning the Schoenberg music that was broadcast last night, I will gladly take it. I shall certainly have some comments of my own to make. Such music does not leave me cold – I wish it did – its effect is very much the reverse' (quoted in Kenyon, 1981, p. 83).

63 This exciting period of BBC history and Edward Clark's role in it has been thoroughly documented in Jennifer Doctor (1999), *The BBC and Ultra-Modern Music, 1922–1936*.

Programme, exhibited a music policy of a rather more nationalistic and insular nature, partly as a consequence of the war. Nevertheless, it was prompted by Schoenberg's death in 1951 to mount a special series of broadcasts of his music in the Third Programme the following year. The result, according to Keller in his 'Bedside Editorial for the BBC',[64] was 'a protracted amateur performance in the worst sense, packed with factual ignorance, musical idiocy and incomprehensible interpretations of the most alarming order'. Having reviewed the Schoenberg series already in *The Music Review*,[65] Keller turned in his 'Bedside Editorial' to a wider criticism of the BBC's impenetrable *modus operandi*, demanding that the Corporation adopt a policy of more openness, particularly with regard to its selection of contemporary music for broadcast: 'we, like the people in an autocratic state, have to depend on rumours ...'[66]

There is also a hint in this editorial that Keller was offended at not being asked to make a more direct contribution to this series, despite spending 'many an hour on gratis advice and information ... in reply to backstage enquiries from actual and potential contributors to the series'.[67] The BBC's files of this period show that, since his offer to talk on Freud in 1946, he had made at least one other unsuccessful suggestion to the BBC, in 1951.[68] His papers also show that he had taken part in BBC Audience Research surveys in the 1940s, and he was, of course, a regular radio reviewer, concerned with the quality of talks as well as of broadcast music,[69] so it is likely that he was keen to begin broadcasting himself. However, as Donald Mitchell remembered later, 'the mass media, including the BBC of course, did not hasten to open their doors to us during those years. I'm not suggesting that

64 *Music Survey*, June 1952.

65 'The BBC's Victory over Schoenberg', *The Music Review*, May 1952.

66 Keller had earlier considered creating a permanent column in *Music Survey* called 'The Fourth Programme' which would be devoted to criticism of the BBC. This was necessary because, he noted, 'the BBC never replies to criticisms. This is what a genius mag. should do.' These remarks are contained in handwritten notes on the performance of *Zaide* at the Crosby Hall, Chelsea, on 5 December 1950, which Keller thought ought to be given on the Third Programme (CUL Keller Archive).

67 It seems that the BBC had made a deliberate decision not to have too much input from well-known 'Schoenbergians' in the series: hence the selection of Tippett as general editor. Erwin Stein had offered his services, pointing out that he was the 'oldest pupil alive' of Schoenberg, but Leonard Isaacs was wary of what he called 'subservience to the small group of fanatical apostles of Schönberg' (letter from Stein to Herbert Murrill, 26 August 1951, BBC WAC Composer's file: Arnold Schoenberg, 1943–62; memorandum from Isaacs to Murrill, 11 September 1951, BBC WAC R27/500/6 Third Programme, 1945–57.)

68 A proposal was made to Leonard Isaacs in January 1951, but since Keller's initial letter of 20 January is missing, the nature of the suggestion is unknown (BBC WAC Talks Contributor File: Hans Keller, File 1, 1946–62).

69 The June 1952 issue of *Music Survey* which contained Keller's 'Bedside Editorial' also printed a transcript of 'the one talk in the BBC's series which will turn out to be of lasting value', Mátyás Seiber's 'Composing with Twelve Notes'.

one was suppressed or censored; but one was not encouraged.'[70] This picture is supported by two letters which Mitchell received in 1953 from Roger Fiske, then Music Talks Producer at the BBC. These were a genuine attempt on Fiske's part to be helpful, and to explain to Mitchell how he could make his style more acceptable for broadcasting. However, 'I think it is only fair to tell you that, when I came into this job, I was given the opinion of various people in the Third Programme on music speakers generally ... But I am afraid you were one of a number of people I was "warned about".'[71] Since Fiske specifically mentions both the Britten symposium and *Music Survey* as examples of the 'altogether too self-confident, over-assertive and indeed over-aggressive' criticism which he felt was unsuitable for broadcasting – 'I don't think the Third Programme is really the place for aggressive criticism' – it is likely that Keller's name had had a 'warning' appended to it too.

Keller's attacks on his critical contemporaries, many of whom were BBC contributors or on the Corporation's staff, probably made things even more difficult. *Music Survey* received a public reprimand for 'transgress[ing] the generally observed maxim that dog does not eat dog' from Frank Howes, probably the most exalted critic at the time, in view of his position on *The Times*.[72] Keller clashed repeatedly with Howes, challenging his anonymity (in common with other newspapers, *The Times* then referred simply to 'Our Music Critic', which Keller complained left Howes unaccountable and gave his personal prejudices the authority of fact) and, more importantly, his negative opinion of Schoenberg. After Howes delivered his verdict on Schoenberg, Keller proceeded to pounce on every error of fact that followed, and even invoked the force of the Critics' Circle when *The Times* refused to publish his corrections.[73]

---

70 *Music Survey* (1981), preface, n.p.

71 Letter from Roger Fiske to Donald Mitchell, 1 July 1953 (BBC WAC Talks Contributor File: Donald Mitchell, File 1: 1946–62).

72 Howes' review appeared in *The Times* under the 'Our Music Critic' label which Keller so disliked, and reads as follows: 'The two [aesthetic and historical issues] are found together in a new English quarterly, that has almost surreptitiously made its appearance on the scene, *Music Survey*, edited by Mr Donald Mitchell and Mr Hans Keller. If history takes the larger share of its space, the critical part, including the usual section devoted to reviews of books, music, and records, is lively. In a leading article on Stravinsky in the current number Mr Charles Stuart lays about him in fine controversial frenzy, which is healthy for aesthetic discussion, but the same sort of treatment applied to reviewing transgresses the generally observed maxim that dog does not eat dog' ('Musical Journals: Some Newcomers', *The Times*, 3 March 1950, p. 7).

73 Keller first involved the Critics' Circle when *The Times* refused to publish the following letter which he sent them on 16 November 1955: 'Sir – Reviewing the Juilliard Quartet's performance of Schoenberg's third string quartet, your music critic suggests (November 16) that "Schoenberg in this quartet is not using a serial technique." In point of fact, the work is written in serial technique from the first note to the last. I submit that your readers ought to be offered a chance to reconsider your music critic's qualifications for his confident pronouncements on Schoenberg's stature as a composer in the light of this basic blunder. What would they say if a writer informed his readers that Beethoven did

One of Keller's most notorious attacks on his fellow critics was 'Schoenberg and the Men of the Press', which *Music Survey* published in March 1951, and there is some evidence at this point that even *Music Survey*'s backers were beginning to get nervous.[74] Among the critics criticized in this article were Frank Howes (of course), Gerald Abraham (who later joined the BBC as music editor of *The Listener* and then Assistant Controller, Music) and Winton Dean. The fact that this last was 'a valued contributor', as Keller put it, to *Music Survey* did not make him immune from criticism. Keller's passion for factual accuracy made him just as rigorous with *Music Survey*'s own contributors, whose work he edited ferociously. Donald Mitchell recalled how Keller's 'idiosyncratic editorial techniques' had changed the journal's character:

> I doubt if I should have arrived on my own account at the editorial style that came to characterize *Music Survey*. Hans, remember, came from another culture and quite another intellectual tradition. His astonishing linguistic ability enabled him to look at English from the outside and perceive potentialities not immediately apparent to those whose mother-tongue English was. It was a linguistic confrontation I found entirely fascinating. Then there were two other rather un-English qualities I believe Hans brought to our editing – discipline and rigour. This meant that everything had to be considered at the deepest level, from the content of a contribution to the distinction between commas Roman and italicized … those were qualities that we tried to make characteristic of the paper as a whole and which we also tried to encourage our contributors to develop in or for themselves. When they were absent, I suppose we tried to write them in.

Keller continued:

---

not use a key in his fifth symphony, and proceeded to criticize the composer's creative faculties out of existence?' Keller refused to see that this letter might have been unnecessarily inflammatory, stating simply that 'if the integrity of criticism is to be upheld in practice, a critic who refuses to acknowledge a basic factual error must be censured' (letter to Matthew Norgate, Hon. General Secretary of the Critics' Circle, 6 December 1955). The following year, he took issue with another of Frank Howes' articles, 'Serial Technique: Why it Attracts Composers' (*The Times*, 16 January 1956); again the paper refused to publish corrections, and Keller again referred the matter to the Critics' Circle. The Circle wrote to *The Times* on 18 April 1956, supporting Keller and requesting corrections – without success. The row dragged on throughout 1956, at the end of which Keller tried to persuade the Circle to take *The Times* to the Press Council. The result of this is not known.

74 Among Keller's papers is a carbon copy of a letter dated 21 October 1950 from Keller to 'Kath and David' [Livingston]: 'As a matter of both artistic and editorial principle it is quite out of the question for me to agree to withdrawing my article on SCHOENBERG AND THE MEN OF THE PRESS. In short, either we go ahead with it or I resign completely from MUSIC SURVEY to which I shall not, in that case, contribute in the future. As I will prove to you when we next meet, there is no personal ill-feeling at all involved on my part; I understand you and you don't understand me and that is all' (CUL Keller Archive).

> Indeed, and joyfully so … We spent immeasurably more time … on editing other people's pieces than on our own writing. In fact, quite often we virtually had to rewrite entire pieces. That was the hardest part of the job, I should think.[75]

Not surprisingly, some of the contributors were less than happy about this. Geoffrey Sharp, for example, was extremely offended to find one of his reviews spattered with editorial inserts marked 'HK',[76] and Ernest Chapman threatened to shoot the editors over their corrective footnotes to their contributors' articles, alongside their tolerance of American usage:

> The next time that I read that a piece of music 'totalizes seventy-two measures' I shall come round to Oakfield School with a loaded revolver, and if I die as well as you it will be well worth while. For pity's sake, what does it mean in PLAIN English? And PLEASE let Editorial footnotes to other people's contributions stop with the present issue. It's a temptation – but it MUST be curbed.[77]

This concern for accuracy and the barrage of detailed information with which Keller backed up his arguments (which had struck Mitchell so forcibly when reading his early reviews) may be due in part to his early experience as a scientific writer in psychological journals. Years later Keller still felt that, as a writer, he was more a scientist than an artist. The distinctive quality of his style of writing English also sprang partly from the self-consciousness of one who has learned the language as an adult, and this, while enabling him to play cleverly and effectively with linguistic conventions, sometimes made his play rather heavy-handed. Although his style loosened in later years, particularly as he sought to avoid unnecessary jargon, his early writings were sometimes felt to be abstruse and rather wordy, and he does seem to have enjoyed linguistic virtuosity for its own sake. Geoffrey Sharp's criticism quoted above of the 'faffs of verbosity' in 'The Musical Character' is a typical example of the way in which Keller's writings were sometimes received by his colleagues in the early 1950s. Keller indignantly refuted any suggestion that he wasted words, replying to Sharp that 'my toughest style … was due to *extreme compression* … What you don't realize is that if you roll five sentences into one the latter is bound to be longer than each of the five would have been.'[78]

---

75 *Music Survey* (1981), preface, n.p.

76 'Salzburg and Bayreuth', *Music Survey*, **4**/2 (February 1952), pp. 426–30. Donald Mitchell wrote to Keller on 24 February 1952, 'I enclose a rude letter from Sharp received this morning … you might care to send him a line in view of the offence he seems to have taken over those editorial inserts.' Sharp's letter is not extant.

77 When this letter was printed in *Music Survey* (**2**/4, p. 282), it appeared duly footnoted by the editors.

78 Letter to Geoffrey Sharp, 5 January 1953. At the beginning of his writing career, however, Keller was more open to criticism of his style, as can be seen, for example, from his response to William McNaught's (editor of *The Musical Times*) rejection of 'Britten and Mozart' because of its 'awkward and often obscure' use of language (letter

Aside from his skills as a writer, his taste for controversy, his endless chronicling of and commenting on all that was new in musical life,[79] and the depth of the musical knowledge from which his writing sprang, it was the arresting and unusual nature of some of the ideas which Keller put forward in his idiosyncratic articles which made him such a potent figure in the 1950s. Some of his insights were the result of his enthusiasm for thinking across conventional genre divisions to produce, for example, an examination of Gershwin's rhythmic character alongside that of Stravinsky,[80] or a demonstration of what Schoenberg's serial techniques owed to Mozart.[81] The latter article is also an example of one of those standard lines of thought which he most often crossed: historical period. In his early character-comparison of Britten and Mozart, Keller had already signalled his intention to 'counteract the current over-emphasis on the historical aspect of music' and throughout his life he continued to alert his readers to the dangers of music history. As well as its irrelevance to musical thought – 'musicians and historians have nothing in common,' he once declared in a radio lecture[82] – he found the very nature of history unnerving: 'As a scientific thinker, I find the discipline of history frighteningly haphazard, an inevitable victim of the personal equation.'[83]

His most original essays of all, however, were those in which he applied his psychoanalytical knowledge to music, even to details of musical structure. For example, observing the 'triple slip' which Mozart makes in his autograph and catalogue listing of the opening of the *Figaro* overture, Keller cites Freud's finding that such a repeated error 'points to heavy unconscious motivation', and suggests that it could represent 'a guilty reaction to, a "denial" of, a belated modulation to the dominant', thus highlighting the 'uniquely unconventional' form of the piece, as well as the thematic significance of the 'slipped' note itself.[84] In the Gershwin and Stravinsky essay cited above, Keller presents a striking picture of Stravinsky's downbeat rhythms 'swimming upstream', as the 'sado-masochistic element

---

from McNaught to Keller, 14 February 1947, CUL Keller Archive). Keller responded, 'My style seems to vary, for some of my stuff is supposed to be well written, according to various editors' comments. I suppose the "obscure" variety links up with (a) my mother tongue being German, (b) the strong influence on my boyhood of German philosophy' (handwritten pencil draft of Keller's response to McNaught: it is not clear whether this letter was ever sent. CUL Keller Archive).

79 Most notably, in this period, in *The Music Review*; in columns like 'First Performances and their Reviews', 'The Half-Year's New Music and the Half-Year's Film Music' (with their tabular assessments) and 'The New in Review'.

80 'Rhythm: Gershwin and Stravinsky', *The Score*, June 1957.

81 'Strict Serial Technique in Classical Music', *Tempo*, September 1955.

82 Mendelssohn's Quartet Op.13', public lecture, with illustrations by the Dartington String Quartet, given in Bath in November 1976, and broadcast on Radio 3 on 14 June 1978.

83 Unpublished review of Martin Cooper (ed.) (1974), *The New Oxford History of Music, Vol. X: The Modern Age: 1890–1960* (CUL Keller Archive).

84 'A Slip of Mozart's: Its Analytic Significance', *Tempo*, Winter 1956–57.

in Stravinsky's creative character' results in 'a state of statically intense tension which, on the deepest level, is achieved through his opposing the flow of rhythm by rhythm itself.' And in a *tour de force* on various aspects of 'Key Characteristics'[85] Keller includes an intriguing speculation about why F minor, Haydn's typically tragic key, so often assumes the character of mock tragedy in Mozart's work:

> Mozart's admiration for Haydn was boundless, reinforced by personal friendship and Haydn's own admiration for him, and untinged – as far as reliable information goes – by hostility. Psychoanalysis has taught us, however, that where there is a father (figure), there is hostility towards him, overt, suppressed, or repressed by great love. Is it too fanciful to assume that the ironisation of F minor was a subtle means whereby Mozart's unconscious allowed itself to discharge its ambivalence, which would have been absolutely intolerable on the conscious level?

When the BBC's first invitation to Keller to give a radio talk finally came at the end of 1955 from Julian Herbage, the editor of the Home Service programme *Music Magazine*,[86] the topic which was chosen – Mozart's musical personality – shows the interest which his psychological writing about music had aroused. In this talk, Keller reveals Mozart's musical personality by contrasting it with a very different one. Rejecting the usual Mozart–Beethoven contrast on the grounds that 'Beethoven soon came to talk a very different language from Mozart's', Keller turned instead to another opposing character who could be compared 'on the basis of a common language and ... of mutual influence': Haydn. After examining their very different treatments of similar thematic material through a series of string quartet examples, Keller concluded that 'Mozart's outstanding and singular character trait ... is his urge and capacity to express and define opposite emotions at one and the same time – a spiritual kind of universality'.

This talk was broadcast on 5 February 1956, as part of the last of three special editions of *Music Magazine* commemorating the bicentenary of Mozart's birth. The anniversary year also saw the publication of a large number of essays on Mozart by Keller, prominent among which were two extended analytical studies: his chapter on 'The Chamber Music' was published in H.C. Robbins Landon and Donald Mitchell's *Mozart Companion* (1956),[87] and 'K. 503: The Unity of Contrasting Themes and Movements' appeared in two parts in *The Music Review*.[88] During the writing

85 *Tempo*, Summer 1956.

86 Julian Herbage was no longer on the permanent staff of the BBC at that time, having left his post as programme planner in 1946. Since then, he had continued working for the Corporation in a freelance capacity, retaining an important role in the planning of the Proms (until Glock's arrival) and continuing to edit *Music Magazine*.

87 Robbins Landon and Mitchell (1956), pp. 90–137.

88 *The Music Review*, February 1956 and May 1956.

of these two pieces, it became clear to Keller that he was moving towards something quite new: ‘The ultimate aim of the present method of analysis is to get at the heart of the music by dispensing with verbal accounts altogether.’ The BBC was to play a crucial role in the realization of this idea, and it was this, as will be seen, which finally brought him into the Corporation as a full-time member of its staff.

Chapter 2

The Birth of Functional Analysis

This chapter is concerned with what has been aptly described as the ideological centre of Keller's work.[1] Whether functional analysis (FA) is in fact his most important contribution to the understanding of music is debatable, as is the significance of his wordless scores as a method of musical analysis. But to Keller himself it was without doubt the core of his enterprise, its wordlessness the symbol of his belief in music's autonomy. On another level, it was also effectively his gateway into broadcasting.

In terms of Keller's radio work, wordless functional analysis was crucial. First, it was conceived specifically for broadcasting, and was an imaginative and exciting use of radio. Second, all the early scores were commissioned by the BBC, and Keller built up a good relationship with the Music Department there, particularly with the Music Talks Producer, Roger Fiske, whose post he assumed when he himself joined the staff. Third, functional analysis elicited significant and early interest from William Glock, who both published and commissioned wordless scores, and who, in his later role as the BBC's Controller of Music, was to be instrumental in bringing Keller on to the staff. Fourth, it was through FA that Keller also established a fruitful relationship with the German radio station, Norddeutscher Rundfunk, for whom he was to broadcast regularly in years to come.

Finally, it can also be said that functional analysis set the seal – even before he joined the Corporation's staff – on Keller's identification with the BBC's Third Programme. Years later, FA still came to many minds as an example of something particularly 'Third Programme-ish' – something esoteric, intellectual, and of extremely limited appeal. That this was far from Keller's intention is beside the point; although he thought that the method would bring musical analysis to a wider, non-music-reading audience, it was never seen by others as something for the ordinary man. In this context it is significant that FA first went on air in 1957: the Third Programme's tenth anniversary celebrations the year before, coupled with the subsequent substantial cuts in its broadcasting hours, meant that its staff were highly conscious of the Third's particular identity and mission, even as they were aware that this mission was increasingly open to question. When the BBC's Head of Music, Maurice Johnstone, picked out the broadcast of FA No. 1 to form the highlight of a 'Third Programme Evening' for broadcast in Germany early in 1958, it was an indication that FA was then considered one

1 See Wintle (1986), p. 352.

of the glories of the Third. The danger of this close identification was that, after the Third's demise, FA might be seen as part of its fatal problem.

Around 1956, Keller produced a number of substantial theoretical articles on Mozart's music.[2] His love for Mozart dated from his childhood, but this group of writings was undoubtedly prompted by the celebrations marking the bicentenary of Mozart's birth. His contribution to *The Mozart Companion* was a commission specifically for the bicentenary; the other pieces sprang either from this work ('Strict Serial Technique in Classical Music' and 'The Unity of Contrasting Themes and Movements'), or from Keller's frustration with other 'appreciations' which Mozart had been offered that year ('The *Entführung*'s "Vaudeville"') – or indeed from both ('A Slip of Mozart's').

Compared with traditional descriptions of the sublimity, balance and perfection of Mozart's music (or 'the accumulation of Taste, of Spiritual and Balanced twaddle' as Keller puts it[3]), Keller's articles are startling, even setting aside his characteristically vigorous style. His demonstrations of Mozart's use of creative disintegration, involving such 'modern' techniques as progressive tonality and serialism, were new and exciting; his use of Freudian method and terminology, although familiar by now, was still provocative to some; and statements like 'Schoenberg was Mozart's unconscious serial pupil'[4] seemed deliberately to court hostility.

The basic concern of these essays is unity: what makes a great work perceptibly an integrated whole, despite thematic, harmonic and structural contrast or disruption? Further, why are these contrasts more striking in great works than in lesser compositions? Taking the model of Freud's analysis of the 'latent' content of a 'manifest' dream, it was Keller's intention to demonstrate the latent unity that lies behind manifest contrasts. Moreover, he also sought to show that the level of diversity was directly proportional to the strength of the unity underlying it. The greater the work, the stronger its unity – and therefore the more exciting its contrasts. As Keller puts it: 'Great music diversifies a unity; mere good music unites diverse elements.'[5] The two articles which Keller himself cites as his first two written functional analyses are the *Mozart Companion* chapter and the K.503 analysis, 'The Unity of Contrasting Themes'. These two pieces, particularly the latter, are dominated by minute thematic analysis, demonstrating how a whole work can be shown to have grown from a single idea. Although the Mozart essays of this period as a whole show clearly that Keller was concerned with

2 'The Chamber Music', in *The Mozart Companion* (1956); 'Strict Serial Technique in Classical Music', *Tempo*, Autumn 1955; 'K.503: The Unity of Contrasting Themes and Movements', *The Music Review*, February 1956 and May 1956; 'The *Entführung*'s "Vaudeville"', *The Music Review*, November 1956; 'A Slip of Mozart's: Its Analytic Significance', *Tempo*, Autumn 1955.

3 'The *Entführung*'s "Vaudeville"', *The Music Review*, November 1956, p. 304.

4 'Strict Serial Technique in Classical Music', *Tempo*, Autumn 1955, p. 24.

5 'The Chamber Music' (1956), p. 91.

questions of unity which were broader than this, it is true that it is thematic unity which is principally demonstrated by functional analysis (to the extent of Keller deeming the internal coherence of a monothematic movement too obvious to require analysis[6]).

This kind of work provoked much comment and criticism. Among the critics, Eric Blom in *The Observer* was particularly negative. As editor of the fifth edition of *Grove's Dictionary of Music and Musicians*, published in 1954, Blom had written there of Keller's work that 'it remains to be seen ... whether he will influence criticism more positively than he has hitherto done by largely destructive methods'. Now that Keller was developing a positive theory of his own, Blom was not inclined to be very merciful. 'If anybody ever succeeds in making me hate Mozart's music, it will be Hans Keller's boast to have done so,'[7] he wrote after the publication of *The Mozart Companion*. Keller, Geoffrey Sharp and the pianist Paul Hamburger all took part in the correspondence which followed this article, and Blom himself wrote two further pieces on the subject. His principal objection was to Keller's finding serialism in Mozart: 'The chapter in *The Mozart Companion* seems to show Mozart as acceptable only where he justifies Schoenberg,'[8] he wrote, adding that he suspected that 'Mr Keller is rapidly approaching a state of mind that will not allow him to see greatness in any music he cannot analyse as being "serial", at any rate in some rudimentary way, and thus pointing forward to and thereby justifying twelve-tone music'.[9] Keller did his best to correct this picture of his work:

> There has been a great deal of commotion about the alleged role which serialism, that *bête noire* of most critics, plays in my analytic approach. Mozart does employ serial devices, and in certain definable circumstances even applies the note-row method very strictly, but the basic principles of latent unity which I have tried to formulate do not contain any reference to serialism nor, of course, do I consider it a criterion of the music's value.[10]

Keller seems to have been rather upset by Blom's criticisms, as it appeared to him that 'everybody who hasn't read my studies keeps talking about Blom'.[11] He was particularly worried that such negative criticism of his recent work might upset his negotiations with the BBC for a functional analysis broadcast.

During his early psychological researches in the 1940s, although he wrote little on music, Keller had developed the idea that musical and conceptual logic were not only different, but diametrically opposed. 'Musical mental

6 See FA No.1 (Mozart's Quartet in D minor, K.421).
7 'The New Approach,' *The Observer*, 8 April 1956, p. 10.
8 Ibid.
9 'Tethered Fancy,' *The Observer*, 15 April 1956, p. 14.
10 Letter to the editor, *The Observer*, 29 April 1956, p. 10.
11 Letter from Keller to Walter Todds, 26 May 1956 (BBC WAC Talks Contributor File: Hans Keller, File 1: 1946–62).

processes,' he thought, 'represent a bewildering picture of psychic phenomena largely isolated from the rest of mental life.'[12] His earliest writings on music – under titles such as 'Manifestations of the Primary Process in Musical Composition' and 'Dream-Work and Development in Sonata Form' – are attempts at linking musical processes with those of the unconscious mind, and thus explaining his Schopenhauerian sense of the singularity of music in Freudian terms.[13] It was not until 1972, however, that he published anything on this subject, when he wrote that 'music is the one art which … has actually rationalised the primary process [of the unconscious] with its displacements, condensations, representations through the opposite'.[14] But this division between musical and conceptual processes, with the consequent difficulties inherent in trying to discuss music in words, was something which he had long felt acutely. In 1951, he described it thus:

> Every honest and musical writer on music knows the paralyzing state of 'having something to say', for whenever we really have something to say about a musical content, we find that we can't say it: unfortunately one cannot express music criticism in terms of music.[15]

It was during the writing of 'The Unity of Contrasting Themes and Movements' for *The Music Review* that Keller realized that there might be a way of doing just that. So, on 28 April 1956, he began what was to be a long correspondence with Dr Roger Fiske, the BBC's Music Talks Producer, proposing a radical new application of his analytical method. Keller's initial letter was as follows:

> XYZ: THE UNITY OF CONTRASTING THEMES
>
> Under this title ('XYZ' stands for the work to be analysed), I propose an hour's broadcast, wordless throughout, which would attempt to analyse a work or movement of your own choice according to my method of analysis as demonstrated in the recent *Mozart Companion* and *The Music Review* for February and May (*K.503: The Unity of Contrasting Themes and Movements*). With a ten minutes' interval in the middle, this experiment would not, I think, prove too exhausting for Third Programme listeners.
>
> At the end of Part I of the last-mentioned study (MR, February '56, p.58), I have pointed out that 'The ultimate aim of the present method of analysis is to get at the heart of the music by dispensing with verbal accounts altogether.' I

12 From the incomplete manuscript of 'Studies in the Psycho-analysis of Music', the first of what Keller had intended to be 'a series of articles' (CUL Keller Archive).

13 This is the subject of his only surviving writings on music from the first half of the 1940s. Unfortunately, these manuscripts survive only in fragmentary form (CUL Keller Archive).

14 'Why This Piece is about *Billy Budd*', *Listener*, 28 September 1972.

15 Review of Schoenberg's *A Survivor from Warsaw*, *Music Survey*, June 1951.

> think I have meanwhile arrived at a stage where such a demonstration would easily be possible.
>
> The best analytic object, probably, would be a very well known classical movement. In the case of an orchestral movement, I should need (a) records and (b) a pianist, preferably Paul Hamburger, who is familiar with my method. In the case of, say, a string quartet, a 'live' body of players would be very welcome: they could do both the exposition of sections, themes etc. and the actual analysing.
>
> Not a word need be spoken, though the announcer may perhaps have to say an introductory word or two; in addition, an introduction in THE LISTENER and/or the RADIO TIMES would be useful, but nowise indispensable. For the rest, the sections played and repeated, the analytic extracts and outlines demonstrated, and the placing and length of pauses between the various 'exhibits' would make the trend of the analysis quite clear. Every problematic or surprising point would be demonstrated twice over, and time would be allowed for the listener to become conscious of his objections which – so far as they could be foreseen – would be taken into account in what one might call the 'modified recapitulation' of the first demonstration.
>
> Like music itself, my method is more easily 'played' than described.[16]

It seems that this letter arrived on Fiske's desk unheralded by any previous discussion. Of course, Keller did know personally several people at the BBC, to whom he may have talked about his ideas (including Walter Todds who worked in the same department as Fiske), but there is no evidence that he did so. He had certainly not sounded out Fiske's opinion, as he appears not to have known that Fiske was then away from the BBC for several months on an extended period of leave. The letter was therefore passed to Walter Todds, who met Keller to discuss it a few weeks later, and was sufficiently impressed with the idea to wish to take it further. Keller, suspecting that the number of people in the BBC who had actually read his recent analytical work would be outnumbered by those who had heard of Eric Blom's reviews of it, sent Todds a copy of a favourable review of his *Mozart Companion* chapter 'in case those who are going to decide on this proposed programme are interested in critical reactions'.[17]

'Those who are going to decide' must have done so favourably, for contract negotiations were in progress by June, and two months later Keller was already being asked by Todds, 'How goes the Unity of Contrasting Themes?'[18] Keller admitted that he had only just started on the project, having had to cope with a few unexpected commissions,[19] but added that a

16 BBC WAC Talks Contributor File: Hans Keller, File 1: 1946–62.

17 Letter from Keller to Walter Todds, 26 May 1956 (BBC WAC ibid.). The review which Keller enclosed was by Andrew Porter (*London Musical Events*, May 1956, p. 29): 'Perhaps the most exciting chapter of all is Hans Keller's on the chamber music …'.

18 Letter from Todds to Keller, 28 August 1956 (BBC WAC ibid.).

19 These included his second talk for the BBC, a review of the thirtieth festival of the International Society for Contemporary Music, which was broadcast on the Third Programme on 19 July 1956. Keller also reviewed the festival for *The Music Review* and *The Musical Times*.

contract for it 'w'd stimulate me into a frenzy of activity'.[20] Unfortunately, agreement on the fee was not reached for several more months, and as late as May 1957 Keller was still feeling that 'the Copyright Dep. do not appreciate the total amount of work involved'.[21] Indeed, he himself may have underestimated it, for although he promised the first five minutes of the score 'as soon as possible' in October,[22] the BBC was still without an initial submission in January 1957, when Roger Fiske returned. This meant that the broadcast could not without difficulty be included in the Third Programme's schedule for the second quarter of 1957, at which Todds had been aiming. Keller was apologetic – 'I hate to be unpunctual'[23] – but agreed to postpone the programme until the third quarter.

The BBC's files do not record any discussion of which work was to be the subject of the analysis, and it is therefore not clear when the decision to choose Mozart's Quartet in D minor, K. 421, was made, nor who made it. However, it is likely that the work was chosen by the BBC, as Keller had invited them to do in his original proposal, since he was particularly keen to stress the universal application of his method: 'I think it is much better if I don't choose the work, in order to preclude any possibility of special pleading on my part. It is, after all, my submission that FA applies equally to all masterpieces, the only condition being that one must understand the work.'[24]

Keller's multifarious commitments continued to delay his start on the analysis, and in the end he could find the time required only when he went on holiday. The first part of the score was therefore written during a three-week skiing trip in February/March 1957. He did not send it on to Fiske for at least a week after his return, until he had had a chance to check it against the authentic edition and 'played every single point to a pupil and/or colleague in order to see whether the demonstration is clear enough'.[25] The final shape of the analysis – very different from the original idea which he had expressed in his 28 April letter – was now evident: the four movements of the quartet would be played, linked by analytical interludes which would demonstrate the unity of the contrasting themes within and between the movements. Keller also proposed a break in the middle, although at this stage he envisaged it as being 'between the andante & the minuet, i.e. before the return to the tonic'.[26] The section of the score which Keller sent in this initial submission is not preserved in the BBC's files, but it would appear from the verbal description which accompanied it[27] that it consisted of the

20 Postcard from Keller to Todds, 2 September 1956 (BBC WAC ibid.).
21 Letter from Keller to Fiske, 30 May 1957 (BBC WAC ibid.).
22 Postcard from Keller to Todds, 17 October 1956 (BBC WAC ibid.).
23 Letter from Keller to Fiske, 19 January 1957 (BBC WAC ibid.).
24 Letter from Keller to Fiske, 5 October 1957 (BBC WAC ibid.).
25 Letter from Keller to Fiske, 30 March 1957 (BBC WAC ibid.).
26 Ibid.
27 Ibid.

first analytical interlude (linking the first two movements), pretty much as it eventually appeared in the published version.

Fiske responded immediately and positively, although

> needless to say, my liking for the part you have so far done doesn't stop me wanting to argue with you on one or two points! For instance, if a classical work is the better for a relationship between its two themes, it must conversely be the worse if no such relationship can be shown. Or has the thing got nothing to do with values? ... Another thought that assails me is that early Haydn symphonies and quartets often use the same theme for the opening subject and the allegedly contrasted one on the dominant. Does this make them better or worse? Does the relationship, to have its maximum musical effect, need to be sub-conscious?[28]

Keller replied to Fiske's questions in considerable detail:

> Unity is a condition, not a criterion of value. The criterion is the widest possible variety on the basis of absolute unity ... A monothematic sonata movement is not, as such, better or worse than a polythematic one. The thematic dimension is not the only one in which variety can be achieved. Much great Haydn is more monothematic than much great Mozart, but it is also, proportionately, more diversified in respect of key schemes and harmonic structures ... Your question about unconsciousness ('sub-consciousness' is not, psychologically speaking, a legitimate term) is far more difficult, the answer far more complex. For one thing, it depends on the character of the composer: much that Mozart could not have achieved consciously, Beethoven could not have achieved unconsciously. But there certainly has to be a minimum of unconsciousness, if only because consciously, you can't think of everything. Also, consciously you tend to overdo unity at the expense of possible variety. Even a great master like Brahms was guilty of over-thematicism in his most exclusively conscious moments, don't you think? The theory of functional analysis is by no means complete, but at the present stage I suspect that a genius's variety is in any case based on a far-reaching repression (and consequent unconsciousness) of the underlying unity, tho' there are considerable individual differences; the background unity may or may not have been conscious to begin with.[29]

It was agreed that such questions could usefully be aired in a *Listener* article to accompany the broadcast. From the start, Keller had felt that such an article would be helpful 'for those who are interested in the wider implications',[30] but he insisted that words were not necessary for listeners to be able to understand the analysis: 'this acoustic analysis ought to be more easily comprehensible than the actual music; if it isn't, I have failed. After all, I'm merely trying to make the implicit explicit.'[31] Perhaps conscious that

---

28 Letter from Fiske to Keller, 2 April 1957 (BBC WAC ibid.).
29 Letter from Keller to Fiske, 11 April 1957 (BBC WAC ibid.).
30 Letter from Keller to Fiske, 30 March 1957 (BBC WAC ibid.)
31 Ibid.

his recent written analyses had been considered 'difficult' – indeed, he himself was later to say that it was their becoming 'unreadable' which had impelled him towards his wordless method[32] – he sought to reassure the BBC that the new experiment had quite a different purpose (and a larger potential audience). Although he had recently analysed the same quartet in *The Mozart Companion*, he attributed different functions to his written and wordless methods: 'there [in *The Mozart Companion*], I tried to solve the most difficult questions, whereas in the present context I want to solve the most important ones.'[33]

Fiske discussed the possibility of a *Listener* article with music editor Gerald Abraham, who responded enthusiastically: 'this sounds a fascinating idea of Keller's'.[34] 'The Musical Analysis of Music' duly appeared the week before the scheduled transmission.[35] Keller's primary purpose here seems to have been to appear accessible: there are repeated reassurances to the reader that 'there is nothing esoteric about functional analysis … the analytic score should in fact be far easier to understand than Mozart's own … I have kept [the score] as short and elementary as possible'. He wrote a longer preview to the broadcast for *The Music Review*[36] dealing with some of the wider issues and making more explicit the links between the broadcast and his earlier verbal analyses, specifically that of K. 503 which had appeared in the same journal the previous year.

Keller completed the rest of the analytical score within a month after sending Fiske the original submission, and the BBC then needed to decide how it was going to be performed. In later analyses, scoring became an important issue to Keller: he described it in 1974 as 'a fundamental part of the analysis'.[37] At this stage, however, he was modest in his expectations of what the BBC could afford in the way of performers, originally suggesting gramophone records and a pianist, while adding wistfully that 'in the case of, say, a string quartet, a "live" body of players would be very welcome'.[38]

32 See 'Problems in Writing about Music', *Times Literary Supplement*, 10 September 1969.

33 Letter from Keller to Fiske, 30 March 1957 (BBC WAC ibid.).

34 Undated postcard from Abraham to Fiske, [June 1957] (BBC WAC ibid.). Abraham later wrote to Keller, telling him 'I look forward with the keenest interest to your programme. I expect you know about Schumann's *deliberate* use of a "controlling" idea for a work – the idea itself never actually appearing' (letter from Abraham to Keller, 13 August 1956, CUL Keller Archive). Keller found it 'interesting that Schumann, who was realistically afraid of going to pieces, was concretely conscious of the unity of his contrasting themes where others weren't' (letter from Keller to Fiske, 13 September 1957, BBC WAC ibid.).

35 *The Listener*, 29 August 1957.

36 'Functional Analysis: Its Pure Application', *The Music Review*, August 1947.

37 Memo from Keller to Robert Layton, 11 October 1974 (CUL Keller Archive). At this time Keller and Layton were proposing the broadcast of a Functional Analysis of Beethoven's Fifth Symphony, which Layton suspected would founder on financial grounds. Interestingly, Keller embarked on a piano quintet version (of which he only wrote a few bars) of his ninth Functional Analysis, of Mozart's A minor piano sonata, K. 310.

38 Letter from Keller to Fiske, 28 April 1956 (BBC WAC ibid.).

The BBC agreed to a live quartet, although initially only scheduled them to play the analytical interludes, with the complete movements of the actual work being provided by a gramophone recording of the Amadeus Quartet. In a letter to Fiske of 11 April, Keller had suggested getting together 'an ensemble of young talents', in which he himself would play the viola, but Fiske explained that 'we should have to use a professional quartet and not an ad hoc group. We could not use you yourself, or the young cellist you mention, unless you went through the rigours of an audition.'[39] Eventually Fiske proposed the Aeolian Quartet and, since they had recently broadcast K. 421, he put to Keller their offer to play the complete work as well as the analysis: 'it's just a matter of your preference between having the same acoustic for your bits and Mozart's or a contrasted acoustic with, possibly, a slightly better performance on the commercial disc. I really don't mind in the least myself which you choose. I think I once told you that I thought a contrast would help the listener but I am less sure of this now; possibly it would be preferable not to have sudden jerks in quality.'[40] Keller agreed: 'I think a complete performance of my programme by the Aeolian Quartet is preferable from every essential point of view and I am delighted to hear that this will be possible.'[41] The recording took place on 26 June 1957 after only one rehearsal, which slightly disconcerted Keller, who had hoped for a more detailed preparation which he would have supervised himself. He attended only the last hour of this one rehearsal, and despite having told Fiske beforehand that 'I certainly don't want to intrude',[42] he subsequently felt that 'the fact that the Aeolian rehearsed, to begin with, without me, did more harm than good'.[43] The final performance was a disappointment to him: 'Not a v.

39 Letter from Fiske to Keller, 23 April 1957 (BBC WAC ibid.). The 'young cellist' was probably Dori Furth, whom Keller was coaching at the time.

40 Letter from Fiske to Keller, 22 May 1957 (BBC WAC ibid.). The earlier letter which Fiske refers to was that written on 4 April 1957, in which he says, 'I am inclined to think that we should not attempt to match up the quality of the complete movements and the quality of the passages played in the studio. In fact, I suspect we should make quite sure that the listener knows immediately when we are switching from one to the other.' In the event, this did prove to be a problem, and the comment in the Audience Research Report on the first analysis that some listeners 'were quite at sea as to where Mozart's music ended and the analysis began' was to be echoed in the reports on most subsequent FA broadcasts. Roger Fiske reported this to Keller on 9 April 1958, after the broadcast of FA No. 2: 'It is quite certain that many people listened without a score and most of these were a bit foxed as to where Beethoven ended and you began, and they found this confusing. I wish we could think of some means of making this clear next time.' Keller's former psychological colleague Margaret Phillips confessed to him that she had had the same problem: 'Knowing the music so little I never knew when I was hearing the original & when the analysis!' (letter from Phillips to Keller, 15 April 1958, CUL Keller Archive).

41 Letter from Keller to Fiske, 27 May 1957 (BBC WAC ibid.).

42 Ibid.

43 Letter from Keller to Fiske, 5 October 1957 (BBC WAC ibid.).

good interpretation of my score, but c'd be worse,' he wrote to Geoffrey Sharp.[44]

The programme was broadcast on the Third Programme at 9.50 pm on Saturday 7 September, 1957. According to the BBC's audience research,[45] it was listened to by 0.2 per cent of the adult population and by 11 per cent of the Third Programme Listening Panel, who awarded it an 'appreciation index' of 69, noticeably higher than the current average for Third Programme chamber music broadcasts:

> By far the larger proportion of the sample audience were very much interested in this broadcast: they thought the idea original and ingenious, even revolutionary. It had many fascinating possibilities, particularly as a form of radio technique ... There were a large number of requests for a repetition of the broadcast and for similar treatment of more familiar and symphonic works, 'to prove the theory' added some. From the minority of the sample who were not particularly enthusiastic ... came a number of suggestions. They asked for ... some verbal signposts, or 'at least a few words for the weaker brethren' ... Several wished they had armed themselves with a score, or that the programme had been timed earlier as they found themselves 'unable to make the necessary effort for sustained concentration' so late in the evening. ... 'This kind of thing needs a highly trained musical ear' was the considered conclusion of one small disappointed group.[46]

For such a new idea, this was a very encouraging report. The majority of listeners were enthusiastic, or at least intrigued, and the minority who were not tended to blame their own musical inadequacies. Keller received a number of fan letters, and professed himself 'very happy about the reactions' to the broadcast and eager 'to utilize the prevailing atmosphere and to satisfy the requests for "more" as soon as possible.'[47] Fiske reported that the BBC had also received 'several nice letters about your broadcast, including one from Robert Donington'[48] and drew Keller's attention to a favourable review by Colin Mason which had appeared in the *Manchester Guardian*.[49] Keller, eager to see what his critical colleagues had made of his experiment, had naturally seen this already and (just as naturally!) found it wanting: 'as unperceptive as it was favourable' he

44 Letter from Keller to Sharp, 30 June 1957 (CUL Keller Archive). This disappointment was not universal. Clifford Curzon thought the performance 'had so many beauties ... that I rather suspected that one H.K. had been doing a bit of coaching!' Letter from Curzon to Keller, 12 December 1957 (CUL Keller Archive).

45 BBC WAC R9/6/69 Audience Research: Programme Reports.

46 Ibid.

47 Letter from Keller to Fiske, 13 September 1957 (BBC WAC Talks Contributor File: Hans Keller, File 1: 1946–62).

48 Letter from Fiske to Keller, 13 September 1957 (BBC WAC ibid.). These letters are no longer extant.

49 'Music Better Than Words for Analysing Music: Experiment in Mozart on the Third', *Manchester Guardian*, 9 September 1957, p. 4.

complained.[50] 'The relations he finds wholly convincing are less close than the ones he doesn't. He always commits the same mistake: where a relation shown consists of a complex of elements, he picks out one element and finds it strange.'[51] Keller was particularly annoyed at Mason's suggestion (with which Fiske was rather taken) that future broadcasts of Functional Analyses should be followed by a critical discussion. 'The thought of a discussion after the playing of a piece of functional analysis horrifies me. Half the success of my method would thus be undone. It is the dream of every contemporary musician to cross the bridge into amateur land. The discussion would chase me back ... What made me so particularly happy about my broadcast was its success with people who normally have no technical musical interests.'[52]

Keller was disappointed to find that Mason's was the only review to appear in the daily newspapers after the broadcast. It was, of course, the summer holiday season, as he had earlier pointed out to Fiske (no doubt to improve the case for a repeat): 'It is only a pity that so many potential appreciators were on holiday.'[53] However, when the second broadcast of FA No. 1 and then FA No. 2 likewise elicited no response from the papers, Keller began to feel that he was being deliberately ignored. He wrote to Donald Mitchell that it was 'interesting, incidentally, the critics' (I mean dailies') complete silence ab't FA No. 1 and (so far as I know) No. 2, except for Colin, whose notice was at least semi-psychological anyway. Not that I'm complaining (heaven help me when they do start on it), but considering the effect the method has had, my colleagues' form of revenge seems primitive, even for them.'[54]

Keller's two previewing articles in *The Listener* and *The Music Review* both elicited contributions to their respective correspondence columns. These letters all tended to be critical, and Keller was frustrated that none of their authors seemed to have heard the broadcast.[55] He was not disheartened, however, recalling later that, apart from the Incorporated Society of Musicians conference response the following December (of which more below), these letters represented almost the only negative reactions to his first wordless score.[56] Indeed, there was much to encourage him. The BBC

50 Letter from Keller to Fiske, 13 September 1957 (BBC WAC ibid.).

51 Letter from Keller to Fiske, 17 September 1957 (BBC WAC ibid.). Colin Mason later wrote a Functional Analysis of his own, on one of the Bartók quartets, which the BBC at one time considered for broadcast (according to a letter from Fiske to Keller dated 14 October 1958).

52 Letter from Keller to Fiske, 17 September 1957 (BBC WAC ibid.).

53 Letter from Keller to Fiske, 13 September 1957 (BBC WAC ibid.).

54 Letter from Keller to Mitchell, 7 March 1958 (CUL Keller Archive). Keller had probably been expecting some comment from Eric Blom in particular.

55 One correspondent to *The Listener* wrote in again to say that he had heard the broadcast and had based his comments as much on that as on the article; a fact which was not obvious from his original letter.

56 See 'Wordless Functional Analysis: The First Year', *The Music Review*, August 1958.

repeated the broadcast on 11 December the same year, and then selected it to be broadcast again as part of a showcase 'Third Programme Evening' being put out by Norddeutscher Rundfunk in Hamburg.[57] William Glock published the score of the analysis in his journal *The Score*[58] and invited Keller to write one or two new analyses for the Dartington Summer School of Music.[59] Walter Legge wrote to Keller in October to suggest producing FA gramophone records,[60] and Universal Edition appeared 'very interested' in publishing scores.[61] Also, Denis Brearley, the General Secretary of the Incorporated Society of Musicians, invited the Aeolian Quartet to perform the Mozart analysis again on 31 December at the Society's sixtieth annual conference in Stratford-upon-Avon. Brearley was enthusiastic about functional analysis and wrote to Keller shortly after hearing the first broadcast to ask for permission to have the analysis played at the conference: 'I ... am sure that it would be of the greatest interest to our members.'[62] Unfortunately, this optimism proved unfounded, and the analysis was greeted with 'considerable and heated opposition', as Keller later wrote in *The Music Review*.[63] 'Mr Keller certainly put the cat among the pigeons', agreed Ernest Bradbury in his conference report, 'but he, as readers know, is an able controversialist, well able to look after himself'.[64]

Bradbury's report doesn't give details of any specific criticisms, but if the negative reaction of the conference was anything like those of the *Listener* and *Music Review* correspondents, it consisted more of resistance to the basic idea of functional analysis than any engagement with this particular score. This lack of specific comment enabled Keller to dismiss some of his critics as neurotic: 'what amounted to a wave of anxiety was all they could produce by way of reaction to the mere idea of wordlessness.'[65] On the other hand, although he rejected all Mason's suggestions, there is evidence that Keller was keen to receive comments on specific details of his score. One criticism which he did accept (made by both Fiske and Oliver Neighbour) was that the transition to the slow movement was not

57 Indeed, Keller was apparently told by the Head of Music at NDR that the BBC's Head of Music, Maurice Johnstone, had considered the functional analysis to be the 'pièce de résistance' of the whole evening (as Keller told Fiske in a letter of 24 January 1958, CUL Keller Archive).

58 *The Score*, 22 (February 1958), pp. 56–64.

59 See below, p. 48.

60 Letter from Legge (Columbia Records) to Keller, 4 October 1957 (CUL Keller Archive).

61 Keller mentioned this to Fiske in a letter of 18 December 1957 (BBC WAC ibid.). He told Fiske that he was 'dawdling' as he felt that 'time is on my side' and he wanted a publisher 'to show the intensest interest if he wants it now'.

62 Letter from Brearley to Keller, 7 October 1957 (CUL Keller Archive).

63 'Wordless Functional Analysis: the First Year', *The Music Review*, August 1958.

64 *Musical Times*, March 1958, p. 144.

65 'Wordless Functional Analysis: the First Year', *The Music Review*, August 1958.

clear.[66] Keller complained that this passage had been 'incomprehensibly played' by the Aeolians,[67] but he did concede that it was probably too compressed anyway and, in the published version of the score, signalled his intention to revise that passage and 'insert an "ossia"'.[68] The 'ossia' idea may have come from a comment of Oliver Neighbour's, who thought that the different speeds at which individual listeners could follow the analysis posed a fundamental problem for FA: 'The advantages of sound over a written analysis are great, but they are only felt if the analyst judges the cottoning-on speed of his audience correctly. Now it happened that, as well as being in step with you, I was both slower and faster than the presentation on different occasions ... In reading an article, of course, you stop as long as you like where you are puzzled or disagree, and can skim the bits that are obvious to you.'[69]

All in all, the reaction to their first foray into wordlessness satisfied the BBC that the experiment was worth continuing, and Roger Fiske told Keller that he was willing to record the next analysis 'any time you have a score ready'.[70] In fact, Keller had been thinking about FA No. 2 for some time, and he had already sent a new idea to Fiske before the broadcast of FA No. 1. At that stage, the BBC naturally wanted to wait and see how the first analysis was received, especially as Keller's new thoughts appeared to have taken a radical turn: 'With undue haste (in view of this year's 20th anniversary of Gershwin's death), I suggest a very different application of functional analysis, this time to The Melodic and Rhythmic Style of George Gershwin.'[71] After quoting an episode from David Ewen's biography *A Journey to Greatness*, in which the ten-year-old Gershwin first hears Dvorák's *Humoresque*, Keller went on to explain his proposed programme: 'After a very brief introduction quoting from this passage, *Humoresque* would be played, whereupon my score would [examine] rhythmic and melodic influence, including the diatonic assimilation of the tonal

---

66 Letter from Neighbour to Keller, 8 September 1957 (CUL Keller Archive); Fiske's comment was presumably oral: Keller refers to it in his letter to him of 17 September. Keller was not very receptive to all of Neighbour's comments, however, telling him that 'the flight of the grumble-bee has taken place in an unsealed envelope without the aggression dropping out' (letter from Keller to Neighbour, 11 September 1957, CUL Keller Archive).

67 Keller to Fiske, 17 September 1957; Keller to Neighbour, 11 September 1957.

68 'Wordless Functional Analysis No. 1', *The Score*, February 1958. In Keller's introduction to the score here, he makes it clear that 'it is not, however, the final version'. Apart from the 'ossia' mentioned above, 'the full version I have had in mind from the outset contains two further analytic developments'. This full version never appeared, and Keller later seems to have regretted that this first version of FA No.1 remained the only example of his wordless analysis available in print for the next 25 years, as he regarded it as 'frankly, rather primitive' (letter to Mrs C.L. van den Berg, Musicology Department, University of South Africa, 14 April 1984, CUL Keller Archive).

69 Letter from Neighbour to Keller, 8 September 1957 (CUL Keller Archive).

70 Letter from Fiske to Keller, 25 September 1957 (BBC WAC ibid.).

71 Letter from Keller to Fiske, 2 July 1957 (BBC WAC ibid.).

penta-scale. I sh'd not confine myself to Gershwin's "serious" works, but sh'd devote much attention to the masterpieces that are his songs for various musicals.'

Keller probably first came across Gershwin's music through his film-music reviewing and in recent months had been involved in a detailed study of it, publishing his first major article on the subject in June 1957.[72] Although this article is primarily concerned with rhythm, Keller does also discuss the melodic influence of the *Humoresque*, in similar terms to his letter to Fiske: 'The unobtrusively pentatonic opening of the Dvorák with its subsequent diatonic assimilation, and the momentarily flattened third followed by the cadentially gapped seventh, are an unmistakable basis for Gershwin's melodic style with its subtle interplay of a more or less hidden tonal penta-scale … of hexachords and "blue" notes on the one hand, and diatonic implications, rejoinders, and contradictions on the other.'[73] Since April, Keller had also been in correspondence with other sections of the BBC's Music Department about a possible programme of Gershwin's popular songs.[74] This idea initially aroused interest at the BBC, and for a short while it looked as though both Gershwin projects might go ahead. Keller felt that they would complement each other, but he could see that the BBC might consider it 'too much of a good thing'; if this were the case, he told Fiske, 'I should – needless to say – immediately drop the recital idea in favour of FA'.[75]

LEEDS METROPOLITAN UNIVERSITY LIBRARY

In the end, neither project materialized (although the idea of a functional analysis of Gershwin's songs did bear fruit many years later in a programme which Keller made with Lionel Salter for the European Broadcasting Union in 1969).[76] It appears that Horace Dann, the BBC producer with whom Keller had been discussing the proposed recital, privately lacked any enthusiasm for it.[77] After trying unsuccessfully to persuade Keller to convert it into an

72 This essay takes most of its examples from film versions of the musicals: 'Rhythm: Gershwin and Stravinsky', *The Score*, June 1957.

73 Ibid.

74 Keller initially wrote to Richard Howgill, Controller, Music, on 27 April 1957, and the minutes of the Music Department meeting held on 29 April record Howgill reading the letter to the meeting, and his colleagues being 'interested in the proposal'. Horace Dann was asked to investigate further with Keller (BBC WAC R27/779/1 Mus. Gen. Music Department Meetings File 2, 1955–62).

75 Letter from Keller to Fiske, 5 October 1957 (BBC WAC Talks Contributor File: Hans Keller, File 1: 1946–62).

76 Described by Keller as a 'utilitarian variation' of functional analysis, the programme consisted of a concert of Gershwin's stage songs, 'linked, not by words, but by momentary interludes, musical phrases which would throw common structural and stylistic characteristics into relief' ('Gershwin's Songs on the Third', *Listener*, 25 December 1969). The concert was broadcast on Radio 3 on 29 December 1969.

77 After discussing the idea with Keller for months, he revealed to one of his colleagues his own opinion of Gershwin: 'The lyrics being the drivelling doggerel they are and the accompaniments being as commercial as the Anglo-American alliance in Charing Cross Road can be, I suggest that Hans Keller's idea is not a Music Division Programmes exercise at all' (internal memorandum from Horace Dann to the Head of Music

illustrated talk, which he considered 'the only form of presentation,'[78] he dropped the project. Meanwhile, Keller himself began to have doubts about his proposed functional analysis of Gershwin when he read the reactions to FA No. 1:

> I am no longer sure whether this entirely different application of functional analysis ought to be the *next* step: I am struck by the fact that various people are asking for a functional analysis of a Beethoven quartet, and you yourself, too, mentioned this possibility after the recording of the Mozart. In a word, if everybody wants structural unity in Beethoven, I don't, for the moment, want to do stylistic unity in Gershwin. What do you think? I'm in two minds about it, all the more so since I am burning to demonstrate the potential range of functional analysis (see my *Listener* piece), which again drives me towards the Gershwin idea.[79]

Perhaps not unexpectedly, Fiske replied that he and his colleagues were 'inclined to think that it would be best to establish your methods with a programme about, say, a Beethoven Quartet, before going on to something rather off the beaten track like Gershwin'.[80] Accordingly, and having once again evaded Fiske's invitation to choose the work to be analysed, Keller started work on Fiske's suggestion of Beethoven's Quartet in F minor, Op. 95.

This time, work proceeded quickly and, despite the fact that the analytical interludes were well over twice as long as those of the Mozart, the score was completed and the parts copied in a little over three months. Keller considered Op. 95 'an excellent choice' as a subject for analysis, as 'the contrasts are violent; the work is incredibly short. I thus had the chance to write a far longer, far more complex analysis within about the same total playing time as that needed for the Mozart.'[81] This is not to say, however, that he considered Mozart's structural unity to be simpler to uncover than Beethoven's. Commenting on the requests that had come from listeners for a functional analysis of Beethoven, he wrote, 'The impression seems to have been that Beethoven would prove a harder nut for FA than Mozart. The truth is, of course, exactly the reverse: Beethoven's thematic background unities are usually nearer the foreground than Mozart's, because his conscious intentions were more thematic anyway. But his contrasts often happen within a far narrower space than Mozart's: perhaps this is the reason why people

---

Programmes (Sound), 1 November 1957, BBC WAC Talks Contributor File: Hans Keller, File 1: 1946–62). This memorandum also reveals that Keller had wanted to invite Peter Pears and Benjamin Britten to perform the songs; Mr Dann considered that the project raised too many difficulties 'even on the shattering hypothesis of an acceptance from this exclusive duo'.

78 Ibid.

79 Letter from Keller to Fiske, 13 September 1957 (BBC WAC ibid.).

80 Letter from Fiske to Keller, 25 September 1957 (BBC WAC ibid.).

81 'Wordless Functional Analysis: the First Year', *The Music Review*, August 1958.

think that they are, as such, greater.'[82] The structure of the Op. 95 analysis is broadly similar to that of the Mozart – analytic interludes between the four movements of the quartet, with a three-minute silence in the middle – but there are two major differences: the polythematic finale meant that an analytic postlude was required, and Keller also placed his silent interval earlier in the total structure. During the composition of FA No. 1, his first instinct had been to have the interval between the middle movements; but in the event, he put it between the minuet and its analysis, resuming afterwards with a recapitulation of the minuet's theme. In the Beethoven analysis, despite the middle movements being linked, Keller did place the interval between them, by means of an analytic postlude to the second movement and a prelude to the third. The latter, in incorporating Beethoven's original transition, preserved the link between the movements, while the former provided a parallel to the postlude which followed the finale.

The recording of FA No. 2 took place on 12 February 1958, this time with the Pro Musica Quartet. They had been recommended to Keller by the publisher and concert agent Howard Hartog, who described them as 'young, enthusiastic, and very willing to be directed'.[83] Keller was very happy with their performance, commenting to Fiske that he would be 'delighted to have the Pro Musica again'[84] in any future quartet FA, despite the fact that they appeared to share the Aeolians' reluctance to rehearse:

> The Pro Musica are ten times better than the Aeolian; the only problems seem to be (a) that they don't know the work well and (b) that they have no time to rehearse. So far I only had one rehearsal (which they wanted to be the only one!), and even then there was no time to hear their version of the work itself: in fact I shan't hear it until the recording. I got another $1^1/_2$ hours out of them … [and] they seem to be very quick on the uptake. But they are very hard-boiled, despite their age, and if we can extend the rehearsal a little on Thurs morning I don't think it will do them any harm.[85]

The programme was broadcast on the Third Programme on 2 March 1958. Again, reaction to it was broadly favourable, although there is a slight but noticeable dip in the enthusiasm of the BBC's audience research report. Only 6 per cent of the Third Programme Listening Panel (and 0.1 per cent of the population at large) heard the broadcast, and the 'appreciation index' awarded was 63, around the average for Third Programme chamber music broadcasts at that time. Although there were still a good many very happy

---

82 Ibid.

83 Letter from Keller to Fiske, 10 October 1957 (BBC WAC ibid.).

84 Letter from Keller to Fiske, 15 March 1958 (BBC WAC ibid.).

85 Letter from Keller to Fiske, 10 February 1957 (BBC WAC ibid.). In print, Keller described the Pro Musica as 'a delightfully inexperienced body' ('Wordless Functional Analysis: the First Year', *The Music Review*, August 1958).

listeners – 'A heaven-sent opportunity to hear and re-hear, analyse and compare!' was one comment[86] – that section of the audience which had had a 'somewhat diminished enjoyment' (in the BBC's words) was larger. This report also shows the appearance of a small rump of completely negative reactions, with comments such as 'so much twaddle' or 'to hell with functional analysis!'.

It is, of course, perfectly possible to explain this more muted report as the inevitable loss of the initial goodwill that any new project attracts; and in any case, reports of future analyses were to show higher scores and larger audiences. Moreover, the fact that the Beethoven quartet itself appeared to be less well-known than the Mozart probably narrowed the appeal. Roger Fiske was quite happy with the report, concluding that 'there is no doubt that it was a success,'[87] and the responses which came from other sources were very good. 'At my end,' Keller told Fiske, 'reactions to FA No. 2 have again been very gratifying. Best of all, Liebermann wants to do it separately in Hamburg.'[88]

Rolf Liebermann, Head of Music at Hamburg's Norddeutscher Rundfunk, had shown a deep interest in functional analysis right from the beginning, and had written to Keller about it as early as October 1957, although at that stage he had not had an opportunity either to hear FA No. 1 or to see the score. Not without some difficulty, Keller managed to get a BBC tape of the broadcast sent to NDR, to which Liebermann reacted with great enthusiasm.[89] Keller's relationship with NDR underwent a slight hiccup, however, when he found out in December that the BBC tape of the Aeolians' original performance of FA No. 1 was to be broadcast in Hamburg as part of NDR's 'Third Programme Evening'. To judge by his letter to Keller of 18 December, Roger Fiske (who knew that Keller was in correspondence with NDR) seems to have thought that Keller knew all about this arrangement; perhaps Liebermann, in a similar way, assumed that the BBC would have told him. Keller felt he was being presented with a fait accompli. 'Things have been happening very much over my head, and I am unhappy,' he told Fiske. 'Please help. You say "I know" that Hamburg will be broadcasting my FA No. 1, but in fact your letter is the first thing I hear about it. From the outset, I told Liebermann that if they wanted [FA], I wanted a new performance.'[90]

When he had calmed down, Keller decided that a rebroadcast of the BBC

---

86 BBC WAC R9/6/69 Audience Research: Programme Reports.

87 Letter from Keller to Fiske, 9 April 1958 (BBC WAC Talks Contributor File: Hans Keller, File 1: 1946–62).

88 Letter from Keller to Fiske, 15 March 1958 (BBC WAC ibid.).

89 Keller seems to have found this rather surprising, in view of his own negative reviews of Liebermann's music (of which, with characteristic bluntness, he reminded Liebermann at the outset of their correspondence about FA; see 'Wordless Functional Analysis: The First Year', *The Music Review*, August 1958).

90 Letter from Keller to Fiske, 19 December 1957 (BBC WAC ibid.).

tape (despite its unsatisfactory performance and the negligible repeat fee he was offered) was better than no German broadcast at all. This was fortunate, as the programme was very well received in Hamburg and proved to be the start of a long and fruitful relationship with NDR. Shortly after FA No. 2 had appeared on the Third Programme, it too was taken up by NDR, and this time Liebermann invited Keller to Hamburg to supervise rehearsals for a new performance in May. Keller considered this 'rather ironical, considering that this time I shouldn't have had any objection to our tape being used,'[91] but he certainly appreciated the lavish resources which the German station appeared to have. A handsome fee, plus two whole days of supervised rehearsals with a distinguished quartet (the Hamann Quartet) provided a striking comparison with conditions at the BBC, and Keller lost no time in pointing it out to Fiske. Two months later, Liebermann completed his halo as an enlightened patron by commissioning a series of three new functional analyses of Haydn quartets for the 150th anniversary of Haydn's death.[92] 'Liebermann is a man of the very rarest calibre,' wrote Keller, gratefully. 'His plans for my future FAs on NDR are more ambitious than mine were.'[93]

Interest in functional analysis was meanwhile spreading in the musical press. By the time of the NDR recording in May, *The Musical Times*, *The Music Review*, *Musical Opinion*, *London Musical Events*, the *Schweizer Musikzeitung* and the *Basler Nachrichten*[94] had all commissioned articles on the subject from Keller (although some of these may have required a little prompting, to judge by a letter which Keller received from the editor of *Musical Opinion*: 'Dear Keller, Thanks for your card. I have not the foggiest notion what 'wordless functional analysis' is.').[95] Indeed, Keller was most industrious when it came to publicizing his new method, offering articles to all his regular journals, responding quickly to all commissions and correspondents, and generally fanning the flames of any interest he could find. Having already presented his theories once in *The Music Review*, he

---

91 Letter from Keller to Fiske, 15 March 1958 (BBC WAC ibid.).

92 The three Haydn quartets which Keller analysed for NDR were Op. 50 No. 5, Op. 20 No. 1 and Op. 76 No. 2. They were all recorded and broadcast in Hamburg in January 1959.

93 'Wordless Functional Analysis: The First Year', *The Music Review*, August 1958. However, even NDR was not perfect: later in the article Keller criticizes their sound engineers who allowed some of his textural points to be 'totally submerged by the flood of beautiful sound. One of the engineers seemed terribly offended when I suggested, in the course of the recording, that the sound was awful and had little to do with musical reality; and I didn't have the heart to pursue the matter further because he seemed so proud of the celestial blend he produced.'

94 'The Home-Coming of Musical Analysis', *The Musical Times*, December 1958; 'Wordless Functional Analysis: The First Year', *The Music Review*, August 1958; 'Functional Analysis', *Musical Opinion*, December 1958; 'Wordless Analysis', *London Musical Events*, December 1957; 'Funkionsanalyse – eine neue Analyse der Musik', *Basler Nachrichten*, 29 June 1958.

95 Letter dated 16 April 1958 (CUL Keller Archive).

used his new article there to present a complete history of the development and reception of functional analysis so far. He also encouraged his friends and pupils to write their own analytical scores – a point he emphasized to Fiske after the latter had suggested that Keller might be worried about 'competition' from other analysts:

> I rang 999 when I saw that you envisaged the possibility of my thinking in terms of 'competition' to which I wd have to 'resign myself'. They told me to try MUS 1633 instead. Competition indeed! Two of my students are at this moment writing FA's. Are they 'competing'? Is there such a thing in art or truth-finding? Waiter, get me an ambulance. I asked Robbie Landon whether he'd like to try an FA. He said he wd, but wanted to hear or see 10 of mine first. Am I now trembling because my FA's are adding up & No.10 will soon be reached, whence I shall have to face 'competition'? It's the bad ones I fear (but shan't resign myself to), not the good ones! I'm neither business man nor politician. Waiter, send that ambulance back, I feel better … I shall … forgive you the misinterpretation of my psyche in my dying hour. I trust you will compose an FA on my collected FA's, to be played at my funeral – by way of final competition.[96]

Keller may not have worried about competition, but he was concerned about how his method was perceived. He kept a close eye on the press and was often publicly critical of what was said about his analyses. Although the daily newspapers remained silent so far as reviews of functional analyses were concerned, a few articles on the subject by others did follow Colin Mason's. These ranged from Philip Barford's seven-page discussion in *The Monthly Musical Record* to a light column in *Time* magazine.[97] While Barford's article was merely 'bad but interesting (symptomatic),'[98] according to Keller, the *Time* piece was 'ridiculous … full of distortions, simple untruths, and misquotations'.[99] Nevertheless, the experience of being in the popular press ('Vienna-born Critic Keller, 38, a violinist and teacher, wrote verbal criticism exclusively for years before he decided that words failed him') was not without its enjoyable side, to judge by the number of times Keller referred to it: 'This afternoon a "Time" man is coming round to interview me ab't FA; they're doing a feature about it!' he told William Glock. 'Sounds nice as long as one doesn't read it.'[100] Afterwards he described the afternoon to Margaret Phillips: 'Those TIME people

96 Letter from Keller to Fiske, 18 October 1958 (BBC WAC ibid.). Keller also made efforts to get Geoffrey Sharp to publish his Swiss pupil Hansjorg Pauli's FA of Wolf's *Serenade* in the *Music Review*.

97 Barford (1958); 'Twilight of Twaddle', *Time*, 17 February 1958, p. 42–3. Keller commented on both in 'Wordless Functional Analysis: The First Year', *The Music Review*, August 1958.

98 Letter from Keller to Phillips, 12 April 1958 (CUL Keller Archive). It is not difficult to see why Keller disliked this article, which, although enthusiastic, misunderstands his ideas. Its swipes at Schoenberg must also have irritated him.

99 Ibid.

100 Letter from Keller to Glock, 9 January 1958 (CUL Keller Archive).

interviewed me for about 6 hours and took dozens of photographs.'[101] Unfortunately, despite all *Time*'s efforts, Keller liked the result as little as he had anticipated: 'The *Time* article is out and, needless to say, awful,' he wrote to Roger Fiske.[102]

The question of FA No. 3 was now in discussion between Keller and Fiske. At first, rather than branching out in another direction – Gershwin or otherwise – the most likely candidate was another quartet, this time by Haydn. The BBC gave some consideration to the possibility of relaying an analysis commissioned elsewhere, since as well as the three Haydn scores for Hamburg, an analysis of the *Lark* quartet (Op. 64 No. 5) was scheduled to be performed at the 1958 Dartington Summer School. This had been the subject of protracted discussion between Keller and Glock, as well as some misunderstandings about whether the BBC would be involved, who would commission the score and pay for the copying of the parts, and whether the performance would be given by a professional or student quartet. Eventually, the score was commissioned and copied by the BBC, and the performance at the summer school was given by the newly-formed Dartington Quartet (composed, at Glock's request, of the summer school string teachers, who were all ex-members of the Philharmonia Orchestra). The BBC did not record this performance, but instead invited the quartet and Keller to record in the studio in London a few days later. The recording was postponed, however, when Fiske realized that the Dartington Quartet, having never previously broadcast together, would have to audition. The quartet took an unconscionable time to organize their audition, and so the *Lark* FA did not reach the airwaves for another two years.

FA No. 3, meanwhile, was not to be a quartet after all. Keller and Fiske had both been thinking about the possibility of an orchestral work: 'The remark you dropped the other day ab't "trying my hand at a symphony some time" struck me very forcibly,' wrote Keller to Fiske,[103] who replied that the BBC had 'discussed another FA yesterday and there was a strong feeling that it would be very interesting to do a Mozart concerto. There was also a strong feeling that we should try to scrape up the money to have Curzon if he's interested. Would you like me to sound him on the subject of K. 503?'[104] Keller was delighted. Clifford Curzon, as well as being a musician whom he much respected, had written to him in glowing terms after hearing the first analysis:

> The broadcast was deeply impressive – though perhaps 'moving' is the nearer word. I felt I was participating in some strange creative act – a beautiful and somewhat terrifying experience … The wordlessness I found strangely exciting – especially at the conclusion of the first movement as it began to break up. I was,

101 Letter from Keller to Phillips, 12 April 1958 (CUL Keller Archive).
102 Letter from Keller to Fiske, 15 February 1958 (BBC WAC ibid.).
103 Letter from Keller to Fiske, 4 February 1958 (BBC WAC ibid.).
104 Letter from Fiske to Keller, 30 March 1958 (BBC WAC ibid.).

of course, a little prepared, as I had read two or three times your brilliant and stimulating analyses in the Mozart Companion; but I did wonder just how difficult – or easy – others not so fortunately initiated would have found it to follow without extra-musical help. On the other hand the very absence of the spoken word seemed in some curious way to create its own necessary knowledge as the analysis moved along a new level of experience. (Shockingly unclearly put, I'm afraid!) It was altogether a wonderful pioneer achievement for which we should all be grateful.[105]

Nevertheless, Curzon turned K. 503 down. The work was not in his repertoire and, in any case, he was planning a sabbatical for 1958 and did not want to accept any more engagements. But he did stress how much he appreciated the invitation: 'I should like greatly to associate myself with this valuable pioneer work – work with which I feel a close sympathy ... I do hope you will consider this just a postponement.'[106] Keller therefore suggested to Fiske that 'next year we invite him to take part in an FA of a work of his own choice'.[107]

K. 503 went ahead with Denis Matthews as pianist (with the Goldsbrough Orchestra, conducted by Charles Mackerras) and was broadcast on the Third Programme on 7 December 1958. In the run-up to this broadcast, Fiske considered further some of the suggestions from listeners which had emerged in the BBC's audience research. Apart from the perennial problem of listeners being unable to distinguish between the original work and the analytical interludes (Fiske found no answer to that one), he discussed with colleagues and with Keller the possibility of performing the original work complete, either before or after the analysis. Keller himself had earlier suggested a performance of the original work before the analysis, to help listeners who were not very familiar with it.[108] However, the consensus of opinion at the BBC, wrote Fiske, 'was that as your analyses start with the first movement complete, and indeed as each movement is played complete before it is analysed, it might be worth thinking about repeating K. 503 *after* your part of the broadcast, so that people could hear it uninterrupted in the light of the analysis.'[109] Keller agreed 'enthusiastically'.[110]

K. 503 was, of course, the work which Keller had analysed in great detail in his two-part *Music Review* analysis, 'The Unity of Contrasting Themes

105 Letter from Curzon to Keller, 12 December 1957 (CUL Keller Archive).
106 Letter from Curzon to Fiske, 2 April 1958 (CUL Keller Archive).
107 Letter from Keller to Fiske, 11 April 1958 (BBC WAC ibid.).
108 Keller made this suggestion in relation to the possibility of a Haydn analysis (Letter to Fiske, 15 March 1958, BBC WAC ibid.), because Haydn's music was at that time less well known to radio listeners than that of Mozart or Beethoven. Indeed, it was one of William Glock's conspicuous achievements as Controller in the 1960s that he vigorously and successfully promoted Haydn.
109 Letter from Fiske to Keller, 9 April 1958 (BBC WAC ibid.).
110 Letter from Keller to Fiske, 11 April 1958 BBC WAC ibid.).

and Movements',[111] and the score of FA No. 3 does show several points of similarity with the earlier essay. Having analysed the work recently in detail may have given Keller the confidence to experiment further, for Roger Fiske noticed that Keller's technique had developed rather differently this time, resulting in a more continuous analytic score. Keller (wrongly) took his comments to be criticisms and hastened to explain:

> I would draw your attention to the advantages of what one might call a structural analytic build-up; for instance, in the old primitive style, it would have been impossible to arrive at a stage in the course of the analysis where you could combine the 4 basic contrasts of a movement within a continuous and valid musical structure of about 10 bars, without adding a note of your own. This is what happens between bars 210 & 220: the focal point of the analysis' 1st part. Of course it's 10 times easier to write an analysis in the old style. But the continuity which you then sacrifice (if you can otherwise achieve it) is actually part of the background unity you want to show.[112]

Fiske had also found the experience of working on FA with a conductor much easier and less time-consuming than working with the quartets. Keller leapt to the quartets' defence: 'FA no.3 is incomparably easier to play than the 4tet scores. For one thing, with my eye on the clock, I suppressed all but the most basic points, so the comparison is not really fair at all on the 4tet players ... For another thing, string quartet phrasing is in itself far more difficult and inevitably more differentiated than orchestral phrasing ... In sum, I should say the opposite was true – *other things being equal*, orchestra cum conductor is the more difficult and time-robbing proposition.'[113] 'I suspect,' wrote Fiske in reply, 'that in an amiable way you prefer disagreement to agreement.'[114]

There were further amiable disagreements over FA No. 3. In November, Keller took issue with the BBC's publicity sheet for the broadcast, which he complained was 'totally inaccurate' and would 'do immeasurable harm to my method'.[115] Apart from its unscientific title ('Subconscious Mozart'), it suggested that the musical contrasts which Keller examined were only 'apparent', it described the analytic score as 'excerpts', and said that Keller had chosen to analyse that particular concerto because 'it best illustrates his theory'. The offending sheet had not been written by Fiske, of course – indeed he had not even seen it – but Keller did not know who else to contact. After this debacle, Keller also pointed out one or two minor points about the *Radio Times* billing, which he wished to have corrected by the programme's announcer. He pleaded that he was not just being pedantic, but realized that

111 *The Music Review*, February 1956 and May 1956.
112 Letter from Keller to Fiske, 22 November 1958 (BBC WAC ibid.).
113 Ibid.
114 Letter from Fiske to Keller, 24 November 1958 (BBC WAC ibid.).
115 Letter from Keller to Fiske, 28 November 1958 (BBC WAC ibid.).

he might be trying Fiske's patience – his letter to Fiske of 4 December contains a large blank space in the middle, and a parody of the FA interval announcement:

> A THREE-MINUTE SILENT INTERVAL IS INSERTED HERE FOR THE RECREATION OF THE ADDRESSEE, WITH OPTIONAL PRAYER THAT HE SHOULDN'T CONSIDER ME A TIRESOME BORE.

Fiske had only just sorted out these problems, when Keller raised another:

> Dear Roger,
>
> I always find myself writing rude letters to you which have nothing to do with you. However, there it is; I hope you enjoy them.
>
> What is it this time? I have now concluded my own listener research. While the reactions of those who listened to FA No.3 on VHF have made me very happy, the reactions of all the others have made me very unhappy: they couldn't hear a thing, or hardly a thing, for there was enormous interference.[116]

The Daventry transmitter had developed a fault on the night that FA No. 3 went out, affecting Keller's broadcast and all the programmes which followed. Keller felt that this made a clear case for a repeat: 'If the BBC had a heart, it would consider a repeat an absolute must. I shall let you know in good time if I decide to take this to the House of Lords. If so, I shall conduct my own case, and shall claim £9,753/15/11d. damages, so p'hps we can settle the matter out of court.'[117] Fiske promised to mention his point to the programme planners, but doubted whether it would be considered sufficient grounds for putting the programme out again: 'we would have to repeat the whole evening if it were.'[118] Keller countered this by arguing that the disruption was more damaging to his programme than to the others, because 'mine depended on the listener's taking in the unexpected all the time, by way of continuous experience.'[119] The BBC remained unmoved, however, so Keller persuaded Fiske to arrange a private playback at Broadcasting House for those of his friends who had been unable to hear the broadcast.

The BBC's audience research report, as Fiske described it to Keller, 'said much as before. A substantial majority much enjoyed themselves and a substantial minority thought you could prove anything came from anything. One writer undertook to prove that the whole of Brahms came from "Three Blind Mice".'[120] Despite the transmitter problem (which, interestingly

116 Letter from Keller to Fiske, 18 December 1958 (BBC WAC ibid.).

117 Ibid.

118 Letter from Fiske to Keller, 31 December 1958 (BBC WAC ibid.). Leo Black has pointed out that there would also have been a contractual problem with repeating an orchestral concert (oral communication).

119 Letter from Keller to Fiske, 1 January 1959 (BBC WAC ibid.).

120 Letter from Fiske to Keller, 27 January 1959 (BBC WAC ibid.).

enough, is not mentioned in the report), audience figures were up again (0.2 per cent of the general population and 12 per cent of the Listening Panel), as was the appreciation index (66). Informal reactions, too, were highly satisfactory and seemed to suggest that the audience for FA was still growing. Keller was now pleased to number professors of music among his fans: 'A man called Page rang me today; Prof. of Music at Victoria, New Zealand ... In view of FA, he says, he wants to "go back to school" and study with me', he told Fiske.[121] Princeton University also approached him, asking for the loan of FA tapes. NDR, as well as their forthcoming Haydn series, repeated their broadcast of FA No. 2 in December (and Keller went to Broadcasting House to listen to it, as he thought reception would be better there). The three Haydn scores he had written for Hamburg were to get another performance too, as William Glock scheduled them to be played at the 1959 Dartington summer school. In addition, Glock asked Keller to write a new analysis for the summer school that year.[122] Finally, the general manager of the Holland Festival, Peter Diamand, wrote that he found functional analysis fascinating and 'would feel very proud if the Holland Festival were the first European Festival to launch it'.[123] 'I have decided to feel elated,' wrote Keller to Fiske.[124]

When Clifford Curzon heard the K. 503 analysis, he wrote to Keller, 'I think the Mozart *splendid*',[125] but jokingly reproached him when they next met for his unfaithfulness in working with another pianist. Keller took him seriously and wrote next day to Fiske to urge the BBC to send Curzon a formal invitation to perform the next FA. He also hastened to smooth things over himself, telling Curzon:

> I only half understood your joke last night, but when Milein told me about your immediately preceding conversation, I began to fear that you might have meant it half seriously ... I hope you have not misunderstood the situation in any way, nor need I tell you how intensely I have been looking forward to our collaboration.[126]

But Curzon had not been in the least offended:

> My dear Hans, I was leg-pulling shamelessly! But I would develop this into a fine

121 Letter from Keller to Fiske, 18 December 1958 (BBC WAC ibid.).

122 This was FA No. 9, and the work analysed was Mozart's Piano Sonata in A minor, K. 310. It was performed twice at the 1959 summer school, once by Susan Bradshaw and once by Susan McGaw.

123 As reported by Keller to Fiske, 5 January 1959 (BBC WAC ibid.). FA No. 1 was scheduled to be performed at the Holland Festival on 12 July 1959 by the Netherlands Quartet, but was postponed until 1960 at the last minute.

124 Ibid.

125 Letter from Curzon to Keller, 21 December 1958 (CUL Keller Archive).

126 Letter from Keller to Curzon, 1 November 1958 (CUL Keller Archive).

art if I thought it could be used always to provoke such a delightful letter as yours of this morning! Forgive me; I'm truly repentant.[127]

He offered several suggestions of piano concertos to be analysed: Mozart K. 595 and K. 488, Beethoven No. 4 and Brahms No. 2 ('though this would be surely too long'[128]). The BBC did not want to do another Mozart concerto straight after K. 503, so Keller embarked on Beethoven's Fourth.

Keller's collaboration with Curzon was a very happy one, and produced his favourite analytical score. At last he had a performer thoroughly committed to his method. 'I shall await your score eagerly,' wrote Curzon to Keller in March, 'and I shall probably plague you horribly nearer the time. I am so greatly looking forward to our work together.'[129] His letter goes on to raise with Keller a point made by Schnabel (his teacher) about thematic relationships in the work (whether bar 102 in the first movement was a premonition of bars 47/8 of the slow movement). Keller was very interested:

> Schnabel's question raises a problem about which I have thought a great deal – not only in the case of this c'to, but in many similar instances. So far as functional analysis is concerned, I always ruthlessly exclude relations of this kind, even though they would be very effective – superficially so. But FA is concerned with background unity of contrasts, not with foreground resemblances whose structural significance is, to me, doubtful. I shd even go so far as to say that if one had drawn Beethoven's attention to the passages you mention ... [he] wdnt have been at all pleased. On the highest level, these things seem to me a step in the wrong direction – away from the greatest possible variety (on the basis of an all-embracing unity).[130]

Keller told Curzon that he was 'happier abt this collaboration than I can say,' and he wrote in the same vein to Roger Fiske: 'Curzon's insight is fantastic, as is his ability to do what he wants to do. This is the kind of collaboration I've been dreaming of ever since No. 1. I suppose it's platitudinous to say that there is all the difference in the world between a first-rate artist and a great one, but one is human enough to rediscover the fact when one's own work is involved.'[131]

The recording was scheduled for April 1959 and, in view of Curzon's commitment to the project, Keller made another suggestion: 'This is the kind of conscientious approach I have always dreamt of, and it strikes me that we might utilize it towards a new experiment. You may remember that you had yourself intended to make FA No. 3 a live performance before an invited audience.'[132] Fiske agreed that the Beethoven programme should be

127 Letter from Curzon to Keller, 3 November 1958 (CUL Keller Archive).
128 Ibid.
129 Letter from Curzon to Keller, 31 March 1959 (CUL Keller Archive).
130 Letter from Keller to Curzon, 2 April 1959 (CUL Keller Archive).
131 Letter from Keller to Fiske, 7 April 1959 (BBC WAC ibid.).
132 Letter from Keller to Fiske, 26 November 1958 (BBC WAC ibid.).

transmitted live in this way, but Curzon inadvertently upset the arrangement by accepting an engagement at the Festival Hall for the evening on which the BBC had planned to broadcast the FA. However, the problem was not insurmountable, as Fiske told Keller, 'because we can equally well record it in Maida Vale with an audience, just as though it were live. Indeed, this is an advantage, for all your countless admirers can then hear it again in their homes a few days later!'[133] The concert was therefore given at Maida Vale on 20 April 1959, with Stanley Pope conducting the London Symphony Orchestra,[134] and it was transmitted on the Third Programme on 6 May, as 'Functional Analysis No. 8'. This nomenclature might have confused some listeners, since the last analysis heard had been No. 3 (No. 4, the *Lark* quartet, was still unrecorded and Nos 5, 6 and 7 were the series of Haydn scores for Hamburg).

Keller had been anxious about his audience when he saw that the broadcast was timed to go out at the same time as a popular symphony concert on the Home Service. However, despite his gloomy prediction that 'both orchestral concerts will have to content themselves with relatively small audiences',[135] the number who listened to FA No. 8 was far larger than that for any of the previous broadcasts (0.4 per cent of the general population and 19 per cent of the Third Programme Listening Panel heard the programme). One reason for this was undoubtedly the combination of a well-known soloist with a popular orchestral work, and many listeners commented on the 'magnificent' performance of Curzon and the LSO, which gave them great pleasure 'even when they failed to find the analytic passages either comprehensible or helpful'.[136] The appreciation index, however, was the lowest of the four broadcasts so far (62), although the comments recorded were similar to those of the previous report:

> The majority of the sample audience found Hans Keller's analysis of Beethoven's Fourth Piano Concerto interesting and enjoyable in some degree. A small group considered the idea 'monstrously impertinent' and a presumptuous interference with a great work. A larger number, while admiring the ingenuity and invention displayed, felt that Dr. Keller's labours were futile and added nothing to an understanding of the music. Many listeners, however, were convinced that the broadcast had much to offer an attentive audience and, although quite a few regretted that their own inadequate musical knowledge and powers of

133 Letter from Fiske to Keller, 27 January 1959 (BBC WAC ibid.).

134 Sir Adrian Boult was originally proposed as conductor. Keller was cautious: 'I'd be delighted if he were delighted, genuinely so. How does one find out? He's a man who is more generous with his sympathies than with his interests' (letter from Keller to Fiske, 2 February 1959, BBC WAC ibid.). Although he did not conduct this performance, Boult did manage later to convince Keller of his sincere interest in FA, as Keller told Glock: 'Amongst FA's most recent adherents, incidentally, I am happy to count Sir Adrian Boult' (BBC internal memorandum to Glock, 8 March 1960, CUL Keller Archive).

135 Letter from Keller to Fiske, 2 May 1959 (BBC WAC ibid.).

136 BBC WAC R9/6/69 Audience Research: Programme Reports.

> concentration prevented them taking full advantage of it, there were frequent expressions of gratitude for so stimulating and rewarding an experience.[137]

Keller reported to Fiske that, from his point of view, the broadcast had been 'again very successful, and I have received various invitations'.[138] One of these was from the Guildhall School for Music and Drama, who wanted to arrange two performances of one of the quartet scores. Keller also told Fiske of new articles which he was writing about FA, this time for *The Chesterian*, *The Music Review* and *London Musical Events*.[139] Fiske found the extent of Keller's literary production on the subject rather ironic: 'Your numerous articles on FA seem to contradict your theory that the thing stands on its own feet without the help of words, but you will, I am sure, have no difficulty in proving your own consistency.'[140] Keller's defence arrived by return of post: 'As for the theoretical basis of my FA articles, they are guided missiles. Their target is the conceptual frame of mind produced by all those profound analyses which everybody writes about and nobody reads – a strong frame about nothing.'[141]

The theoretical basis of functional analysis was something which had been occupying Keller's mind for some time. In his previewing articles to FA No. 1, he had already promised a fuller theoretical discussion of his new method: 'I hope to give a tolerably complete account of what is becoming a theory of unity in a book on criticism on which I am working'.[142] This book was *Criticism: A Musician's Manifesto* for which Keller had been under contract to André Deutsch since 1954. The book was already late and its proposed contents seem to have strayed somewhat from the original intention (which was an account of what music criticism should be, complete with 'anti-models' provided by his fellow critics). By 1959, Keller seems to have concluded that the theory of functional analysis did not really sit very happily within a critique of contemporary music criticism, for among his papers is a carbon copy of a proposal for a separate short publication dealing solely with FA:

FUNCTIONAL ANALYSIS

A book of 10,000–20,000 words on –

(1) FA's short history;

---

137 Ibid.

138 Letter from Keller to Fiske, 13 June 1959 (BBC WAC Talks Contributor File: Hans Keller, File 1: 1946–62).

139 'A New Critical Language', *The Chesterian*, Summer 1959; 'Wordless Functional Analysis: the Second Year and Beyond', *The Music Review*, May 1960 and August 1960; 'Hans Keller on his Wordless Functional Analysis', *London Musical Events*, May 1959.

140 Letter from Fiske to Keller, 23 June 1959 (BBC WAC ibid.).

141 Letter from Keller to Fiske, 26 June 1959 (BBC WAC ibid.).

142 'The Musical Analysis of Music,' *The Listener*, **58**/1483 (29 August 1957), p. 326.

(2) what it is not (countering prejudiced reactions);
(3) what it is: a new critical and analytic language. It hasn't happened before, which is why it may not be easy to appreciate that it has happened. Its basic contribution is 'a new level of musical experience' (Clifford Curzon). How so: the answer to this question –
(4) – to be given in concrete terms, with reference to
  (a) the attached gramophone record of FA No.9 (Mozart's A minor Piano Sonata, the analysis written for piano 5tet);
  (b) the score of the analysis, reproduced in this chapter by way of music examples.

> As I mentioned before, I am preparing a book on 'Criticism: A Musician's Manifesto' for André Deutsch (to be finished by December 31). Deutsch has first option on any subsequent book, and his permission would have to be sought to go ahead with this plan. I do not think there would be any difficulty: he once said to me that he was not interested in specialized books.[143]

Neither this book nor *Criticism: A Musician's Manifesto* was ever written, nor do any drafts of them survive. When Keller did eventually write a book on criticism, some twenty years later,[144] he gave some explanation of his difficulties with *A Musician's Manifesto*. The book on his theory of unity, however, remained unwritten, and his silence unexplained. In 1957, he had written that, where the theory of FA was concerned, 'the more practice precedes it the better. Ideally, by the time the theory comes to be fully written, it ought to strike the musician as almost a platitude.'[145] Perhaps a sufficient body of practical demonstrations of FA never accumulated, before Keller's theory of music grew beyond the original theory of unity.

Another possible problem might have been uncertainty as to the nature of the audience for functional analysis. A description which Keller gives (in a letter to a friend) of his ideal addressee as 'a highly educated musician – educated musically, not academically – without professional prejudices and preoccupations'[146] does not seem to be easily reconcilable with his often-expressed desire to appeal to ordinary music-lovers. In fact, it is rather like a picture of a typical Third Programme listener. Nevertheless, Keller would have been more than happy to see his analyses transferred from the Third to the Home Service. In his second survey of the development of functional analysis for *The Music Review*, he recorded his regret that 'performances of

---

143 The proposal is dated 28 May 1959 and is unaddressed. It is not known for whom it was intended, nor, since there is no other correspondence on the subject extant, whether it was ever actually sent (CUL Keller Archive).

144 *Criticism*, which, although it was written in 1976, was not published until after Keller's death (Faber and Faber, 1987).

145 'Functional Analysis: Its Pure Application', *The Music Review* **18**/3 (August 1957), pp. 202-6.

146 Letter from Keller to Dr Tischler, 15 December 1958 (CUL Keller Archive). This description is of Dr Tischler himself: 'you are my addressee, one of my ideal ones,' Keller told him.

functional analyses tend to be relegated to the Third Programme sphere ... Wordless functional analysis is to be understood like – indeed as – music. It follows that it is the kind of analysis which, while gratifying Third Programme needs, makes the Third Programme approach unnecessary so far as the musical analysis of non-Third-Programme music is concerned.'[147] It is clear from this that Keller intended to have it both ways and to be understood on as many different levels as was the music he was analysing. However, the BBC did not share this view to the extent of programming functional analyses anywhere other than on the Third Programme. When the decision to repeat FA No. 1 was made, it had crossed Keller's mind that the repeat could be placed on the Home Service. He was aware that this was not really likely (asking Fiske 'is this a silly question because Home is out of the question?'[148]), although at that time the BBC did quite often repeat the Third's successful experiments on the Home Service. After the broadcast of FA No. 3, Keller wrote to Julian Herbage, the editor of *Music Magazine* (at that time a Home Service programme), to suggest a mini-analysis (13 minutes) for his programme, to mark the 150th anniversary of Mendelssohn's birth. One possible subject, he suggested, might be one of the *Songs Without Words*, 'whose title wd thus acquire a double meaning'.[149]Although he did not take up this offer, Herbage was interested in functional analysis, and later commissioned Susan Bradshaw to give a *Music Magazine* talk on the subject to coincide with the broadcast of the *Lark* quartet FA.[150]

Music Magazine apart, Keller's correspondence with the BBC over functional analysis was nearly all with Roger Fiske, whose post of Music Talks Producer gave him a fair amount of autonomy (as Keller later put it, 'the Music Talks Producer at the BBC is rather a separate radio station ... nobody has much of a chance or desire to interfere with him'[151]). It is therefore not easy to gauge how widespread was the interest in functional analysis elsewhere in the Corporation. There were at least several very interested individuals, however, and the most enthusiastic of these was Deryck Cooke, who published 'In Defence of Functional Analysis' in *The Musical Times* shortly after the Curzon broadcast.[152] In this article, Cooke was responding specifically to a critical letter which had appeared in *The Musical Times*, but it might be indicative of the general opinion in the BBC's Music Department that Cooke's view of FA's reception is rather more negative than the upbeat picture painted by Keller in his own articles (and in his letters to Fiske). 'The opponents of Functional Analysis are many and

147 'Wordless Functional Analysis: the Second Year and Beyond – I', *The Music Review*, February 1960.

148 Letter from Keller to Fiske, 5 October 1957 (BBC WAC ibid.).

149 Letter from Keller to Herbage, 18 December 1958 (CUL Keller Archive).

150 Broadcast on the Home Service on 6 March 1960.

151 *1975* (1977), p. 20.

152 Cooke (1959).

vocal; its supporters, so far as I can see, are few', wrote Cooke, before going on to present his defence in the shape of a thematic analysis of Beethoven's Seventh Symphony. Keller was extremely pleased by Cooke's support, describing him later as one of 'the earliest and the most enthusiastic, the most unqualified and indeed concretely understanding supporters of wordless – though not only wordless – functional analysis'.[153]

Keller gained another, particularly influential, supporter on the BBC's staff when, on 3 May 1959, William Glock was appointed Controller of Music. Despite their many differences of opinion (which were exacerbated later by the experience of working together), Glock and Keller had an enormous amount of respect for each other as musicians. It is therefore not surprising that, almost as soon as he had arrived at the BBC, Glock should have asked Keller if he was interested in joining the staff. On 26 May, Glock had lunch with Third Programme Controller P.H. Newby and, as he told Keller afterwards, 'I ... recommended you strongly'.[154] At Glock's suggestion, Keller also had a talk with Newby a couple of days later. What Newby thought of Keller on that occasion is not recorded – he was later to describe Keller as a genius[155] – but Keller's impression of Newby was apparently 'very favourable'.[156] When the BBC's Appointment Board met for the formal interviews at the end of June, both Glock and Newby were there, and Keller reported afterwards to Roger Fiske that he had found the Board 'eminently suitable for interviewing me'.[157] Significantly, as far as functional analysis was concerned, it was Fiske's job as Music Talks Producer for which Keller was applying.

Fiske was due to retire at the end of the summer of 1959. In view of his own interest in the job, Keller was naturally anxious that Fiske should see the long-delayed *Lark* FA through to transmission, or at least recording, before his departure. 'Just imagine I get your job,' he wrote, 'and the first thing I do is to record FA No. 4 for 17 hours on end: the BBC won't remember that the score was commissioned $1^1/_2$ years ago and that the broadcast is more than a year late. I'll be out by the back door in no time, & there is no espresso bar

153 Review of Deryck Cooke's *Vindications*, *Music Analysis*, July 1983.

154 Letter from Glock to Keller, 27 May 1959 (CUL Keller Archive).

155 'If I had to answer the question, "Have you ever met anyone whom you think was a genius?" I would say "Yes", and it would be Hans Keller.' (P.H. Newby, interviewed by Humphrey Carpenter; quoted in Carpenter, 1996, p. 204).

156 Letter from Keller to Glock, 30 May 1959 (CUL Keller Archive).

157 Letter from Keller to Fiske, 9 July 1959 (BBC WAC Contributor's File: Dartington String Quartet, File 1, 1958–62). Keller went on to describe the interview to Fiske, telling him that Newby had asked him, Pilate-like, 'What is truth?', to which Keller says he replied, 'I said that was a loaded one to ask me on a Monday, and that if I knew what truth was I wouldn't keep talking about it, which would be a great loss to our culture.' Keller then footnotes this: 'This version of Keller's answer is identical with the one he quotes in his Memoirs, vol.x. On the other hand, it bears no resemblance to the one quoted in the Reports of the BBC Appointment Board, 1959. Future investigators may be able to solve this textual mystery. Ed.'

in Great Portland Street either... On the other hand, if I don't get the job, why should I forgo the pleasure of recording one more FA with you? Kindly note that I mean this sentence.'[158] Unfortunately, events conspired to prevent this one last collaboration. The Dartington Quartet had now based themselves in Devon, thus increasing the cost of a recording, and before anything was arranged, their cellist left the quartet. By the time they had found a new cellist, and the BBC's Artists Committee had met to discuss whether they should go through another audition, Roger Fiske had departed and Keller was the BBC's new Music Talks Producer.

'I said at the interview that I shouldn't step down from FA in any way; I shd say so again if I got the job', Keller had told Fiske.[159] The BBC seemed to be quite happy with this, and Keller was apparently 'guaranteed at least two FA broadcasts per year'.[160] It is all the more surprising, therefore, to find that the *Lark* FA (which was finally broadcast on 11 March 1960) was, with one exception,[161] the last to be broadcast on the BBC for 18 years. More surprising still is that, after 1963, Keller wrote no more analytical scores for 15 years. This was despite an unfulfilled commission in May 1961 from the publishers Augener Ltd to write a series of analyses of Beethoven piano sonatas for publication,[162] and another from the BBC for an FA of Beethoven's Fifth Symphony (the work was Deryck Cooke's suggestion), which Boult and the London Philharmonic were scheduled to record in December 1961. There was also a series of invitations and commissions from music festivals at that time: the Holland, Aldeburgh, Redcliffe and Tilford Bach festivals all featured FA performances in 1960–63. It is hard to believe that all this interest simply dried up.

Functional analysis was of crucial importance to Keller and remained so – in theory. He continued to describe it as 'right at the centre of my life's work'[163] for the rest of his life, but the fact remains that he completed only one new score after the early 1960s.[164] The reasons for the long hiatus which

158 Ibid.

159 Ibid.

160 Letter from Keller to Ian McIntyre, Controller Radio 3, 18 November 1980 (CUL Keller Archive). That Keller may not have been entirely confident of the efficacy of this guarantee is shown by the long letters on the subject (dated 1 September and 31 August 1959 respectively) which he sent to William Glock and S.S. Gilbert, Assistant Establishment Officer (Sound), on his arrival at the BBC, enquiring anxiously how the BBC's future commissioning of FAs was going to work in practice.

161 The exception was an analysis of Mozart's Clarinet Quintet, K. 581, written for the Hampton Music Club and broadcast on the Third Programme on 4 March 1962.

162 Letter from Ernest Chapman of Augener to Keller, 10 May 1961 (CUL Keller Archive). The sonatas which Keller was to analyse were Op. 2. No. 2 in A, Op. 57 in F minor and Op. 110 in A flat.

163 Letter to Ian McIntyre, Controller Radio 3, 18 November 1980 (CUL Keller Archive).

164 Mozart Quintet in G minor, K. 516, broadcast on Radio 3 on 4 November 1978. Two further analyses (of Mozart's quartet K. 156 and piano quartet K. 478), dating from the 1980s, survive in fragmentary form in CUL Keller Archive.

ensued in Keller's composition of analytical scores are probably very complicated. Publicly, Keller tended to gloss over it, but, privately, he gave two reasons why he stopped writing analyses. Although he did not complain of this at the time, he told his BBC colleague Robert Layton in 1974 that 'The long pause which has intervened in my composition of FAs was, frankly, caused by my resentment at the few performances, public and/or radio, which each new FA received: one or two per country; then people (including the BBC) wanted a new one.'[165] Indeed, after the first functional analysis had received four performances in quick succession and a great deal of critical attention, it must have been disappointing that the BBC, for example, never offered any of the other analyses more than a single broadcast. Keller also confessed more than once to unease over possible conflicts caused by his own membership of the BBC's staff: he didn't want it to seem as though he was abusing his position or that his staff membership was helping his method along. He was always very sensitive on this point and, of course, it didn't help that it was Roger Fiske's job that he was taking over when he joined the BBC in September 1959, so that if functional analysis broadcasts were to continue, he was going to have to produce them himself.

Another reason for the lack of new analytical scores during most of Keller's BBC years was probably simple pressure of work, particularly after 1965, when he took on the additional job of chairing the working party which planned the European Broadcasting Union's international concert season. More fundamentally – and perhaps unconsciously – the emphasis of what he called his theory of music later moved away from the rather narrow demonstration of thematic unity towards exploring another compositional principle, which he had touched on in his original *Music Review* article: 'the simultaneous suppression and definite implication of the self-evident'.[166]

This shift in emphasis does not amount to a completely new direction in Keller's thought: the elements of what he later called his theory of music can be found in his earlier writings. That the shift was probably unconscious can be inferred from his continuing to use the same terminology – music should be analysed 'two-dimensionally', in terms of its 'foreground' and 'background'. However, whereas in the 1950s 'the foreground is diversity, the background unity',[167] in the 1970s he defined his theory as follows:

> Within the context of my theory, 'background' means ... the sum total of well-defined expectations which the composer creates in the course of a structure, but most of which are never met: they are as thoroughly suppressed as they are implied. Instead ... we hear meaningful contradictions, again well defined as

165 Internal memo to Robert Layton, 4 September 1974 (CUL Keller Archive).

166 'K. 503: The Unity of Contrasting Themes and Movements', *The Music Review*, February 1956 and May 1956.

167 'Functional Analysis', *Musical Opinion*, December 1958.

such, of what we have been led to expect, and the sum total of these contradictions I shall call the foreground of the composition.[168]

The words 'the sum total' are important: as Keller so often demonstrates, there are different kinds and levels of background material. These are particularly strikingly shown in his later work, but an early example appears in his K. 503 analysis, when he invokes the second act finale of *Figaro*, to show that 'the latent compositorial background is, at the same time, a manifest, historical background'.

Keller's later work deals with a range of wide formal issues (the combination of different forms, the splitting of their functions, and the development of new types of sonata contrast) which go far beyond his original 'theory of unity'. Perhaps his earlier assertion that 'as soon as you have analysed the unity of a great work, its variety explains itself'[169] was no longer enough: as he explained to Roger Fiske, 'The thematic dimension is not the only one in which variety can be achieved. Much great Haydn is more monothematic than much great Mozart, but it is also, proportionately, more diversified in respect of key schemes and harmonic structures.'[170] Faced with monothematicism, however, functional analysis was silent: 'My first functional analysis ... did not need an analytic postlude because the finale is monothematic (variation form), which means that it does not contain contrasting themes whose unity has to be demonstrated'.[171]

It could be said, of course, that after the composition of several analytical scores, Keller had made his point, although this was not an idea which he himself would consciously entertain. It was probably a combination of the awkwardness of producing the broadcasts himself – 'I didn't want to create the impression that I was misusing my BBC position'[172] – together with the excitement and challenge of a new job, which caused Keller's functional analysis enterprise to stall, distracting him at what may have been a crucial moment. Meanwhile, his analytical approach was to develop beyond the demonstration of thematic unity into something not so easily expressible using his wordless method. If this does account for his silence, it is a sad irony that, in joining the BBC (which was after all FA's 'mother station' as he later put it[173]), Keller had manoeuvred himself into a position which entailed the loss of something so important to him.

168 *1975* (1977), pp. 136-7.

169 'The Chamber Music' (1956), p. 91.

170 Letter to Roger Fiske, 11 April 1957 (WAC Contributor File: Hans Keller, File 1, 1946-62).

171 'Functional Analysis', *Musical Opinion*, December 1958.

172 Letter from Keller to Humphrey Burton, Head of Music & Arts, BBC Television, 11 December 1980 (CUL Keller Archive).

173 Letter from Keller to Ian McIntyre, 3 December 1980 (CUL Keller Archive).

Chapter 3

From the Third Programme to the Music Programme

In joining the BBC, Keller was entering an organization which has spent most of its short existence engulfed in continual change and self-examination, despite enjoying a position of security and public esteem unparalleled in an institution so young. While its lofty ideal of 'public service broadcasting' has, throughout its 75 years, remained almost unquestioningly accepted at home and widely admired abroad, the Corporation itself seems increasingly to live in a state of chronic insecurity. In all its periodic upheavals, the BBC has always anticipated criticism, responding to scarcely-voiced threats and pressures with an almost neurotic alacrity.

Internal BBC politics are therefore a fascinating study and Keller, hyper-sensitive to the nuances of collective life, became increasingly embroiled in them during his time on the staff. There is a clear difference, however, in the way in which he was involved during his second decade as a staff member when compared with his first. The turning-point, as he himself identified it, was the BBC's publication of its 1969 policy document *Broadcasting in the Seventies* and the unprecedented wave of internal protest which that provoked. Looking back over the difficult years which followed, Keller concluded that the BBC seemed to have suffered at that point 'an abrupt change of corporate personality such as is well known in the history of collectivity'.[1] This impression was strengthened for him by the departure, around the turn of the decade, of three significant figures for whom he had had a high degree of respect: Controller of Music, William Glock; Third Programme Controller, Howard Newby; and, of course, Director-General, Sir Hugh Greene. 'The people in charge in the Sixties proved capable of accommodating, indeed desirously provoking, individual thought,' wrote Keller after his retirement, contrasting this with the increasingly sterile working relationship he had with their successors.[2]

1 'Fare Better, BBC', *The Spectator*, 30 June 1979.

2 Ibid. Sir Hugh Greene retired as Director-General in 1969, but stayed with the BBC as a member of the Board of Governors for a further two years. Keller praised the way in which 'individual thinkers, minds of "sincerity and vision" (Greene's words), anti-collectivists, downright dissidents were appointed to important posts' during his tenure. 'In fact, one almost felt that he admired one in proportion as one disagreed with him – and one's sense of responsibility was, of course, strengthened by what I would describe as his

However abrupt the changes heralded by *Broadcasting in the Seventies* may have seemed at the time, it is nevertheless possible to trace their origins back many years, and it is important to do so in order to set Keller's later battles in context. As will be seen, the central issues which concerned Keller about *Broadcasting in the Seventies* were the loss of the Third Programme and the move towards 'generic' broadcasting. However, the Third had been the subject of strong criticism almost since its inception, and its very existence was seen by some (among them Reith himself) as an unwelcome type of generic programming.[3] Moreover, the extensive review of sound broadcasting with which the BBC greeted the Third Programme's tenth anniversary in 1956 had many parallels with *Broadcasting in the Seventies*, and the resultant drastic cut in the Third's broadcasting hours in 1957 was the subject of public and private arguments very similar to those which surrounded the final axe in 1969. In effect, the Third was already living on borrowed time when Keller arrived at the BBC.

Like the National Health Service and the provision of universal secondary education, the Third Programme was born out of that extraordinary period of idealism, altruism and national solidarity which followed the Second World War. As a result, perhaps, of the relative cultural deprivation of the war years – the blackout restrictions on live theatre and concerts, the effect of the paper

---

imaginative trust in one's disloyalty ... To work in the BBC in his decade was, as a result, sheer paradise, and one knew it at the time – when I coined the phrase "the good young days", because I knew that once they were past, they'd be recognised as the best old days ever, never ageing, ever new' (unpublished letter to the editor of *The Listener*, 16 October 1980, CUL Keller Archive). William Glock retired from the BBC in 1972, and the 'elementally artistic collaboration' ('Fare Better, BBC', *The Spectator*, 30 June 1979) which Keller enjoyed with him (particularly in their early days on the staff) was not repeated with his successor, Robert Ponsonby. Howard Newby did not retire until 1978, but in 1971 he relinquished control of the Third Programme (by that time Radio 3) to become Director of Programmes, Radio. His successor as Controller, Stephen Hearst, a television man and a definite broadcasting 'professional', was regarded with deep suspicion by many in the Music Department. On a personal level, Keller's relations with both Ponsonby and Hearst seem to have been reasonably cordial – he used to attend football matches with Hearst, and recorded in his January 1973 diary that 'Robert P ... I like v. much as a human being' – but many of their opinions were anathema to him and his clashes with both were frequent. Leo Black has suggested that one contributory cause of Keller's problems with his BBC managers was that 'he had no experience of military service, while both Controllers with whom he was most involved in the early 1970s, Robert Ponsonby and Stephen Hearst, had been in the war ... Howard Newby had taught in Egypt then, which could help explain his very different approach to working with subordinates' (letter to the author, 1 February 2000). Keller did attempt to enlist into the British Army during his internment, but was classified as medically unfit (CUL Keller Archive).

3 Reith was committed to the ideal of one voice speaking to the whole nation and disliked dividing listeners into classes. His thoughts on the Third Programme are recorded in the Beveridge Committee's report of 1951, in which he says, 'The Third Programme, positively and negatively, is objectionable. It is a waste of a precious wavelength. Much of its matter is too limited in appeal, the rest should have a wider audience' (Home Office, 1951, Appendix H, p. 364).

shortage on publishing, and the relentlessly cheery morale-raising tone of most popular entertainment, including wartime radio – there was also a clear surge in the popularity of all the arts at that time. Concerts were packed, book sales soared, cinema queues stretched as far as the eye could see, and there was a significant broadening of interest in contemporary culture. Along with the rest of the country, the BBC had long looked forward to the rebuilding of a new and better world to assuage the horrors of war; in which radio could play a vital role as civilizer, educator, national unifier and international reconciler – indeed, in the words of one internal BBC report from 1942, it was thought by some that radio could become 'the prime re-educative agency of the post-war world'.[4] The accent was therefore on serious, improving broadcasting, but (with one eye on the preservation of its monopoly) the Corporation also stressed the importance of maintaining a universal provision: there was to be something for everyone in the new BBC. A good illustration of the BBC's perception of the determinedly reconstructive national mood on the eve of peace is found in a speech which its Director-General, William Haley, gave at the end of 1944:

> The most hopeful thing in the world today is the zest and eagerness with which the British peoples are arguing about the future. The controversies, even the squabbles, now proceeding are an astonishing tribute to the stamina of this nation in the sixth year of a grim and arduous war. The British peoples might be excused if they felt a trifle tired; if they had come to the conclusion that victory in itself was enough. But not at all. Victory is now everywhere recognised only as a beginning. It is the great preliminary. It is what we manage to build following the exertions of these six long years that really matters. Of nothing is that more true than of broadcasting.[5]

Although Haley is rightly regarded as the father of the Third Programme, the idea of a separate cultural radio network was not entirely new. As early as 1924, the minutes of the new BBC's Control Board recorded a suggestion that 'highbrow education and better class material' should be covered by a separate network.[6] Unlike the situation in 1945, it seems that this idea did not arise out of any perceptible public pressure then for more culture on the air – indeed, there was not always a welcome for those 'highbrow' programmes which were already available. In 1925 even one of the BBC's own board of directors complained to Reith that he was broadcasting 'too many uninteresting items, such as Elizabethan music, new fangled songs, weird quartettes and quintettes, groaning Chamber Music, quite unappreciated by

4 Undated report written by Robert Reid, North Regional Publicity Officer (BBC WAC R34/578/1: Policy: Post-war Planning, General and Numbered Documents, 1941–42).

5 William Haley, Speech given to the monthly meeting of the Radio Industries Club on 28 November 1944 (BBC WAC R34/580, Policy: Post-War Planning, Programmes). This speech was one of two public statements which Haley made about the BBC's plans for post-war broadcasting, the other being at the Cardiff Business Club on 15 March 1945.

6 See Briggs (1965), p. 27.

the public, readings from unknown poets, etc ... also talks on subjects which are of no interest to 99% of the listeners'.[7] Kate Whitehead makes the interesting suggestion that these first thoughts of a cultural programme were more probably seen 'as a way in which the serious programmes could be hived off into another station leaving the popular service free to "entertain"'.[8]

There were other ideas for separate channels offering different types of material put forward over the next decade or so, but they all foundered on Director-General John Reith's immovable vision of one unifying national radio network, which would educate and entertain the whole country, irrespective of class and education. Reith left the BBC for the chairmanship of Imperial Airways in 1938, and the reorganization of radio which took place at the beginning of the war brought a significant new alternative for listeners. The Forces Programme, a light entertainment service, went on air in 1940 and rapidly became as popular with audiences at home as it was with the troops for whom it was designed. Although few realized it at the time, its content was little short of a revolution in BBC thinking, carrying profound implications for peacetime broadcasting. One contemporary who did appreciate this was the radio critic (and later BBC producer) Grace Wyndham Goldie, who wrote of the Forces Programme in *The Listener* that 'the whole attitude of the BBC to its audience is for the first time reversed. For the first time the quality of the programmes is being decided from below rather than from above ... These are concessions which it is going to be difficult to withdraw.'[9]

Therefore, when the BBC came to consider its plans for radio broadcasting after the war, it faced demands for alternatives to the Home Service from both sides. The majority of listeners wanted a light service like the Forces Programme to continue, and a minority – but, it was argued, an articulate and influential minority – wanted something much more serious. The BBC's charter was due to expire at the end of 1946 and the Corporation knew that it would have to begin negotiations about its renewal as soon as the war was over. It was clear that the plans they put forward would have to satisfy both requirements: the provision of a light service was essential in order to preserve the BBC's monopoly in the face of suggestions about competing Corporations or 'sponsored' programmes; and a cultural or educational service would help convince the powers-that-be that the monopoly was in worthy hands.

One of the strongest arguments in favour of the BBC's monopoly was, of course, its impressive war record, so it is not surprising that Haley should have chosen to open his earliest public statements about the future of post-war broadcasting with a reminder of the glorious recent past:

---

7 Letter from Burnham to Reith, 7 December 1925 (quoted in Carpenter, 1996, pp. 3–4).

8 Whitehead (1989), p. 7.

9 Goldie (1940).

> It is a story of which this country can be proud. It is a story which, so far as broadcasting is concerned, cannot be paralleled in any other country in the world. It is a story which could not have happened if Britain had had a different system of broadcasting, if there had been no BBC.[10]

The BBC's wartime activities had also influenced many European countries towards copying the British system of broadcasting, as Haley pointed out to MPs at a meeting in March 1945:

> Neighbouring countries during the war had been profoundly impressed with the value of conducting broadcasting under a national authority as a result of the part played by the BBC in the life of Occupied Europe.[11]

Despite all this, the spectre of possible competition was already throwing its shadow over the BBC. At his meeting with the MPs, Haley was asked 'whether it would not be possible, side by side with this BBC plan, to have one or two other Corporations running sponsored programmes in order to introduce an element of competition',[12] and he was acutely aware that 'the one drawback that is sometimes charged against the BBC is that its monopoly robs the listener of the fruits of competition'.[13] Haley's answer, apart from to cite technical difficulties which meant that the BBC needed all available wavelengths for its own plans, was to introduce a system of internal competition into the BBC's own programme planning. Thus was born the BBC's division between 'Planning' and 'Supply', one of the many curious features of the Corporation's administrative structure. As time went on, it became the cause of considerable frustration in the Music Department, and created an anomaly which was not resolved on Radio 3 until John Drummond united the roles of Controller Radio 3 and Controller Music in 1987.

Haley's original idea was based on the model of a newspaper editorship. He himself was a newspaper man, having come to the BBC from the *Manchester Guardian/Evening News* Corporation via Reuters press agency, and when he left the BBC it was to take up the editorship of *The Times*. He saw his network controllers as the editors of a coordinated set of newspapers. Rather as in the *Manchester Guardian*'s relationship with its sister paper, the more popular *Manchester Evening News*, the BBC's three networks would compete with each other for the listeners' attention, yet the competition would be limited by their widely differing styles. If an idea was rejected by one 'editor', it might well be successfully offered to another. The supply

10 Speech given to the monthly meeting of the Radio Industries Club on 28 November 1944 (BBC WAC R34/580, Policy: Post-War Planning, Programmes).

11 Minutes of meeting between Haley and the Broadcasting Sub-Committee of the Tory Reform Committee, 8 March 1945 (BBC WAC ibid.).

12 Ibid.

13 Speech given to the monthly meeting of the Radio Industries Club on 28 November 1944 (BBC WAC ibid.).

departments, of which Music was one, therefore worked for all three networks – and, in the early days of television, for both media. The opportunity for conflict between the network controllers, with responsibility for programme planning, and the Controller, Music, in charge of music policy, grew as generic broadcasting meant that one network, Radio 3, increasingly became identified as 'the music channel'.

In 1946, however, music was to be found on all three networks, which were differentiated not by the forms of their material, but by what was referred to as their 'brow-level'. As Haley saw it:

> We do not intend that the three Programmes shall be rigidly stratified. Rather will they shade into each other, their differences being in approach and treatment rather than in range of content … The classical music in the Light Programme will, we hope, be attractive enough to lead listeners on to the Home Service; the Home Service should lead on to the Third Programme.[14]

In a later interview, Haley gave an example of the sort of thing he meant:

> I would want the Light Programme to play the waltz from *Der Rosenkavalier*. Then about a week or ten days later I would hope the Home Service would play one act – the most tuneful act – of the opera. And within the month the Third Programme would do the whole work from beginning to end, dialogue and all.[15]

Thus the three programmes were not supposed simply to cater for existing classes of listener, but actively to encourage the public up the cultural scale. It was believed that Third Programme material would inevitably broaden its appeal in time, as listeners became familiar with artistic delights which they had previously had no opportunity to experience. 'I have always believed,' said Haley,

> that every civilized nation, culturally and educationally, is a pyramid with a lamentably broad base and a lamentably narrow tip. And … I devised these three programmes with the idea that we would have a Light Programme which would cover the lower third of the pyramid. We would have a Home Service which would take more than the middle third, take everything up to the tip. And then we'd have a Third Programme. Now it has been said that this was stratifying or segregating listeners into classes. Well, it was in a way, but that was only the start; it was not meant to be a static pyramid. And my conception was of a BBC through the years – many years – which would slowly move listeners from one stratum of this pyramid to the next.[16]

---

14 Haley, 'The Home Programme Policy of the BBC', policy document submitted to Board of Governors, 4 July 1946 (BBC WAC R34/420, Policy, Home Services, 1944–47).

15 BBC Oral History Project: Sir William Haley interviewed by Frank Gillard; transcript corrected by Haley and dated by him 4 April 1978 (quoted in Carpenter, 1996, p. 9).

16 Ibid.

The trouble was that the new system of internal competition worked against this idealistic vision. Haley later admitted that he had made 'a very big mistake' in giving his programme heads such complete editorial control, with no cooperative mechanism in place to coordinate planning:

> This idea that we would slowly narrow this pyramid, and get the base smaller and smaller, and the middle and peak larger and larger, was obviously against the interests, as they saw it, of the programme heads. And therefore they never really got down to a very active co-operation.[17]

In the event, the Light Programme, in terms of audience figures, was simply too successful, and it seemed that many listeners were sinking down Haley's cultural pyramid, rather than making their way upwards. Even the Home Service's audience share began to cause concern (it dropped in one year from more than half to just over a third of the total radio audience) and there was some anxiety that this former voice of Reith's unified BBC was beginning to be 'ground between the upper and nether millstones of the Third Programme and Light Programme respectively', losing 'in listeners to Light Programme and in prestige to Third Programme'.[18]

Although it was hoped that the Third Programme's audience would steadily increase – 10 per cent of the listening public was the aim – any help or explanation for fledgling highbrows was notably absent from its schedules, as the original brief specifically excluded any form of adult education. The work of encouraging listeners up the cultural pyramid was the task of the other Programmes, with the Third assuming that its audience would be 'already aware of artistic experience and will include persons of taste, of intelligence and of education'. These persons were further defined as being 'selective not casual, and both attentive and critical. This programme need not cultivate any other audience, and any material that is unlikely to interest such listeners should be excluded.'[19] As the Third's newly-appointed Controller, George Barnes, explained to listeners in the special supplement to *The Listener* which marked the launch, the BBC had to choose between those 'who find popular exposition often condescending' and those who, 'like Prom. audiences, want their programmes to have notes':

> Compromise on this issue antagonises all. We shall therefore provide the programme and not the notes. There will be few 'hearing aids' for listeners to the Third Programme. We hope that our approach will be at once sensitive and adult;

17 Ibid.

18 Letter from Norman Collins to Lindsay Wellington (Controllers of the Light Programme and Home Service respectively), 26 November 1946 (BBC WAC R34/420 Policy: Home Services, 1944–47).

19 George Barnes, draft statement of intent for Programme C, 14 January 1946 (BBC WAC ibid.).

> that our audience will enjoy itself without crutches and will satisfy its desire for knowledge without a primer.[20]

This was the policy which led to charges that the Third was exclusive, pretentious and intellectually snobbish. Yet, when the BBC began to change its mind ten years later and replaced some of the Third's broadcasting time with adult education, self-help and 'minority interest' programmes, the results were disastrous, as the following contemptuous parody shows:

> Here you can learn how to acquire a taste for old glass; quite easy, you know, and all done in a dull little talk lasting a quarter of an hour. Or how even you, with your rather modest income ... can become a collector of pictures; rather bad ones of course, but think of the fun of it; lots of boring little prints, all alike.[21]

The original 'no crutches' policy was fundamental to the philosophy of the Third Programme. The works of art which it displayed were to speak for themselves and, moreover, were to be given the room to do so. Hence the generous repeats and *Listener* reprints, and Haley's policy – which he described as being 'the heart of the Third Programme' – that there should be no fixed points cluttering the schedules, and nothing should ever have to be cut:

> I said, 'No, not on your life, no fixed points. The people in charge of it all shall have a completely blank open space of up to five hours every night, night after night. And if they want five nights to do something in, then have five nights.' And that was agreed. And I said, 'It follows from that that everything the programme does shall be given the time that the man who created it or wrote it or composed the music thought was necessary ... There'll be no cuts.'[22]

Another policy, which produced complaints that the Third was not only pretentious but deliberately obscure, was Haley's dictum that it 'can live only by experiment'. Alongside its quest for the highest international standards in the presentation of established classics, the Third sought to become a force of 'artistic and cultural importance', a creative forum which would revitalize contemporary culture, 'secure the goodwill of writers, composers, and performers, as well as of listeners', and give 'unequalled opportunity' to new talent. It also hoped that the new standards of performing excellence which it would broadcast would influence artistic life throughout the country 'to raise the level of performance in the concert hall and on the stage and platform'.[23]

---

20 Barnes (1946a), pp. i–ii.

21 Laslett (1958). Laslett was a Cambridge academic and former BBC Talks producer who in 1957 led the public campaign against the cuts in the Third Programme's airtime.

22 BBC Oral History Project: Sir William Haley interviewed by Frank Gillard; transcript corrected by Haley and dated by him 4 April 1978 (quoted in Carpenter, 1996, p. 8).

23 Haley, 'Draft for Board', 18 June 1946 (BBC WAC ibid.).

As with the original decision to expand the BBC's services after the war, the policy of encouraging artistic experiment is not without some foundation in the BBC's consciousness of possible criticisms of its monopoly status. As Haley put it, 'perhaps the strongest artistic argument against monopoly broadcasting is the tendency of all big institutions to accept what is safe. England is sprinkled with municipal buildings safely designed in the neo-Georgian manner, each admirable to its purpose but barren in its influence.' Haley was prepared to take risks in pursuit of this, acknowledging that 'experiment presupposes failures, and we can afford to fail ... What we cannot afford is to play for safety.' The 'no fixed points' policy was itself a risk in broadcasting terms, as it gave listeners no routine or regularity in their listening, and required on their part a careful attention to the columns of the *Radio Times* to find what they wanted.

This resulted in the kind of planning which Keller, in later years, defended with passion. There was no sense in which such a Third would ever become a background, or a comfortable habit, and its audience could not be taken for granted. Such material which, by common consent, required fixed points, like the principal news broadcasts, was regarded as outside the province of the Third, so much so that E.M. Forster, reviewing the Third Programme on its fifth anniversary, wrote that it was 'not ... concerned with the present', gazing instead 'Janus-faced ... with tranquillity into the past ... [and] with ardour into the future'.[24] As Keller saw it, 'News and traffic information are one thing, intellectual and aesthetic experience another. The one has to be available at fixed points, the other has to be offered as an object of free, deliberate, considered choice, if the listener's intellectual autonomy is to be respected.'[25]

Yet, as Keller also pointed out, the Third Programme had a particular shape of its own. It was not only a series of interesting and important programmes, but, at its best, each evening made sense as a whole: 'The Third Programme had a rhythm, which manifested itself throughout an evening, so that you could listen a whole evening without, however, using it at any stage as a background.'[26] Those who worked for the Third felt very strongly about the importance of its distinct identity, which they felt was often misunderstood by their colleagues elsewhere in the Corporation. For example, a suggestion made in 1950 that the Home Service programme *Music Magazine* ought to be transferred to the Third was opposed by Third Programme staff not because of any problem with its content, but on the grounds that the programme's structure was incompatible with the Third's.

> The whole Third Programme is in its way a magazine. All our attempts are towards making it more coherent, more of a unity. The magazine type of

24 Forster (1951), pp. 539–41.

25 'Broadcasting in the 'Eighties', *The Spectator*, 10 July 1976.

26 'Hans Keller in Interview with Anton Weinberg', ed. Mark Doran, *Tempo*, 195 (January 1996), pp. 6–12.

programme is appropriate we feel to a broadcast service which is itself fragmented and broken up into distinct compartments. For us it has the character of miscellaneity, which is what we are always trying to avoid.[27]

In the Third's early days, its principle of no fixed points, no cuts and no fade-outs – no matter how long the overrun – was such a great contrast to the stopwatch nature of the other networks as to seem cavalier, and criticism of the Third's unpredictable schedules appeared several times in the press: one paper dubbed the Third 'the Timeless Wonder'[28] and another featured a mocking cartoon in which a haughty-looking Third Programme producer in evening dress upbraids a departing musician: 'Oh, by the way, Mr. Pontifex, you finished absolutely exactly at nine-thirty – don't you think that's just a trifle regional?'[29] To Haley, however, such criticism was to miss the point of the whole great enterprise:

Let it often make mistakes. Let it often under-run and over-run. Let it remember always that it is an experiment, even an adventure, and not a piece of routine. Let it arouse, and not seek to muffle, controversy. Let it enable the intelligent public to hear the best that has been thought or said or composed in all the world. Let it demonstrate that we are not afraid to express our own culture or give our people access to the culture of others. Let it set a standard, and furnish an example, which will not only raise the level of our own broadcasting but in the end affect the level of broadcasting in other lands. Let it be something which has never been attempted hitherto in any country.[30]

The BBC marked the tenth birthday of the Third in 1956 with a series of celebratory broadcasts, ten new works commissioned from ten different composers,[31] and the publication in book form of a selection of its most famous talks, edited by the Programme's then Controller, John Morris.[32] In the spring of that year, Morris gave a paper on the development and influence of the Third Programme to the International Meeting of

27 Memorandum from Christopher Holme, 29 March 1950, quoted with approval by Harman Griesewood, Third Programme Controller in a memorandum to Alec Robertson (original *Music Magazine* presenter), 12 June 1950 (BBC WAC R27/236 Music General: 'Music Magazine' file 1, 1941–54).

28 *Daily Express*, 3 October 1946.

29 *Punch*, 4 December 1946.

30 William Haley, quoted by Rex Keating in 'Third Programme problems in certain underdeveloped areas', UNESCO Reports and Papers on Mass Communications, No. 23, December 1956.

31 These were Kenneth Leighton's String Quartet, Boris Blacher's *Fantasy for Orchestra*, Phyllis Tate's *The Lady of Shalott*, Peter Racine Fricker's Cello Sonata, Jacques Ibert's *Bacchanale*, Anthony Milner's *The Harrowing of Hell*, Alun Hoddinott's Septet, Vagn Holmboe's *Symphonic Metamorphosis: epitaph*, Andrzej Panufnik's *Rhapsody* and Goffredo Petrassi's *Invenzione concertata*. They were almost all premiered by the BBC in the autumn of 1956.

32 Morris (1956b). None of the talks selected is on music.

Cultural Radio Programme Directors held by UNESCO in Paris,[33] where he was surrounded by paeans of praise for the Third from his European colleagues, most of whom were engaged in attempts to emulate what they saw as the BBC's astounding success. Indeed, the very name, 'Third Programme', is used throughout the speeches as a synonym for cultural broadcasting, with delegates referring to 'Third Programme-type broadcasts' or 'creating a Third Programme' in their own countries. Radio Italiana had even gone so far as to name its own cultural network 'Terza Programa'.

The picture at home was not quite so rosy. Even by the time of the Third's fifth birthday in 1951, the post-war surge of interest in matters cultural appeared to be already on the wane. By 1956, it was clear that Haley's cultural pyramid was never going to narrow its base, and the Third Programme would not realize anything like its original aim of capturing 10 per cent of the radio audience. What prompted the BBC into a major re-examination of its whole sound broadcasting output, however, was the rapid (and, by some, unforeseen) growth of television broadcasting[34] – and, what was worse, the speed at which the BBC lost its monopoly in this area. After commercial television went on air in 1955, most were convinced that commercial radio would not be far behind, a prospect which the BBC viewed with what could almost be described as corporate terror. Already Radio Luxembourg, which began broadcasting in English in 1951, was a threat to the popularity of the Light Programme, and the total radio audience was in any case wilting under the pressure of television.[35] The BBC feared that by the time its charter next came up for renewal in 1962 its audience share would no longer justify the universal licence fee. Concluding that 'the loss of its monopoly in broadcasting has very much reduced the BBC's power to manipulate programme policy in the interest of social and cultural

33 Morris (1956a).

34 The broadcasting of the Coronation in 1953 contributed enormously to the spread of television.

35 However, television and Radio Luxembourg were not the only causes of the decline in the BBC's radio audience, which had peaked in 1948: the conclusion of the BBC's own audience research department was that 'Television and … Luxembourg … are by no means responsible for all the reduction in listening. Indeed the average BBC sound audience had already fallen by 20% before either of these two causes *could* have had any appreciable effect' ('The trend of listening since the war', report by R.J.E. Silvey, 4 January 1957, BBC WAC R34/1022/3 Policy: Future of Sound Broadcasting in the Domestic Services Working Party). During the meetings which the Working Party on the Future of Sound Broadcasting had with BBC staff in 1956, the interesting suggestion was made by a Mr Thornton that British radio suffered much more than American radio from competition from television simply because, at this date, most British homes were not centrally heated; the two apparatuses were therefore usually kept in the same room. 'In the U.S., where the whole house was heated, the television set was normally in the sitting room, and a number of small portable radio sets were found all over the house' (Minutes of meeting held on 6 December 1956, BBC WAC R23/950 Policy: Working Party on Sound Broadcasting AHS – Minutes).

aims',[36] the BBC prepared to begin abandoning Haley's great vision. A cynical view of the Corporation's thought-processes is given by the former producer and principal protester Peter Laslett:

> Now, so the case went, the support of the highbrows in 1962 was foreordained; they could not possibly back the commercial broadcaster against the BBC in sound or vision. Therefore in order to keep as many listeners as possible and as much support among the mass audience, those who elect members of parliament, the BBC must begin looking carefully at audience figures, cut (or perhaps abolish?) the Third Programme, drop or make inconspicuous everything which looked like an audience loser.[37]

Pragmatic retrenchments, as opposed to visionary expansions, are very often driven by committees rather than individuals, and so the BBC's 1956–57 review, like the later *Broadcasting in the Seventies*, was a rather more complicated process than that of 1944. The report submitted in January 1957 by the working party set up to examine the future of radio broadcasting was the result of 25 meetings and 44 consultations with other members of staff. Nevertheless, the role of certain individuals in this process was crucial, most notably that of the working party chairman, Richard D'Arcy Marriott. Marriott, the former Controller, Northern Ireland, had just arrived as Assistant Director of Sound Broadcasting, and he began discussing the need for review immediately with the Director of Sound Broadcasting, Lindsay Wellington. Wellington was impressed by Marriott's arguments and submitted them in October 1956 to the Director-General, Sir Ian Jacob, recommending that they merited immediate and detailed investigation. The Future of Sound Broadcasting in the Domestic Services Working Party which was set up as a result carried out its extensive review in a remarkably short period of time, so that Marriott, as chairman, was able to present its conclusions to the Governors a mere two months later.

Marriott's starting point appears to have lain in his observation of the development of television, from which he drew two basic lessons. First, he was clear that television was undoubtedly going to be the dominant medium, on which 'the BBC's reputation and possibly its very existence are going to depend'. This would mean that an increasing proportion of the BBC's resources would have to be concentrated in television, which would probably require a contraction of the services offered by radio, one of whose objects would henceforth be 'to serve TV'.[38] Second, he was struck by the 'remarkable equanimity' with which the general public accepted the idea of commercial television. 'The main defenders of our monopoly were to be

36 BBC WAC R34/1021, Policy: The Future of Sound Broadcasting in the Domestic Services, Report, 1957.

37 Laslett (1958).

38 Marriott, untitled memorandum, July 1956 (BBC WAC R34/1022/2, Policy: Future of Sound Broadcasting in the Domestic Services Working Party).

found in the House of Lords and other strongholds of "the Establishment",' he pointed out, 'not among the majority of people in the country', a large percentage of whom now preferred to watch the new service. The paternalistic BBC had traditionally had too little respect for the tastes of the majority of its audience, and was now paying the price: 'If the BBC had been firmly grounded in the affections of its listeners, it is possible that commercial television would never have come into being.' The Corporation ought to ask itself, therefore, whether it was giving the people what they required:

> It is a salutary discipline to ask ourselves what would happen if commercial radio were to be established tomorrow. Could we confidently say that we could hold our audience, because we were giving them what they wanted from us, particularly in the field of entertainment? And if we could not, would it be because we were unable to do so or because we did not choose to do so? Neither case would be one that it would be easy to defend publicly.[39]

These were radical thoughts, but Lindsay Wellington, for one, was of the opinion that they ought to be taken seriously. He drew from his discussions with Marriott two points which he believed were fundamental to the sort of new policy they were considering, and presented them to Sir Ian Jacob:

> (a) the need to abandon the BBC's traditional belief that it can compel listeners to attend to 'better things', or should attempt to do so;
> (b) the need to abandon finally any pretence of competition between the three Sound programmes.[40]

Marriott had been able to show, by analysing radio schedules 'horizontally' rather than 'vertically' (that is, considering what was offered to the listener at any one moment of time, rather than the content of each separate network), that 'for a great part of the time two of our three programmes are catering for 10% of the population, leaving one programme to provide for the remaining 90%'. He provided several examples:

> There is nothing unusual in Home Service broadcasting Dvorák's Stabat Mater while Third carries a talk on metaphysics and a recital from the Edinburgh Festival, leaving Light to satisfy the rest of the audience; or to quote a case discussed recently, while Home Service offers a symphony concert and Third a Henry James play, Light is broadcasting a Sherriff play, which at least half of the population will have neither the leisure nor the inclination to listen to. Recently Light Programme mounted two interesting programmes on the Suez crisis ... one of them coincided [on the Home Service] with a discussion on Appeasement and

39 Marriott, 'Sound Broadcasting Policy', October 1956 (BBC WAC ibid.).

40 Wellington, 'Memorandum to Director General: Future of Sound Broadcasting', 18 October 1956 (BBC WAC ibid.). Attached to this memorandum is a statement on 'Sound Broadcasting Policy' prepared by Marriott.

> the other with recollections of Virginia Woolf, while Third was offering material that would certainly not reach beyond the 10% … Can it be right that we should devote twice as much attention to the educated section as we do to the great majority of our audience?[41]

Wellington agreed that it was not right. 'The whole output of Sound Broadcasting should cease to be so heavily weighted in favour of the highly educated and serious minded,' he wrote to the Director-General.[42] Privately, to Marriott, he gave an interesting analysis of why the BBC's educative mission was proving unworkable:

> There was general growing agreement in the 19th century that 'the people' should have 'the best' – working-class leaders joined with Liberal aristocrats in clamouring for this. What was missing was any working-class experience (on a mass scale) of 'the best'. Once this was experienced through the BBC it became clear (around 1950) that 'the people' didn't desire 'the best' at all. So, much of the Reithian/Haleian preconceptions are now proved to be false assumptions.[43]

In the course of the many discussions which followed, reducing the BBC's radio provision to two networks was frequently considered, with the Third being the usual candidate for execution. It was concluded, however, that, given the number of sound-only licences still in operation, a full service should continue to be provided at least in the short term, while the BBC continued to observe the evolving relationship between radio and television. Nevertheless, the working party felt that the BBC's 'extravagant' cultural broadcasting had to be curtailed in some way, and recommended a 50 per cent cut in the Third's airtime.

Though the eventual cut was marginally less drastic, reaction from outside the BBC was dramatic. Well before the plans were announced, the Third Programme Defence Society (later renamed the Sound Broadcasting Society) was founded by Peter Laslett, a Cambridge academic and former BBC talks producer, and Peter Needs, a London schoolteacher, and, with backing from the press, it gathered together supporters at a remarkable rate. Since these supporters included people like T.S. Eliot, Laurence Olivier, Michael Tippett and Ralph Vaughan Williams, the Corporation had a difficult defence job on its hands. The BBC's official announcement of its plans in April was followed by almost universal condemnation in the press, whose correspondence pages were filled with multi-signature protest letters from famous intellectuals, and even prominent former BBC employees like

41 Ibid.

42 Ibid.

43 Unsigned memorandum, probably from Wellington to Marriott, discussing a draft which the latter had prepared for the Director-General, headed 'Notes' and dated 5 October 1956 (BBC WAC ibid.).

Sir Arthur Bliss and Sir Adrian Boult.[44] A petition signed by 130 Members of Parliament was collected in the House of Commons and, in the debate which followed, the BBC's failure to consult its Advisory Council (of which several MPs were members) was deplored. Marriott may have been surprised by the vehemence of this chorus of protest, for while he had noted with surprise, when scanning press reaction to the Third's tenth anniversary, that 'there is no demand, as there might have been, from the middle- and low-brow press for the Third Programme to be abandoned', he thought this was the result more of 'a general national characteristic of approving cultural monuments which have no connection with our own lives'[45] than any positive engagement with what the Third was actually doing.

There is no evidence that Hans Keller took any part in this prolonged public debate on the Third. In view of his evident interest in radio and the prominent role he played in the protest at the next BBC review, this is perhaps surprising. At the time, however, Keller's protesting energies were concentrated on campaigning for the abolition of capital punishment, in which cause he was remarkably assiduous, collecting record numbers of signatures to the petition in support of Sidney Silverman's bill.[46] Of course, he was not yet on the staff of the BBC, but even if he had been, he would have found there a very different atmosphere from the internal rebelliousness provoked by *Broadcasting in the Seventies*. In 1957, the member of the BBC's staff who wrote that 'I would be ashamed if what was conceived in war as an act of faith were jettisoned by the Corporation as an act of despair'[47] was in the minority. Most staff appeared to acquiesce in the cutting of the Third, and the Controllers of the other two networks actively recommended its abolition. Even John Morris, the Third's Controller, didn't

44 One particular letter, which appeared in *The Times* on 26 April 1957, 'carried the authority of a proclamation of the reigning monarchs of English letters' according to an American journalist writing a few years later (see Mehta, 1963), signed as it was by Lord Beveridge, Arthur Bliss, Adrian Boult, the Bishop of Chichester, T.S. Eliot, E.M. Forster, Christopher Fry, John Gielgud, Victor Gollancz, John Masefield, Harold Nicolson, Bertrand Russell, V. Sackville-West, Ralph Vaughan Williams, and Peter Laslett. The *Daily Mirror* was less impressed, referring to the signatories as 'fifteen Third Programme fans. They include … a Peer of seventy-eight, another Peer of eighty-four, a poet getting on for seventy, a composer of eighty-four, a writer in his seventies, a bishop of seventy-four.'

45 Marriott, 'Press Opinions on Third Programme Tenth Anniversary', undated memorandum (BBC WAC R34/951/1, Policy: Working Party on Sound Broadcasting, AHS's papers).

46 In January 1956, Peggy Duff, Secretary of the National Campaign for the Abolition of Capital Punishment, wrote to thank Keller for his efforts: 'Congratulations on the lists you have sent us. No-one else has sent us so many names … You hold the record and nobody looks like wresting it from you' (letter from Duff to Keller, 2 January 1956, CUL Keller Archive).

47 Unsigned undated memorandum to the Director of Sound Broadcasting (BBC WAC R34/1022/3, The Future of Sound Broadcasting in the Domestic Services: Working Party, 1956–57).

seem to be inclined to fight for it, conceding instead that it 'needed drastic pruning', and even offering it as the most suitable candidate for the axe, should the BBC decide to reduce radio to two networks. 'If it were decided it cut it out,' he advised the working party, it should be done by 'reducing its hours gradually and then merging it with Home Service.'[48]

John Morris's appointment as Controller of the Third Programme in 1953 at the age of 57 (with only three years to go before retirement, although in the end he stayed on for five) was taken by some, even at that early date, as an indication that the closure of the Third might be imminent. Described by his predecessor, Harman Grisewood, as 'a nice fellow', but 'an office man',[49] Morris turned out to be an uninspiring Controller and the view of the Third which he presented to the working party contrasted rather sharply with one which they received at another meeting a few days later: 'Mr Newby said that the future of sound lay with the Third Programme.'[50] An opportunity to put this to the test came in 1958, when John Morris retired and Howard Newby, at the age of 40, was appointed to succeed him.

Howard Newby, novelist and 'uncommon egghead',[51] was, like William Haley – and Hans Keller – an autodidact, whose range of interests and knowledge was considerable, if often understated. His appointment encouraged the battered ranks of Third Programme staff and their supporters to feel that the BBC was now committed to what was left of its cultural broadcasting, particularly since the very post of Controller, Third Programme, had alone been spared abolition in the streamlining of radio's administration; Home and Light were subsumed under the central hierarchy, while the Third was allowed to keep its independence a little longer. 'A quiet, unworldly sphinx-like man',[52] who nevertheless, 'when you knew him better ... emerged as a very sharp man with a wry sense of humour',[53] it seems that Newby was greatly appreciated by those with whom he worked. He was, says John Manduell, 'an immensely civilized person',[54] a judgement with which Robert Layton agrees: 'I think of him as the most civilized boss I've ever worked for and I admired him enormously.'[55] Brian Trowell, in charge of opera on radio from 1967 to 1970, also thought that Newby was 'outstandingly perceptive and intelligent in the way he handled us'.[56] He got on well with the Music Department, as Lionel Salter recalls: 'The

48 Minutes of the working party meeting held on 9 November 1956 (BBC WAC R34/950, Policy: Working Party on Sound Broadcasting, AHS – minutes 1956–57).

49 Harman Grisewood, interviewed by Humphrey Carpenter, 1 July 1994 (quoted in Carpenter, 1996, p. 130).

50 Minutes of the working party meeting held on 14 November 1956 (BBC WAC ibid.).

51 According to the *Manchester Guardian*, 4 November 1958.

52 Mehta (1963), p. 119.

53 Ernest Warburton, quoted in Carpenter (1996), p. 190.

54 John Manduell, interviewed by Humphrey Carpenter, 30 March 1995 (quoted in Carpenter, 1996, p. 244).

55 Robert Layton, oral communication, 11 November 1996.

56 Trowell (1972).

programme meetings we used to have with Howard Newby were enormous fun'[57] – not least, for some, because of the intriguing spectacle of his arguments with Hans Keller. According to Alexander Goehr, 'Howard Newby ... loved sparring with Hans: they enjoyed each other a great deal;

> Howard had a mischievous side and he used to have a frisson of delight when Hans went off on one of his wilder rampages ... it was a real pleasure, because here was a typical English liberal civil servant of that time, very sharp, but not at all banal – I mean, Howard Newby was not at all banal – looking at this object from outer space sitting opposite him, who was given to the most extravagant speeches, extravagant praise of what he liked, total condemnation of what he did not like. And, you know, Howard would both encourage him and put him down ... Newby was quite imperturbable: [he'd] seen mavericks before – after all, the BBC was full of them.[58]

'I had an immense liking and admiration for Keller,' says Newby, 'though if anyone had heard me say this at the time they would have been amazed, because he used to insult me in public – to a degree that now amazes me – and our rows were tremendous. But he insulted anyone in authority that he could.'[59]

At around the same time as Newby took up his duties as Controller, Third Programme, William Glock was invited to lunch by the then Controller of Music, Richard Howgill, whom Glock had asked for support in his candidature for the directorship of the Guildhall School of Music. Howgill, however, told him that he had a 'better idea' and proposed that he apply instead to take over his own post at the BBC when he retired the following year. Glock says this suggestion threw him into 'a state of some turmoil',[60] which was not alleviated by the BBC's procrastination over the appointment. It was almost a year after Glock's lunch with Howgill that it was officially announced that he would be the next Controller of Music.

'I feel rather as though I were a citizen of Wittenberg in 1536 and Luther had just been elected Pope', was how Walter Legge described his reaction to the news of Glock's appointment.[61] The choice of someone so closely identified with the European avant-garde was a stunning surprise to those who felt that the Corporation's music policy had become conservative and insular during the 1950s.[62] Asa Briggs has drawn a parallel between Glock

---

57 Lionel Salter, oral communication, 10 January 1996.

58 Alexander Goehr, oral communication, 28 November 1996.

59 Howard Newby interviewed by Humphrey Carpenter, 24 May 1995 (quoted in Carpenter, 1996, p. 198).

60 Glock (1991), p. 97.

61 Quoted in Glock (1991), p. 99.

62 This was not a universal view, however. Robert Layton, who arrived at the same time as Glock, says, 'I always joke that the Third Programme was much better before I joined it!' (oral communication, 11 November 1996). David Cox agrees that, in general, the 1950s music policy is now under-rated (oral communication, 17 January 1996).

and the BBC's revolutionary Director-General of the 1960s, Hugh Greene: 'Much that [Glock] said about BBC music policy was similar to Greene's language. Without any prompting, he always spoke of the paramount need for "liveliness"; of the need to turn away from "conventional patterns", of "trying to open up frontiers that would otherwise remain closed", and, above all, of the importance of taking risks. "If you are prepared to put a foot anywhere, then you must be prepared to put it wrong."'[63]

Glock had been involved with the contemporary music policy of the Third Programme almost at its beginning, when in 1947 he was sent by George Barnes (the Third's first Controller) and Etienne Amyot on a tour of the occupied zones in Europe, to 'bring back some news and, where possible, evidence of what had been going on since 1939 both in performance and composition'.[64] It had been an important part of the early Third Programme policy that its programmes should be international in nature, but its contemporary music policy by the time Glock was appointed as Controller was distinctly wary of the continental avant-garde. Glock's arrival changed this, swiftly and dramatically. Not surprisingly, it caused consternation among some of his musical colleagues in the BBC – 'the change was too sudden, and too radical altogether to be easily accepted,' remembers Lionel Salter[65] – indeed, even for those who agreed that some change was necessary, Glock's pace was still dizzying. 'In many ways, I think probably the BBC did need shaking up,' says David Cox, 'but we weren't expecting it quite so violently.'[66] Chief among those who objected to Glock's reforms was his own deputy, Head of Music Maurice Johnstone. 'A battle royal seemed inevitable,' wrote Glock later,[67] and Keller seems to have agreed when he arrived that Johnstone was the principal obstacle to Glock's plans. In a letter to Glock in which he analysed staff opposition to the new policies, he concluded that 'the only strong personality on the other side is Maurice'.[68] Glock decided that Johnstone had to go, and with his departure the following year the post of Head of Music was abolished, and Glock took over its responsibilities.

At the beginning of his tenure as Controller, Glock took a lot of power into his own hands. As well as assuming Johnstone's job of running the Music Department (for which, according to Lionel Salter, he was singularly

63 Briggs (1995), p. 398.

64 Glock (1991), p. 46. Glock went to Munich, Vienna, Prague, Berlin, Hamburg and the ISCM Festival in Copenhagen, had 'great experiences', which included 'thrilling' performances of *Salome* and *The Barber of Seville* in Vienna, and met 'many leading musicians', including Shostakovich and David Oistrakh. He also found a great deal of interest in British music-making 'and so I found myself delivering scores by Tippett, Priaulx Rainier, and many others, and receiving German scores in return which nearly filled a suitcase'.

65 Lionel Salter, oral communication, 10 January 1996.

66 David Cox, oral communication, 17 January 1996.

67 Glock (1991), p. 101.

68 Letter from Keller to Glock, 24 October 1959 (CUL Keller Archive).

unfitted: 'William Glock … was an absolutely dreadful administrator!'[69]), he also took personal charge of the planning of a number of the BBC's most important concerts, most controversially – then and later – the planning of the Proms.

> I found when I arrived at Yalding House, our headquarters, that some of the most creative tasks in BBC music (above all, the planning of the famous Promenade Concerts, or Proms) were delegated to a committee. I had never believed that any great artistic enterprise could succeed in that way, and I resolved to try and establish a new policy by enacting it myself. This meant taking over the Proms and a few other crucial concerts, public and otherwise. My decision about the Proms aroused anger and outrage. I was denounced to the Director of Sound Broadcasting as a Hitler intent on destroying the very foundation of BBC music policy.[70]

Although the concentration of such a wealth of important musical patronage in one pair of hands caused a lasting controversy (Robert Simpson made a very public protest over this issue 20 years later[71]), the excellence of Glock's superbly imaginative programme planning has never been disputed. 'He built beautiful programmes,' says Alexander Goehr,[72] and Lionel Salter agrees: 'He was the most brilliant of programme men.'[73] One of his innovations was the skilful mingling of different styles and periods in a single concert, most notably in the Invitation Concerts which he launched in January 1960. These 'kippers and custard concerts', as Robert Simpson dubbed them,[74] were often given by more than one ensemble and contained the most striking combinations. Byrd and Machaut might be placed alongside Boulez, for example, or Bach and Handel with Schoenberg and Webern; other combinations included Victoria, Bach and Stravinsky, or Dowland, Beethoven and Henze. The opening concert of the series featured the Amadeus Quartet and Cecil Aronowitz playing two Mozart quintets, sandwiching the New Music Ensemble with Boulez's *Le Marteau sans Maître*.

Glock also reorganized the structure of the Music Division, scrapping the network-related Chief Assistants (Chief Assistant Home Service and Chief Assistant Third Programme, for example) and replacing them with Chief Assistants responsible for particular categories of music (Orchestral and Choral Music, and Chamber Music and Recitals), with a team of producers under them. In his early days at the BBC Glock worked very hard at recruiting like-minded musicians to the Corporation's staff, seeing it as

69 Lionel Salter, oral communication, 10 January 1996.
70 Glock (1991), p. 101.
71 See Simpson (1981).
72 Alexander Goehr, oral communication, 28 November 1996.
73 Lionel Salter, oral communication, 10 January 1996.
74 Quoted by Leo Black, oral communication, 4 August 1995.

'essential' to the success of his policies that he bring in new blood.[75] As will be seen in Chapter 4, Keller was the first – and most controversial – of these appointments and, for a while, he and Glock worked closely together. Leo Black, who joined the BBC the following year, remembers Keller as 'certainly the *primus inter pares* among the number twos'[76] at that time. David Cox, who was already at the BBC (in charge of music for the external services) when Glock and Keller arrived, agrees: 'Keller was very much in cahoots with Glock. They used to have long sessions together discussing everything, enclosed in Glock's office.'[77] Although Keller was appointed to an established post, many of Glock's new recruits came into the Corporation in a less formal way, without interviews and on short-term contracts, giving rise to the rather widespread impression that Glock was simply inviting all his friends into the BBC with scant regard for normal procedure. As Glock's successor, Robert Ponsonby, puts it, 'William Glock ... happened to meet them in the street, it seems: "Come on Deryck" or "Come on Hans, come and join the BBC on Monday." I'm not exaggerating too much – there were no boards or competition in those days: these people were invited in!'[78] Nevertheless, Ponsonby admits that the Music Division of the 1960s contained 'a lot of phenomenally gifted people'.

Having appointed the staff he wanted, reorganized the structure of his department and taken personal control of a significant slice of concert planning, Glock was apparently happy to give his staff a fairly free rein with the rest of programme-making, so that those who had dubbed him a 'Hitler' on his arrival found their fears unfounded. Indeed, some of his colleagues have criticized him for being too distant and insufficiently involved in the department's day-to-day work. Personally, he is often described as 'a cold fish' who didn't really know his staff.[79] 'It was very difficult to know what Glock thought about anything,' says Lionel Salter, 'not least because he was very rarely there. You know that he didn't work from the office at all, if he could help it: he worked from his own flat.'[80] Robert Layton describes Glock as 'kindly' but distant: 'He was very remote. But he was very, very absorbed in what he was doing.'[81]

It was not long after Glock's arrival that the BBC decided to launch a new Sound initiative that was to have a huge effect on the Music Department. When the Third Programme's hours were cut in 1957, the missing time had been filled by a new programme, unimaginatively titled Network Three and nicknamed by producers the Fretwork Network because of the hobbies

75 Glock (1991), p. 102.

76 Leo Black, oral communication, 4 August 1995.

77 David Cox, oral communication, 17 January 1996.

78 Robert Ponsonby, oral communication, 14 July 1995.

79 Robert Layton, oral communication, 11 November 1996, and Lionel Salter, oral communication, 10 January 1996.

80 Lionel Salter, oral communication, 10 January 1996.

81 Robert Layton, oral communication, 11 November 1996.

programmes which filled its schedules. Network Three was an example of the BBC's curious confusion of cultural and minority programming: at times (and particularly times of financial stringency) it seems as though the BBC's management viewed the arts as just one among many minorities for whom it had to cater. Network Three, in taking broadcasting time away from this one minority, would now, it was proudly announced, allow airtime for other minorities, such as (according to *Radio Times*) 'the jazz-fancier or the pigeon-fancier, the man or woman who wants to learn, say, Spanish from scratch, the fisherman or cyclist or collector of LP records … the bridge player or the naturalist, the more sophisticated film-goer, the ardent motorist or the enthusiast for amateur dramatics.'[82]

'A piece of appeasement worthy of Neville Chamberlain himself', was Peter Laslett's description of the new service,[83] and it was not long before the BBC began to realize that Network Three was proving to be rather a disaster. Since it was mocked by the press and listened to by even smaller audiences than heard the Third Programme, the BBC urgently sought to replace it. For a solution, Marriott revisited an idea which he had first suggested to Wellington in 1956 at the beginning of the review process:

> There is also at least one other possibility that we should not overlook and which would involve at certain times the use of a third network and that is the provision of a regular supply of good (but not necessarily difficult) music: much like one of the stations in New York, the name of which escapes me.[84]

Thus the Music Programme was born – conceived originally by a non-musician, as William Glock pointed out: 'I do not think any of it originated in the minds of musicians.'[85] Glock himself had considerable reservations about it, fearing the 'danger of musical wallpaper'.[86] Nevertheless, he was interested in the planning opportunities which it provided: for example, when Michael Tippett challenged him to break free of the concept of a series of concerts, 'a few of us met at Yalding House each weekend, and set out to innovate. The idea was to have a clear run of three hours or so, and to construct a small "musical festival"; with a different *leitmotif* every week.'[87] In this way, 'five of us, including Hans Keller, planned the whole of every Saturday morning'.[88]

The Music Programme took its time to reach the airwaves, held up by disagreements with the Musicians' Union over the amount of 'needletime'

82 *Radio Times*, 29 September 1957.

83 Laslett (1958).

84 Memorandum from Marriott to Wellington, 8 October 1956 (BBC WAC R34/1022/2 Policy: Future of Sound Broadcasting in the Domestic Services Working Party).

85 Glock (1991), p. 128.

86 Glock, interviewed by Frank Gillard for the BBC's Oral History Project (quoted in Carpenter, 1996, p. 225).

87 Glock (1991), p. 130.

88 Glock, interviewed by Humphrey Carpenter, 20 November 1995 (private source).

(the use of commercial recordings) which the BBC could have. It was introduced in three phases, finally becoming a full daytime service, seven days a week, in March 1965. Interestingly, the Chief Assistant who planned it (initially John Manduell, with Keller covering the job for a short while at the beginning of 1965 while Manduell was away ill) reported to the Controller of the Home Service and not to Howard Newby. This was intended to keep the service firmly in the 'middlebrow' range. As Wellington's successor, Frank Gillard, warned Glock, 'The Music Programme should not be regarded as a channel for new, difficult and advanced music.'[89]

The Music Programme's audience was carefully monitored by the BBC's Audience Research Department and, as was the intention, it showed a different profile from that of the Third Programme, in being more exclusively middle-class and considerably less selective. This lack of selectivity made it clear that Glock's 'musical wallpaper' fears were not without foundation. Although similar fears were also expressed by several critics, it is interesting that Hans Keller's own opinion at this time appears to have been remarkably sanguine. Commenting on a *New Statesman* article by former producer David Drew, Keller said that, although he himself was 'constitutionally incapable of background listening', not enough was yet known about 'musical perception and cognition' to be able to say that such listening is always a bad thing: 'There is a considerable body of opinion according to which background listening is positively recommendable in cases where there are resistances to the music in question. People who assimilate a musical language pre-consciously may thus learn to absorb the musical substance more readily.'[90]

The difference between this response and the views which Keller expressed on generic broadcasting only a few years later is startling. Here he seems to come close to approving a kind of subliminal instruction which later he would surely have viewed as unethical, insisting as he did that the listener must at all times remain 'master of his mental fate':

> The only influence we are entitled to exert is influence towards increased individual independence, towards the listener's remaining master of his mental fate, rather than towards our mastering it. It follows that news channels apart, all generic broadcasting is unethical: inevitably, it turns music, even speech programmes, into a drug … Mixed programming alone affords the possibility of sharply and meaningfully contrasting programmes which, throwing each other into relief, invite the clearest possible choice.[91]

At no time in all the debate over the changes proposed in *Broadcasting in the Seventies* did Keller note the role which the Music Programme had

---

89 Memorandum from Gillard to Glock, 30 July 1964 (BBC WAC R34/1034/1, Policy: Music Programme).

90 Letter to the editor, *New Statesman*, 8 January 1965, p. 41.

91 'Broadcasting in the 'Eighties', *The Spectator*, 10 July 1976.

1. Hans Keller, *c.*1959. Photo: Brian Seed

2. Hans Keller with William Glock (left) at Dartington, *c.*1958.
Photo: Catherine Scudamore

3. Hans Keller with the Dartington Quartet, *c.*1958. Photo: Catherine Scudamore

4. Hans Keller and Milein Cosman in their Hampstead home, 1961. Collection of Milein Cosman

5. Hans Keller with Huw Wheldon and Michael Tippett during a studio discussion for the TV programme 'Britten at Fifty' in 1963. Photo: BBC

6. Hans Keller in his study, *c.*1958. Collection of Milein Cosman

7. Hans Keller and Milein Cosman with Peter Maxwell Davies and Harrison Birtwistle at Dartington. Collection of Milein Cosman

8. Hans Keller and Milein Cosman with Walter Todds at the Irish Embassy in December 1966. Photo: Lensmen International

9. Hans Keller with Peter Pears at Snape, *c.*1979. Collection of Milein Cosman

10. Hans Keller and Milein Cosman with Anthony Dean (right) at an EBU conference dinner in the late 1970s. Collection of Milein Cosman

11. Hans Keller at the microphone with Denis Matthews. Collection of Milein Cosman

12. Hans Keller talking to Misha Donat at Milein Cosman's Gaudau Arts Centre Stravinsky show in 1982. Photo: Errol Jackson

13. Hans Keller at home in Frognal Gardens, photographed by Milein Cosman

played in the Third Programme's demise, nor did he criticize at the time the fact that it was a 'generic' programme. Music had always played a rather larger part in the Third Programme's schedules than intended (for example, it was supposed to fill 'a third' of the opening schedules, but the actual proportion was 50 per cent), a temptation which increased as successive agreements with the Musicians' Union gradually made music broadcasting cheaper by increasing the use of recordings. Once the Music Programme was on air, it created a huge preponderance of music on that wavelength, which threatened to swamp the Third's more varied programming.

Although Richard Marriott retired from the BBC in the year *Broadcasting in the Seventies* appeared, he did once more play an important role in the development of the new policy. From December 1967 until 15 November 1968, he chaired the Working Group on the Future of Radio that laid the foundations for the ensuing Policy Study Group, chaired by Gerard Mansell, which produced *Broadcasting in the Seventies*. Marriott's original brief had been to make recommendations about the future network structure of BBC radio in preparation for a new allocation of European wavelengths, but he had taken the opportunity to revisit some of his earlier concerns. The intervening years had not changed his picture of radio as television's junior partner, and 'we asked ourselves, as everybody concerned with the future of radio must do, whether we are providing more radio than is really needed'. Once again, he urged the BBC to look at its schedules horizontally, and address the question of the listener's choice solely in those terms. The evidence was, he thought, that listeners were choosing a congenial wavelength, as opposed to particular programmes, and were no longer willing to structure their day around the radio. Generic broadcasting was therefore much more suitable than mixed programming for a medium which, he felt, had 'lost its compulsiveness'. Radio planning ought to be as 'simple and convenient as possible, with the minimum need for reference to the printed programme'. Interestingly, Marriott's report notes that BBC radio had been 'working on this basis for some time'[92] and, in this context, he must have had the Music Programme in mind. Indeed, *Broadcasting in the Seventies* itself cites the Music Programme as its first experiment in generic programming: when announcing the BBC's move towards 'the specialised network, offering a continuous stream of one particular type of programme, meeting one particular interest', it states that 'already BBC radio has moved in this direction, first with the Music Programme, then with the all-pop Radio One.'[93]

To many in Music Division, however, the large increase in broadcasting hours which the start of the Music Programme made available to them was simply a most exciting opportunity. To Keller, it brought a wider sphere of influence (since its planning was left much more to the Music Division than

92 From the Working Party report (quoted in Briggs, 1995, pp. 738–9).
93 BBC (1969), p. 3.

was the case on the Third Programme), as well as an opportunity to produce music talks again, as will be seen. It was undoubtedly the case, however, that Radio 3 was already born.

Chapter 4

Music and Words

'May I say,' wrote Keller in the course of a routine internal report a couple of months after his arrival at the BBC, 'that I am extremely happy here.'[1] Keller's time as Music Talks Producer, despite lasting only seven months, was indeed a memorable one. He himself fondly recalled his huge and 'rather naive' enjoyment of it,[2] as well as the sense of freedom it gave him before he became embroiled in the morally murky waters (as he saw them) of BBC management: 'the Music Talks Producer at the BBC is rather a separate radio station,' he later wrote[3] (a description which he also used of the EBU concert planning committee he later chaired – another aspect of his work which he found very satisfying). Others cite his considerable success in the post: Stephen Plaistow, for example, remembers how, on his own arrival at the BBC nearly two years after Keller had moved on to take charge of chamber music, his colleagues were still talking of the innovations he had made in music talks.[4] The BBC's files of the time also give a vivid impression of the energy and enthusiasm with which Keller took up his new duties, and the flood of highly characteristic ideas which he brought forward.

Despite the brevity of his period in charge of them, music talks have a significant place in Keller's work as a staff member. For the rest of his BBC life, he retained a deep interest in talks policy, continuing to make suggestions and innovations. When the daytime Music Programme went on air in 1964, he took responsibility for its talks (almost certainly at his own initiative), in addition to his other work. Even after relinquishing this charge in 1972, he continued to produce a great number of talks – indeed, they were certainly his principal, if not at times his only, activity as a producer throughout his career. Moreover, the contribution which he made to BBC music talks as a speaker himself is justly famous, and it is therefore interesting to examine his policies and production of others in a medium which he made so much his own.

Keller's abiding interest in talks is also an illustration of what has been

---

1 Memorandum to the Establishment Officer (Sound), 30 November 1959 (CUL Keller Archive). The main subject of the memorandum was a report on Keller's recent publications: it was the custom to report any outside work to the Establishment Officer, and the amount of independent writing which Keller continued to do after his appointment at the BBC was a matter of careful agreement between him and the Corporation.

2 *1975* (1977), p. 20.

3 Ibid., p. 20.

4 Stephen Plaistow, oral communication, 27 July 1995.

described as his 'compulsive verbalising',[5] as it is perhaps surprising that the inventor of wordless functional analysis should have taken so much time away from the specifically musical opportunities of broadcasting to concentrate to the extent he did on talks. Keller was not especially noted as a programme-builder, in the way that Glock was, for example, and he did not do a great deal of actual production of music programmes. His output of talks, on the other hand, was significant,[6] as was his tirelessly meticulous editing of them – a contrast to his approach to music planning, where, according to Glock, he was 'more interested in the general ingredients involved than in deciding on the details'.[7]

Keller took up his new BBC post on 1 September 1959, four months after the arrival of William Glock as Controller of Music. As has been seen, Glock had aroused considerable hostility in some parts of the Music Department, so it was inevitable that Keller, the first new member of staff he appointed, would be viewed with suspicion, even if nothing else had been known against him. Naturally, however, Keller provoked plenty of opposition on his own account: 'In view of what *Music Survey* has done to us, only over my dead body' was apparently Head of Music Maurice Johnstone's reaction to the idea of appointing Keller,[8] and even Glock himself later admitted that it had been his 'most controversial decision'.[9]

In their early years together at the BBC, Glock and Keller worked closely in tandem and, although their relationship was later to deteriorate, they seemed at this stage to share many of the same objectives. In particular, Glock wanted support in his attempt to improve the BBC's representation of twentieth-century music, and Keller, although his understanding of the contemporary scene was ultimately very different from Glock's, certainly

---

5 See Derrick Puffett, in Wintle (1986), p. 388.

6 'Since the Third Quarter of 1970, I have been responsible, in addition to my two official jobs, for about 350 daytime music talks – the majority of a quality which produced reprints in *The Listener*, repeats and requests for repeats in the evening, interest on the part of BBC Transcription Service and Pick of the Week, prominent mention in the BBC handbook, and even requests from Radio 3 to transfer certain talks intended for the daytime to the evening, in view of their importance' (internal memorandum from Keller to BBC Personnel Officer Jock Beesley, 24 February 1972, private source). Although Keller is including here his supervision of daytime music talks, as well as his own productions, he did produce a substantial number of these talks himself.

7 William Glock, in Wintle (1986), p. 379.

8 *Music Survey* (1981), Preface, n.p. 'At the appointments board for my first BBC job, although I was chosen, I was reliably informed that the then Head of Music, Maurice Johnstone, was the first to speak after I had left the room: "In view of what *Music Survey* has done to us, only over my dead body."' Keller's reputation as a vigorous Schoenberg supporter was probably also a factor in this opinion, if Glock's description of Johnstone's musical conservatism is accurate: 'He was a pertinacious and likeable Lancastrian, who in 1959 still dismissed the works of the Second Viennese School in a spirit of almost moral indignation.' Glock (1991), p. 101. Nevertheless, Johnstone had great respect for Keller's Functional Analyses (see Chapter 2, n. 57).

9 Glock (1991), p. 103.

had an equal sense of the importance of this task: 'From the standpoint of promoting contemporary music, which is *the* musical problem of our age, the Controller of Music in a national broadcasting Corporation occupies about the most important position that can be imagined.'[10]

From Glock's point of view, new staff were needed in order to make significant changes to the BBC's repertoire. Keller had long been arguing in print that the BBC was badly in need of a resident modern music expert and, initially, he saw Glock himself as sufficient guarantee.[11] Glock, however, felt that he could not do what was needed alone: 'I knew that, if great things were to happen, it would be essential to recruit some outstanding new members of staff.'[12] Among those who joined the Corporation in Glock's first year was the composer Alexander Goehr, who arrived with David Drew a few months after Keller; he describes the situation as follows:

> At the beginning, when Glock got the job, he wanted to employ some supporters, and the people he approached were old ICA people, basically, people from the ICA committee ... Of course Glock got Keller in, because Keller had great talents, and he got him in as Head of Talks because that's an obvious thing to do – I mean, you didn't have to be a genius to think of that. And once Keller was in, Glock hadn't got so many friends in the BBC, and so Keller was his man. And surely it was Hans who recruited most of the others.[13]

Leo Black, who joined the BBC in 1960, shortly after Goehr and Drew, remembers Keller's recruiting work for Glock – indeed his own appointment was one of the results:

> Glock had asked around about various youngish people who could come in and help him, as he saw it, liven up the place he'd been put in charge of, and clearly the person whose reactions he trusted most was Hans.[14]

Keller was also Glock's ally when it came to dealing with resistance to the changes from long-standing members of the department. A 'private and confidential' memorandum which he sent to Glock a few weeks after arriving shows him keeping his boss informed of meetings held in his absence and analysing personalities and alliances on the other side, concluding that 'the opposition may be much stronger than we care to realize'.[15] Despite finishing his memo 'What a waste of time it all is', Keller probably enjoyed all this politicking enormously, signing himself 'Black Sheep' and relishing a sense of being the underground resistance which was

---

10 'The New in Review', *Music Review*, May 1959.

11 See 'The New in Review: TV music, Mr Salter, and the BBC', *The Music Review*, **20**/1 (February 1959), pp. 71–2, and 'The New in Review', *The Music Review*, May 1959.

12 Glock (1991), p. 102.

13 Alexander Goehr, oral communication, 28 November 1996.

14 Leo Black, oral communication, 4 August 1995.

15 Internal memorandum from Keller to Glock, 24 October 1959 (CUL Keller Archive).

to restore the vital spark to an over-venerable institution. As he announced to his friend, the composer Benjamin Frankel, 'The BBC isn't changing me; I'm changing the BBC.'[16]

Glock has described his musical friendship with Keller as being 'founded partly on our mutual love of Haydn and Mozart ... Hans and I met enthusiastically over the Viennese classics.'[17] Certainly, in the coming years, they were both to do much to restore Haydn's music to the broadcasting schedules. Their differences over more modern music, however, were many:

> I could not enthuse about what I knew of Franz Schmidt, whose works he revered so greatly. He in turn did not respond at all to Debussy, or to most French music. He valued Britten above any limit I could then aspire to, and sometimes he held opinions that were simply outrageous. One example was his startling assertion that 'Gershwin was a better composer than Webern' – as though in purpose and ideals they inhabited the same universe! In general, however, and although we set out in twentieth-century music from different points of the compass – Schoenberg and Stravinsky – I could follow and respect his judgements, antipathetic though some of them may have been.[18]

Glock's and Keller's respective viewing of twentieth-century music through the opposing poles of Stravinsky and Schoenberg may bear a large responsibility for some of their later disagreements, according to Alexander Goehr, who remembers that 'there were times when Hans and William hardly talked to each other, especially on the issue of Schoenberg, because William loathed Schoenberg'.[19] According to Lionel Salter, who was in charge of television music programmes at the time of Keller's appointment and who later became Assistant Controller, Keller's promotion of Schoenberg was just as vigorous inside the BBC as it had been outside and, however 'antipathetic' this may have been to Glock, he did not resist it:

> When [Hans] came in, he annoyed everybody by this mania he had – no other word for it – he was an absolute fanatic about spreading the gospel of Schoenberg ... Schoenberg had been under-represented, but the thing that, I think, rather shocked some of us was the way that William Glock allowed himself to be swayed to such an extent by this barrage from Hans.[20]

Robert Layton, who joined the BBC the day before Glock, gives a similar picture of how Keller's enthusiasm for Schoenberg appeared to his BBC colleagues at the time of his appointment:

> He was regarded as a maverick figure who was an extreme admirer of Schoenberg. I always felt the Schoenberg worship was psychologically a strange

16 Letter from Keller to Frankel, 28 February 1960 (CUL Keller Archive).
17 Glock (1991), pp. 103–4.
18 Ibid., p. 103.
19 Alexander Goehr, oral communication, 28 November 1996.
20 Lionel Salter, oral communication, 10 January 1996.

> phenomenon. We all worshipped various composers (I worshipped some Scandinavian composers) [and] we were all enthusiastic about those causes to which we subscribed. But in Hans' case, Schoenberg could do no wrong, and he really did seem to be totally dedicated. If Schoenberg had given something his imprimatur, that was OK.[21]

Among Keller's very earliest contemporary music talks suggestions was a two-stage project designed to present composers in conversation with the general listener and with each other.[22] The first stage comprised 'a whole hour's Brains Trust on New Music with outside questions' ('"uninstructed", "hostile" questions from the public', as he elaborated later[23]), put to a panel of two or three composers, a performer (Peter Pears) and a publisher (Howard Hartog), chaired by Donald Mitchell. This would be followed by a discussion between a group of composers 'of opposing tendencies' entitled *We, the Player, and the Listener*, the membership of the panel on this occasion overlapping with that of the Brains Trust. Howard Newby, Controller of the Third Programme, suggested that the first programme might go out on the Home Service, and the second on the Third, so Keller put the idea to Leonard Isaacs, Home Service Music Organizer. Isaacs was interested ('in principle I am all for an attempt to close the gap between "contemporary" composers and the general listening public'), but foresaw practical difficulties ('one would probably need five miles of tape for a 45-minute programme'). In addition, the very subject of contemporary music was not one which sat happily in Home Service schedules: 'The programmes in Home Service … which have a hidden didactic purpose have been hitherto almost entirely concerned with the supposedly timorous audience which cannot yet trust itself to listen to a whole symphony concert,' he explained to Keller. Adding dryly, 'but we may progress,'[24] he nevertheless recommended the idea to the Home Service Head of Planning.

On this occasion, however, they did not progress, so Keller put all his energies into his Third Programme composers' discussion. His initial ideas for panellists had been Peter Maxwell Davies, Elizabeth Lutyens, or Mátyás Seiber to represent 'advanced' composers, and Benjamin Britten, Robert Simpson, or Benjamin Frankel[25] to represent 'conservative' ones. It is evident from Keller's subsequent correspondence that the panel was to be built around Britten, and Keller wrote to him on 10 September to try to persuade him to take part: 'You know that *pace* Stravinsky, I regard you as the greatest

---

21 Robert Layton, oral communication, 11 November 1996.

22 The project was outlined first to Glock in a memorandum of 3 September 1959, and then in greater detail to members of the Third Programme Music Meeting four days later. (BBC WAC R51/889/1: Talks: Music and Music Intervals).

23 Annotation by Keller on a memorandum from Leonard Isaacs, 14 September 1959 (BBC WAC ibid.).

24 Memorandum from Isaacs to Keller, 14 September 1959 (BBC WAC ibid.).

25 Keller marked Frankel's name 'not with Lutyens' in view of the law-suit between him and her husband, Edward Clark.

composer alive. I therefore consider it my absolute duty to try and get something out of you, however pessimistic I may feel about my own attempt.'[26] 'My dear Hans,' replied Britten,

> The trouble is that if anyone else but you had asked me to take part in this discussion the answer would have been an immediate and firm 'no'. It is respect, affection and gratitude (for your prompt and stimulating help over the Schubert grace-note) which make me hesitate ... *But* I am not at all sure that I am the person for this discussion. I shall probably say many things which neither you nor I like – being a nervous and therefore accidental speaker.[27]

Equivocal as this reply was, Keller was delighted.

> My dear Ben, I am profoundly grateful – on our musical culture's behalf ... 'A nervous and accidental speaker' is, of course, ideal – *if* he is somebody: inevitably, his accidentals will be essentials; his wrong-note technique, however improvisatory, cannot fail to be right.[28]

Keller's next task was to find the 'opposite pole', an 'advanced' composer who could provide an effective contrast to Britten. Possibly at Glock's suggestion, he first approached Pierre Boulez. He outlined his idea to Boulez in person,[29] so there is no record of exactly what he suggested, but it would appear that he then envisaged a panel of three composers, Britten, Boulez and Mátyás Seiber, to be chaired by Donald Mitchell. He put this personnel to Boulez, who was evidently not impressed: 'A vrai dire, musicalement, je ne respecte que *très peu* de gens, et je ne les vois pas parmi ceux que vous me proposez. Ergo ...'[30] Keller showed this to Mitchell (annotating it 'so there, chum, you're not respected – but at least in excellent company') and sent Boulez a curt reply: 'I am sorry that you respect so very few people musically – an attitude usually confined to bad composers, of whom you are not one.'[31]

Keller's next idea was Roberto Gerhard, but when he mentioned this to Britten, the reply was long in coming and, when it did, discouraging:

> I did not react to the suggestion of Gerhard because I could not and cannot make up my mind as to the possibility of the whole scheme. February, by the way, is no

26 Letter from Keller to Britten, 10 September 1959 (BBC WAC Artist File: Benjamin Britten, File 2).

27 Letter from Britten to Keller, 19 September 1959 (BBC WAC ibid.).

28 Letter from Keller to Britten, 25 September 1959 (CUL Keller Archive).

29 According to the minutes of the Third Programme Music Meeting, 7 October 1959 (BBC WAC R27/885/1: Third Programme Meetings, File 4, 1959–62).

30 'To tell you the truth, I respect only a *very few* people musically, and I don't see them amongst those you have suggested to me' (undated letter from Boulez to Keller, BBC WAC ibid.).

31 Letter from Keller to Boulez, 4 November 1959 (BBC WAC ibid.).

good because of concerts and work and things. I have know [*sic*] Roberto for years, but we have not always hit if [*sic*] off. Don't be worried by all this; I will write again shortly when I see the future a little more clearly.[32]

Keller had one more try, suggesting Elizabeth Lutyens and Richard Rodney Bennett, in addition to Seiber ('at least they are genuine people'[33]), before what must by now have seemed the inevitable refusal came from Britten.

My dear Hans, I rang you up, as I expect you heard, when last in London, to suggest we lunched together, but heard you were in Hamburg. I wanted to tell you personally that I just *can't* do that discussion at the moment. You know I've not been well recently, & I'm having the Devil's own struggle to get this really enormous (in size and difficulty) opera done in time for the Festival next June – fighting against ill-health & depression. I *must* keep what little energy & time I have to think about that, & not add the worry of the discussion to it. I am really very sorry, but fear it's inevitable. Besides I'm so involved in trying to find the right notes that I can't worry about why they are right – or wrong! I will do a talk or something for you next winter.[34]

With Britten out of the picture, Keller seems to have given up the programme. This episode provides an illustration of one of his basic principles: the importance of getting the right people to speak, irrespective of how radiogenic their voices, on the grounds that creative artists are infinitely more worth listening to than the most accomplished professional broadcaster. He was also prepared to take great pains to allow such speakers the freedom to speak naturally, taking on himself the responsibility of producing a coherent programme. For example, when trying to get Stravinsky to give a talk while he was in London, he told him that, 'So far as I'm concerned, you can walk into a studio, talk freely for five minutes, and walk out again. I would then edit the tape to your satisfaction.'[35] In the case of the abortive composers' discussion, he had intended it to be 'as spontaneous as possible, and the possibilities of pre-recording to be fully explored: sometimes the least articulate people are the most articulate when they finally get round to saying something. The thoughtless "professional" radio attitude – take the most articulate speakers, the best broadcasters first – is to be discouraged.'[36] Probably Leonard Isaacs was right to think that this would have meant 'five miles of tape'.

Keller's pursuit of those he considered to be the right people to give talks was absolutely determined. Having decided, for instance, that 'an extra- if not anti-historical short talk' on Schoenberg as a great composer was

32 Letter from Britten to Keller, 26 November 1959 (CUL Keller Archive).
33 Letter from Keller to Britten, 30 December 1959 (BBC WAC ibid.).
34 Letter from Britten to Keller, 11 January 1960 (CUL Keller Archive).
35 Letter from Keller to Stravinsky, 31 October 1959 (CUL Keller Archive).
36 Internal memorandum to the members of the Third Programme Music Meeting, 7 September 1959 (BBC WAC R51/889/1: Talks: Music and Music Intervals).

'urgently needed' and that Oliver Neighbour, previously a reluctant speaker, was the best person to give it, he wrote to him in no uncertain terms:

> I remember your last reaction to my 'short talk' suggestion – but I have to do my duty. There is no other possible speaker, and it would be a pity if The Psychology of Oliver Neighbour (another subject for a short talk) were responsible for there being none at all.[37]

And when Stravinsky visited London in the autumn of 1959, the opportunity for BBC listeners to hear him speak was too important to be missed, as Keller tried to impress upon him:

> I am not asking you whether you have anything to say, because I know you have. But I am imploring you to say it … I don't wish to sound arrogant, or to appear to be lecturing you, but it seems to me that as a great composer, it is your duty to open your mouth before you leave these shores again.[38]

To those he knew better, Keller made more personal appeals: 'You know that I am trying to make music talks as musical as possible; don't withdraw into a corner when I call on you for help,' he wrote to Peter Pears,[39] whom he was trying to persuade to do a programme on the late Erwin Stein's unpublished manuscript, 'Form and Performance'; 'You are the only performer who could do justice to this book.' Having secured Pears' agreement, Keller pursued him relentlessly for the script, writing him frequent letters, sometimes in duplicate ('in case you want to mislay more than one'[40]) and would not accept that a busy concert schedule was any excuse: 'I cannot see the temporal difficulty. Erwin's book is portable; it should be easy for you to jot down the talk at odd moments.'[41]

Sometimes these methods worked and sometimes they didn't – Stravinsky was not prepared to oblige on that occasion, but a programme was eventually extracted from Pears. They do show, however, how seriously Keller took radio as a cultural force, an attitude which he expected other musicians to share. Not only was he completely committed to the task he had undertaken ('I shall put my whole mind and heart into the BBC job,' he had promised Glock on the day of his arrival; 'I am constitutionally incapable of any other attitude, once I have decided that a job is worth while'[42]), but he was convinced that what he was doing was of great importance:

> I have what the 19th century would have called a 'mission'; Kafka would simply

37 Letter from Keller to Neighbour, 3 November 1959 (CUL Keller Archive).
38 Letter from Keller to Stravinsky, 31 October 1959 (CUL Keller Archive).
39 Letter from Keller to Pears, 10 September 1959 (BBC WAC Artist File: Peter Pears, File 6, 1959–60).
40 Letter from Keller to Pears, 24 November 1959 (BBC WAC ibid.).
41 Letter from Keller to Pears, 25 September 1959 (BBC WAC ibid.).
42 Letter from Keller to Glock, 1 September 1959 (CUL Keller Archive).

> have called it a 'mandate' and R.A. Butler would call it a 'job'. If I don't fulfil that, I have, in the eyes of my own conscience, no right to fill this post.[43]

Music talks would henceforth 'concentrate on our musical culture's most burning problems,'[44] Keller decided, and he lost little time in diagnosing what was wrong with existing policy and devising his own, which he presented to the Third Programme Music Meeting a week after his arrival:

> Generally speaking, I can already see that our music talks policy is not sufficiently alert. We are riding, passively, on waves of interesting suggestions, the most interesting of which are taken up. So far, so competent. We need more than competence. Most suggestions are interesting, and an unfortunate number is most interesting. Here lies the danger. Talking time is limited; it is our overriding duty to find the most important people, spheres of interest, subjects, at the risk of dropping many a most interesting suggestion. This is not to say that we should push the potential broadcaster into a passive role. On the contrary, *mutual activity* is the solution. Once we know whom and what we want – what our culture wants – there is plenty of room for suggestions, for free activity on the part of the broadcasters. But we must show enough knowledge and imagination to teach them what to teach us.[45]

One way in which Keller tried to create this 'mutual activity' was to prompt musicians visiting London to talk on whatever issue was of deepest concern to them at the time: 'Is there any point you feel strongly about at the moment?'[46] was a frequent question. Believing that 'in music, there is no intellectual understanding without instinctive understanding',[47] he was much more interested in hearing profound convictions than careful, judicious assessments. He also wanted his speakers to react to issues of the day, and to each other. One example of the latter is the way he treated one of the talks which he inherited from Roger Fiske. Before he departed, Fiske had commissioned Peter Maxwell Davies to talk on 'The Position of the Composer in Britain Today'. Because of its polemical nature,[48] Keller decided to use the talk as the foundation for a debate and commissioned a

---

43 Letter from Keller to John Amis, 5 November 1959 (CUL Keller Archive).

44 Letter from Keller to Murray Schafer, 18 November 1959 (CUL Keller Archive). This declaration of his policy was in response to a suggestion for a talk from Schafer. 'Do you think your material falls into that category?' Keller asked him. 'I don't. But I may be mistaken.'

45 Internal memorandum from Keller to the members of the Third Programme Music Meeting (7 September 1959, BBC WAC R51/889/1: Talks: Music and Music Intervals).

46 Letter from Keller to Ernest Ansermet, 5 October 1959 (CUL Keller Archive).

47 Letter from Keller to Elizabeth Brusa, 4 February 1984 (CUL Keller Archive).

48 Davies' theme was the insularity of most British musicians and their audiences, their 'complete ignorance' of contemporary continental developments and 'the reluctance of English musicians to face up to the problem posed by the legacy of the last century'. Such was the strength of his attack on twentieth-century English music (those brought up with it, he said, 'only like it because they are able to associate it with the past ...

series of 'counter-blows against Davies'[49] from other composers: Alexander Goehr asked 'Is There Only One Way?' on 2 October 1959, and Robert Simpson spoke on 'Composing' on 22 November 1959.[50] Keller then wanted these talks to provoke 'counter-blows' in their turn, and he asked other musicians to listen and respond: 'On Sunday, November 22nd, Bob Simpson will speak on "Composing", by way of reaction to (against) Max's talk. Will you please listen and see whether Bob gives you nightmares; if so, will you immediately ring me in case you have a "short talk" in you without noticing it,' he wrote to Susan Bradshaw.[51]

Another, very different, way in which Keller tried to get more musical dialogue on air was to broadcast musicians rehearsing. He explained this to Peter Pears, who had been wondering 'how practically to get people to play more themselves and sing' and had suggested transmitting 'Mozart Piano 4tets played only by strings, listener to supply piano part.'[52] Keller dismissed this idea on the grounds that 'this is not music-making, and certainly not chamber-music-making, whose *sine qua non* is give and take … One thing I am planning,' he went on, 'is transmissions of chamber music rehearsals, another, transmissions of coaching. On the other hand "people actually teaching over the air" [another of Pears' suggestions], in the sense of addressing themselves to the listener-pupil, without a real pupil in the studio, seems phoney to me, because if you want to educate, you want to e-ducate, and that's impossible with a generalized abstracted student ("the listener"), except in the course of general talks, which is what I'm doing anyway.'[53] Keller had first outlined his rehearsal idea to Howard Newby in September and then took steps to put it into practice when Adrian Boult, who was recording a series of talks on conducting, expressed himself interested and agreed to record a rehearsal of Beethoven's Coriolan Overture. A string quartet rehearsal and performance was also scheduled, but in the end, Keller had changed jobs before either project was transmitted.

One of the most famous of Keller's innovations during his period as Music Talks Producer was the 'short talk'. Formally launched at the end of

---

Those works, so widely and so highly praised, usually show a serious lack of ideas, content and technique; when one compares them with a more serious work by Schoenberg – or even by Bartók – they become unlistenable'), that Keller may have detected a whiff of the British musical self-contempt which he himself had diagnosed only a few years earlier. Davies' script is preserved in BBC WAC.

49 Letter from Keller to Daniel Jones, 3 December 1959 (CUL Keller Archive).

50 Both scripts are preserved in BBC WAC (Goehr's was also reprinted in *The Score* – of which William Glock was editor – vol. 26 (January 1960), pp. 63–5). Goehr took issue with Herbert Eimert's recent definition of contemporary music as inevitably post-Webern; Simpson addressed the importance of content over any particular style, accepting 'all the resources that are available, consonance, dissonance, melody, rhythm, harmony, tonality, atonality, instruments, voices ...' in a talk which quotes Keller twice.

51 Letter from Keller to Bradshaw, 6 November 1959 (CUL Keller Archive).

52 Undated letter from Pears to Keller (BBC WAC Artist File: Peter Pears, File 6, 1959–60).

53 Letter from Keller to Pears, 10 December 1959 (BBC WAC ibid.).

November 1959, this was another proposal which Keller had put forward in his first few weeks at the BBC. Introducing the idea to readers of the *Radio Times*, he described it thus:

> Musicians are not naturally verbose. They tend to express some of their most important views and discoveries not in big books, but by way of their own brand of small talk. Again, musician-critics, though used to expressing themselves verbally, keep private many novel points that do not lend themselves to extensive treatment; in fact, we occasionally find their conversation more enlightening than some of their writings.
>
> With these thoughts in mind, I invited a number of musicians and critics to present a new fact or a new point of view, preferably one which enhanced or disturbed their dreams, in a high-powered, unreserved, unqualified ten-minute talk for the Third Programme. Their response was what I had hoped for ... The listener may like to ask himself whether the musical short talk is an attractive form from his own standpoint. Of course, it depends on the content. But the content depends on the form too: the thoughts expressed in these short talks would probably have remained unexpressed without them.[54]

The first 'short talk' to be broadcast had actually been transmitted some weeks before – Alexander Goehr's 'Is There Only One Way?' Keller was able to make this experimental recording before the idea had been raised at Third Programme Music Meeting because some studio time had become available unexpectedly and Glock encouraged him to 'go ahead and see how it works'. 'I hope you will not think my behaviour cavalier,' wrote Glock apologetically to Newby, 'I think there are considerable possibilities here.'[55] Keller, of course, was very happy with this sort of informal working arrangement, being always impatient with the BBC's byzantine committee structure. Indeed, it was not long before he was trying to find short-cuts: 'I am getting a little tired of Waiting for Wednesday [the day of the Third Programme Music Meetings],' he told Glock and Newby. 'It inhibits my natural tempo, and I think I can get twice as many things done if, as occasion arises, I work by way of memoranda.'[56] He had already complained to Newby about the way the meetings were organized: 'Why no agenda? Ought not the principle to be – a maximum of forward-looking thought within a minimum of time? Forgive me if there are considerations of which, as a new boy, I am unaware.'[57]

On this occasion, Goehr's talk was recorded within a couple of days and broadcast a fortnight later. The broadcast was well received and

54 'Musical "Short Talks"', *Radio Times*, 27 November 1959.

55 Internal memorandum from Glock to Newby, 17 September 1959 (BBC WAC R51/889/1: Talks: Music and Music Intervals).

56 Internal memorandum from Keller to Glock and Newby, 12 October 1959 (CUL Keller Archive).

57 Internal memorandum from Keller to Newby, 25 September 1959 (BBC WAC R27/855/1: Third Programme Meetings, File 4, 1959–62).

recommended for a repeat, with Goehr being commended inside the BBC as 'a potentially good broadcaster and his material was interesting'.[58] This undoubtedly helped the new idea to be accepted, and encouraged Keller to seek experimental broadcasts for future suggestions, as in the case of his unsuccessful suggestion, *The Artist Replies*: 'All I am asking for in the first place is a test case – a single experimental production.'[59] *The Artist Replies* was a very characteristic Keller idea (a theme which appeared again in the second 'short talk' production to be broadcast – Denis Stevens on 'The Music Critic Criticised'[60]) and, as Keller described it to his Third Programme Talks colleagues, carried echoes of *The Need for Competent Film Music Criticism*:

> Under this title, I suggest a monthly feature consisting of artists' replies to critics. The need for criticism in reverse, for artistic criticism of art criticism, is very strongly and widely felt, but so long as broadcasting does not meet it, it will seem chronic rather than acute: newspapers or journals will never employ artists to criticize critics. In my submission, the new feature could develop into a cultural force of profound significance; it could prove more helpful towards the development of art than does criticism itself.[61]

Keller pressed quite vigorously for *The Artist Replies*, resisting one proposal that an element of artistic response to criticism could be included in *Comment*, an existing topical arts programme. Despite Keller's contention that 'neither the organisation nor the scope of *Comment* allow for any development of my idea within its terms of reference',[62] Howard Newby was unwilling to let him develop his proposal further on the grounds that it would have meant the BBC 'taking our cue from the press rather than from art itself and you would inevitably be involved in the BBC obligation to give mangled critics the right of reply (so creating a programme differing from the original intention)'.[63] Newby also wanted to 'wait until the nature of the fortnightly

---

58 Minutes of the Third Programme Music Meeting, 7 October 1959 (BBC WAC ibid.). Goehr was not yet on the BBC's staff.

59 Internal memorandum from Keller to Newby, 29 January 1960 (BBC WAC R51/889/1: Talks: Music and Music Intervals).

60 One of Stevens's main criticisms of his fellow critics was the scarcity of their reviews of broadcast concerts, despite the fact that a far greater proportion of their readership was likely to have heard the radio concerts and therefore be able to take a genuine interest in the reviews. This was in harmony with Keller's view of the importance of radio concerts, and the fact that, from his earliest days as a critic, he had paid significant attention to them. Stevens's script is preserved in BBC WAC.

61 Internal memorandum from Keller to the members of the Third Programme Talks Meeting, 1 December 1959 (BBC WAC ibid.). Keller often circulated his ideas to committee members in advance of meetings because, as he put it on this occasion, 'I want the importance of the idea to sink in before we discuss it.'

62 Internal memorandum from Keller to Newby and the Controller of Talks (Sound), 29 January 1960 (BBC WAC ibid.).

63 Internal memorandum from Newby to Keller, 2 February 1960 (BBC WAC ibid.).

"The Musicians Speak" reveals itself'.[64] Perhaps he felt that this latter programme, in which, as Keller described it to Egon Wellesz, 'outstanding musicians assume the role of critics and react to important topical events',[65] would cover rather similar ground.

Newby may have been right, for there is on file at least one example of Keller's wishing to use *The Musician Speaks* as a forum for a performing artist to criticize the critics. The opportunity to make the issue topical was provided by Walter Legge, the founder of the Philharmonia Orchestra, who, having first excluded critics from one of his concerts, announced that, due to 'the deterioration of the standards of musical criticism in London', he would henceforth 'give our critics a dose of their own medicine by publishing in the programmes of the Philharmonia Concert Society criticisms of their criticisms'.[66] Keller had at that time just relinquished the post of Talks Producer to take over Chamber Music and Recitals, but he drew his successor Basil Lam's attention to Legge's announcement: 'There are possibilities here, don't you think?' Lam agreed and considered treating the subject to a discussion between Legge and critic Martin Cooper. This was not quite what Keller had in mind, and he suggested that Lam might instead 'get a musician on the subject in *The Musician Speaks*'.

The third short talk to be broadcast was Deryck Cooke's on 'The New Musical Philistine', in which he discussed the question of fashionable and unfashionable composers. The subject was his idea and Keller found his proposed treatment of it 'fascinating', as he reported to Glock and Newby.[67] Keller was also impressed by the quality of the final script: 'It is absolutely first-rate,' he told Donald Mitchell, 'I think I can promise you that you will find the talk pure joy.'[68] After the experience of producing Cooke's talk, Keller was eager that his *Music Survey* colleague should also contribute to the short talks, especially since he was beginning to be frustrated by the amount of editing some of his other speakers needed. 'What about doing 19 words per day for your first short talk. I am longing to see another script which I needn't mess about with. The first and latest is Deryck's – on "The New Musical Philistine".'

Keller brought all his rigorous *Music Survey* editing techniques to the production of BBC talks, sometimes spending an extraordinary – some would say inordinate – amount of time revising and refining speakers' scripts. As he wrote to Denis Stevens when commissioning 'The Music Critic Criticised', he wanted them to 'Be concrete. Be short. Be

64 Ibid.

65 Letter from Keller to Wellesz, 8 April 1960 (CUL Keller Archive). Keller was arranging for Wellesz to take part in *The Musician Speaks*, talking on the first English stage production of *Erwartung*.

66 Letter from Legge published in *The Daily Telegraph*, 21 April 1960.

67 Internal memorandum from Keller to Glock and Newby, 12 October 1959 (BBC WAC Contributor File: Deryck Cooke, File 1, 1959–62).

68 Letter from Keller to Donald Mitchell, 18 November 1959 (CUL Keller Archive).

substantial'.[69] Indeed, because of Keller's natural tendency towards aphorism, some scripts which were intended by their authors to make full-length programmes ended up being honed down by Keller into short talks.

There were times when Keller's contributors found his seemingly unending editing wearying. Alexander Goehr, for example, well remembers the tortuous revision process through which Keller took him before 'Is there Only One Way?' went out:

> For these blasted five pounds, or whatever I got paid ... he made me work. I mean I perhaps had to write that five times before he was satisfied ... He put one through a mill, and I wasn't lightly going to give another talk in that series – well, he drove one crazy, you know, again and again! And enough was never enough: he was happy to go on indefinitely and always did in whatever we collaborated on ... he'd go on to the end of time, changing it and improving it.[70]

Robin Holloway also recalls vividly the experience of doing a short talk for Keller some years later. Keller had accepted the talk only 'so long as it was rethought from top to toe'. The process of rethinking is described by Holloway thus:

> The first inspissated draft bears brusque editorial comment ('non sequitur', 'no need to be incomprehensible' etc.) and a distinctive formulation: 'Nature and art: you don't define the fundamental difference. The one only communicates if you project meaning on to it; the other communicates.' After several rewrites I received a letter making nine precise staccato points with, elegantly placed at halftime, the inevitable challenge: 'if I can't write a clear summary of your talk, who can? I bet you (£5, even bet) you yourself can't. Will you accept the challenge? You would be the judge.' 'If you wish,' the letter concluded, 'we'll meet and start knocking it into shape (repeat: shape). It will take hours.' We met; it *did* take hours; and the eventual result is probably not worth the expenditure of his brilliance on my alluvial mud. But this, too, was a lesson, efficacious and unforgettable, which opened up... a potential for writing about music that I have followed ever since.[71]

Goehr agrees about the efficacy of Keller's script-writing lessons: 'If I were able to write English, then I would say I learned to write English from Hans' editing and questioning!'[72]

A letter written to Roberto Gerhard, who was providing a six-minute introductory talk for a broadcast of Webern's Opp. 29, 30 and 31, shows how many queries even the shortest of scripts could elicit from Keller:

> Many thanks for your fascinating script, which I have slightly edited – not so slightly in the case of the Webern quotation, which was incomprehensible as it

69 Letter from Keller to Stevens, 5 October 1959 (CUL Keller Archive).
70 Alexander Goehr, oral communication, 28 November 1996.
71 Robin Holloway, 'Keller's Causes', *London Review of Books*, 3 August 1995, p.10.
72 Alexander Goehr, oral communication, 28 November 1996.

stood (I read it to seven musicians). 'The remotest opposite pole' would be a pleonasm, because a pole is one of two terminal points anyway; and it is most confusing to hear of one pole without a clear definition, or at least implication, of the other. Of course, if you don't like the present version, please amend it. I have also slightly changed round the ensuing sentence, in order to clarify, aurally, the end of the quotation. So much for Query No.1.

> Query No.2: 'Starting from a perfectly classical home-position' is, in my modest submission, far too abstract; the virginal listener won't have the vaguest idea what you are talking about. Could you put in a more concrete phrase? Also, I'd be grateful if it didn't contain 'Starting from', since I've included this in the Webern quotation.
>
> Query No.3: I've left a space here because an emphatic adjective seems to me to be needed to throw the 'misunderstandings' into relief. I leave the question to your judgment.
>
> Query No.4 (p.3): 'His passionate allegiance to … the law by which he abides' is a bit tautological, don't you think? Besides, do you think there will be three listeners who will understand this sentence? PLEASE reconsider!
>
> Query No.5: With great respect, you have pumped more into the single word reason than it can comprehensibly hold. May I implore you to renounce what is, basically, a pun, and render the last phrase more understandable? Again, I have tried it out on various people.[73]

Even after all this, when a speaker finally arrived in the studio with his lacerated script, it was still not always plain sailing, as Keller warned H.C. Robbins Landon before the recording of a set of introductions to Haydn broadcasts in 1959:

> I warn you, Landon: there'll be retakes. If you make mistakes, I'll retake in order to correct them, and if you don't make mistakes, I'll retake in order to get a few fluffs in and make it all sound more natural; besides, you'll find plenty of expression marks in your script, not to speak of all those little changes. In short, you will be pestered as never before, and each snippet will be rehearsed twice. You need not fear a nervous breakdown. Amongst the innovations I am introducing here is a slight extension of the recording team: it now always includes a psychiatrist.[74]

In the studio, according to Lionel Salter, Keller was not really very fluent technically, and tended to leave that side of production to the studio manager. When Keller produced Salter himself in short talks, 'he didn't take an active hand in the production at all'.[75] Alexander Goehr agrees: 'I don't think he

73 Letter from Keller to Roberto Gerhard, 23 November 1959 (BBC WAC Artist File, Roberto Gerhard, File 2, 1953–62).

74 Letter from Keller to Landon, 14 October 1959 (CUL Keller Archive).

75 Lionel Salter, oral communication, 10 January 1996. Salter went on, 'I don't think, honestly, that Hans was technically qualified to do anything like this. I remember that when stereo broadcasting first came in, I received a note from whoever it was in charge of the new techniques, would I nominate people in the department to go on a course for stereo production. And I wrote back and said, "Yes, with pleasure, I'll give you some

liked the studios much'.[76] There was one technical process, however, with which he remembers Keller being most certainly at home – 'He liked the editing channels very much!' This indifference to technical procedures was not a characteristic of Keller alone, however, to judge from Stephen Hearst's impression of music producers in general when he arrived in 1972, after several years in television, to take over the Controllership of Radio 3 from Howard Newby. Music producers – significantly (he thinks) not called producers but 'assistants' – were 'always in the dining room when they should have been in the kitchen'. As an example of this, he remembers a panicky telephone call from the presentation editor during an EBU live relay of an Aldeburgh Festival concert, which was going out to 20 countries simultaneously:

> Cormac Rigby rings me ... and he said, we're under-running by seven minutes, what was he to do? I said, who is the producer; he said, Stephen Plaistow. Where is Stephen? In the audience. They always sat in the audience! They thought the mixing was something else. Now to me this was absolute heresy: the producer was not actually listening to what was going through ... this was left to the technical staff. They were musicologists: they talked of higher things![77]

This question of the 'professionalism' or otherwise of the Music Department was to be a feature of its relationship with the BBC's management in the 1970s (at least in the eyes of the management) and Keller, whose criticisms of the BBC became more and more outspoken as the decade progressed, and who constantly made an issue of the idea of 'professionalism', increasingly became a focus for his bosses' irritation: 'He believed the profession of music producer was a phoney one, and he had enormous influence,' says Hearst. 'And that I will not forgive him for.'

When Glock's reorganization of the Music Department's staffing structure created two new Chief Assistant posts, one responsible for chamber music and recitals, and the other for orchestral and choral music, Keller was appointed to the former. He had wanted the post, had applied for it and, from Glock's point of view, he was undoubtedly the obvious choice. In April 1960 Keller was still his right-hand man, they shared many of the same ideals, and his love and knowledge of the repertoire was indubitable. The post of Talks Producer had a brief interregnum under Basil Lam, until Keller was succeeded formally by Robert Layton, who continued in the job for the next 20 years.

Layton says he got the impression at the time of his own appointment as

names, but some of my people, of course, would like to do a course on mono production – they know nothing about it!" And in my mind was Hans, who didn't know the difference between one microphone and another.'

76 Alexander Goehr, oral communication, 4 December 1996.

77 Stephen Hearst, oral communication, 4 November 1996.

Music Talks Producer that Howard Newby had thought Keller's selection of speakers rather too personal:

> I remember being summoned by Howard Newby, and he said, Hans has, in his day, engaged about three speakers, Donald Mitchell, and – oh, I forget who they were. But he did favour a very small group of chosen speakers. And he said to me that your job is to spread the net as widely as possible. I want you to go out into the universities and try and get as many different viewpoints as possible, and not to reflect views with whom you just have sympathy. Hans was thought to be very partisan, but it was very, very lively, of course.[78]

Alexander Goehr is surprised by this, thinking that, although he could imagine Newby making 'some kind of bar-room remark about the new gang of people whom Hans backed', music talks under Keller were not in any way narrow:

> On the contrary, [in] the old BBC you got the feeling that the same three people were talking uninterruptedly. And in Hans' time you rather got the feeling that the doors had been thrown open to almost anyone who cared to come. It was quite the opposite, because there was no narrowness ... It was magnificent, and Howard surely appreciated it.[79]

There is a sense in which both views are right. Music talks under Keller had certainly moved away from the academic and critic-dominated half-hour lectures of the 1950s. Keller introduced new speakers, some young and most of them composers or performers, and he laid great stress on the importance of hearing musicians themselves speak, rather than their critics. The introduction of the short talks brought a greater flexibility to the schedules and probably meant that more music talks reached the air. They also proved popular (Keller later quoted 'appreciation indices of 84 and thereabouts'[80]) and effective, as he reported to Newby and Glock: 'I note that the short talks are quoted & referred to far more widely than any other'.[81] A lively sense of debate was engendered by the use of more topical subjects, the increased concentration on contemporary music, and Keller's encouraging his speakers to react to each other. On the other hand, Keller's personal stamp is highly visible throughout. Projects like *The Artist Replies* and *The Musician Speaks* were clearly the product of the former editor of *Music Survey* – an impression which was compounded by the presence of several *Music Survey* contributors among Keller's speakers, including more than one appearance from Donald Mitchell. The first few issues of *The Musician Speaks* which Keller produced before Basil Lam took over also show an emphasis on those

78 Robert Layton, oral communication, 11 November 1996.

79 Alexander Goehr, oral communication, 28 November 1996.

80 Undated internal memorandum [*c*. 1964] (BBC WAC R51/889/1: Talks: Music and Music Intervals).

81 Internal memorandum, 8 March 1960 (BBC WAC ibid.).

composers whom *Music Survey* had defended most vigorously: Mátyás Seiber talked about Stuckenschmidt's Schoenberg biography, Susan Bradshaw reviewed the first English performance of Schoenberg's Band Variations, Lennox Berkeley spoke on recent Britten works, and Egon Wellesz reviewed the first English staging of *Erwartung*.

Although Keller undoubtedly made his mark on music talks remarkably quickly, the new schedules were scarcely under way before he moved on, and seven months is a very short time on which to base any kind of assessment. However, his involvement with music talks did not end at this point, for, after the 'initial flush of excitement'[82] about his promotion to head chamber music had worn off, Keller seems to have found it hard to relinquish talks entirely. He continued to make lots of suggestions, on one occasion frightening the BBC's distinguished poetry editor, George MacBeth, away from a project on 'Words and Music' which he had been producing; after seeing a set of ideas for it which Keller had sent to Howard Newby, MacBeth wrote in dismay, 'It is obvious from this list of possible material for the "Words and Music" series that I am quite unqualified to cope with any of the production on this project. It looks to me as if it could be an absolutely first-class scheme, but one which should obviously be handled by someone in Music Department.'[83]

The opportunity for Keller to take a more active role in talks came with the start of the daytime Music Programme, when he put forward a new idea for concert intervals. Hitherto, the Third Programme's policy had generally been to broadcast completely unrelated talks in the intervals of concerts, on the grounds that the concert audience would probably be making itself a collective cup of tea, so the talk would attract a different set of listeners. Thus political, historical and literary talks would often find a place in the intervals of opera and concert relays. The question of what to do with the intervals of concerts in the daytime Music Programme was one which was often discussed throughout the 1960s. The concerts were usually recorded, so the possibility arose of doing without an interval altogether (deemed too tiring in any but the shortest concerts), or having a much smaller break. Since the Music Programme was meant to be less taxing than the Third, some felt that almost all talk should be excluded, resulting in the idea of filling intervals not with speech, but with more music. Like many in the Music Department, Keller viewed the prospect of wall-to-wall music with suspicion, and hastened to put forward an alternative interval idea of his own:

> THE CONCERT INTERVAL
>
> Under this title, a new kind of feature programme could replace the projected interval recital in the Music Programme's Sunday Symphony Concert. The

82 As he described it in *1975* (1977), p. 20.

83 Internal memorandum from MacBeth to Keller, 18 December 1961 (BBC WAC R51/889/1: Talks: Music and Music Intervals).

> interval recital has not proved a success in the past from any point of view; it makes as much sense as an interval symphony would make in a two-part recital.
>
> The new idea would be to catch the attention of a relaxing audience by concentrating on topics that would engage people's interest in the interval if they were at a concert hall: their conversation at the bar or coffee bar should define the field within which the programme is to operate. While any attempt at 'educating' the public should be avoided, their acute or latent curiosity should be satisfied, and the different items of the programme should be sufficiently short for the listener to switch on and off mentally as the mood catches him.
>
> I would point out that in my talks-producing days, some of my 'short talks' reached appreciation indices of 84 and thereabouts: their underlying premises were similar to the present project's.[84]

The idea was approved, and Keller set about producing programmes for the first few Sundays.[85] On the Music Programme's opening day, the afternoon concert was a live broadcast from the Edinburgh Festival (a Schubert and Beethoven recital by Rudolf Serkin), and in the interval listeners heard the Festival's director, the Earl of Harewood, discussing its future with Keller. Two weeks later, Keller could be heard again, talking to Peter Pears about Bach's St John Passion, and the following week he considered the question 'What is Bartók's stature?' with Antal Dorati. A fortnight after that, he appeared once more, talking to Deryck Cooke about Schumann's orchestration. Since Keller could never be described as a diffident interviewer, his repeated appearance led one critic to complain that the discussions were being 'overpowered by Mr Keller'.[86]

In fact, these discussion programmes were not really what Keller had originally intended for the concert interval, as he told John Manduell (who as Chief Assistant, Music Programme, was responsible for its planning) after the Schumann conversation had gone out.

> The programme is alright so far as it goes, but it doesn't go anywhere near its original intention… What I had in mind was a fast-moving magazine programme with relatively short items, strictly functional within the context of the concert, any of which could be listened to, *ad libitum*, by people relaxing and maybe walking in and out during a well-deserved interval.[87]

Although, as inventor and executor of the programme, he admitted to Manduell that 'I have only (or perhaps not only?) myself to blame if the original intention is not realised', he did go on to list a number of practical problems, chief among which was that 'the job needs a great deal of producer effort and quite a bit of microphone journalism on the part of staff

84 Undated internal memorandum [*c*. 1964] (BBC WAC ibid.).

85 The Music Programme initially broadcast once a week, on Sundays.

86 Unsigned editorial, *Strad* **85**/895 (November 1964), p. 235.

87 Internal memorandum, 23 October 1964 (BBC WAC R51/1184: Music: Concert Interval Talks).

members who are able to conduct short, crisp conversations with composers, performers, etc.' Although Keller contended that 'musically competent microphone journalists simply do not exist in the outside world', the increasing frequency of microphone appearances by Music Department staff was beginning to cause concern. The BBC was anxious not to be seen to be taking employment away from writers and musicians, so its policy in this respect had hitherto been very strict: a member of staff could only broadcast when no suitable outside speaker could be found, formal approval had to be sought via a 'staff contribution form', and the staff member had to be paid separately. At a review of Music Department contributions carried out in September 1966 (in which Keller was second to Basil Lam in frequency of broadcasting), the Planning Committee identified daytime talks in the Music Programme as an area of particular concern. Howard Newby's defence of the outstanding merit of the evening Third Programme broadcasts was accepted, especially since they were all coordinated by Robert Layton according to the official guidelines. However, 'we are more concerned about the number of talks (16) given by staff in the Music Programme during this period. I think I am right in saying that these talks are not usually arranged through Layton but at any rate where they are "interval talks" are offered and produced by the Music Assistant responsible for the concert into which they fit. This, if it does happen, is not really an acceptable arrangement.'[88]

Another informal working practice in the production of daytime music talks which was questioned by planners around this time was self-production by the member of staff who was speaking. In a memorandum to the Controller of the Home Service (who was ultimately responsible for the Music Programme), Keller defended this, explaining that, although it arose originally out of staff shortage, it had proved 'eminently successful'. He reassured the Controller that it was only used for recorded programmes, where 'at least one of the speakers has to be an experienced talks producer [and] at least one of the speakers has to be a highly experienced microphone journalist ... Coming down to earth, it is a hard fact that if we decided that every such conversation or discussion should be produced in the conventional sense, "The Concert Interval" would, for the time being, evaporate: we just haven't got the staff. I might add that in my experience, it is better for a good producer to produce himself than to be produced by a bad producer.'[89]

The planners appeared to be appeased by this, although the need for effective control of daytime music talks was a repeated subject of discussion over the next few years. Self-production seems to have continued, in practice if not in theory, for some considerable time, since Ian McIntyre, who took

---

88 Internal memorandum from M.F.S. Standing, Controller, Programme Organisation (Sound) to William Glock, 20 September 1966 (BBC WAC R34/1034/2: Policy: Music Programme, File 2, 1965–76).

89 Internal memorandum from Keller to the Controller, Home Service, 14 August 1964 (BBC WAC R51/889/1: Talks: Music and Music Intervals).

over as Controller of Radio 3 from Stephen Hearst in 1978, cites it as a reason for his view that Radio 3 talks were of a lower quality than those of Radio 4 (whose Controllership he had just relinquished). 'It was certainly true that a lot of music production when they produced each other was a formality,' he says. As a non-musician, he felt excluded from the introverted atmosphere of the Music Department, in which music producers were used to putting each other on air, and he suspected that some listeners might feel the same about this cosy arrangement. 'Sandpit broadcasting' is the way he colourfully describes it: 'quite a high-class sandpit, but basically they were just playing – talking to each other.'[90]

The need for a proper coordinator for the daytime talks was becoming apparent, especially after the Music Programme entered its Phase III (from 20 March 1965 it began broadcasting daily from 8 am until 6.30 pm), and Keller seems to have been angling for this role. Although nothing appears to have been official at this stage, there is evidence of other departments being instructed that 'Chief Assistant (Orchestral and Choral) [as Keller then was] should be informed of any interval talk on a musical theme'.[91] Although it was accepted that the Music Talks Producer could not himself be expected to handle the additional work of all the Music Programme talks, Robert Layton remembers it being suggested to him that he perhaps ought to feel offended by Keller's interest:

> I took no particular interest in the daytime talks ... I thought, well, he wants to do these – I didn't want to build an empire, because you know where empire-builders end up in the BBC! Because it was put to me that Hans was muscling in, doing talks, and that was a kind of oblique criticism of the kind of work I was doing. But that struck me as perhaps being to a certain extent mischief-making on the part of certain colleagues and I just thought that I will get on with what I have to do – I didn't feel it in any way as being a threat. My particular brief was for the old Third Programme and then the evening on Radio 3.[92]

In November 1969, Keller and Peter Dodd, who had succeeded John Manduell as Chief Assistant, Music Programme, discussed the possibility of a new series of interval talks, to be produced by Music Division and to contain material directly relevant to the concert. Dodd then went through his

---

90 Ian McIntyre, oral communication, 15 May 1995.

91 Internal memorandum from Lorna Moore (Chief Producer, Arts Talks) to Mr R.E. Keen, 29 March 1965 (BBC WAC R51/1184/1 Music: Concert Interval Talks). Leo Black has pointed out that, since orchestral concerts were much more often in two parts than were recitals, it would be natural for responsibility for interval talks to gravitate towards Keller's post (oral communication, 31 January 2000). However, on one memorandum where Keller refers to being 'ultimately in charge' of 'The Concert Interval' series, this statement is annotated with a large question mark by William Glock (internal memorandum from Keller to John Manduell, copied to Glock, 23 October 1964, BBC WAC R51/1184: Music: Concert Interval Talks).

92 Robert Layton, oral communication, 11 November 1996.

schedules and sent Keller a list of uncommitted intervals in the first quarter of 1970, asking him, 'Would you consider taking these on for a start?'[93] When Keller outlined his plans, it was clear that his role was to be principally that of a coordinator: the first few programmes were to be produced by Robert Simpson, with Anthony Friese-Greene as interviewer. As for the programmes' general policy, 'Flexibility will, indeed, characterise "The Concert Interval". Sometimes, it will be a magazine programme; at other times, a straight, substantial music talk will be preferred.'[94]

Keller quickly drew a large number of his Music Division colleagues into producing and contributing to the daytime music talks, and their collective output was enormous: some 200 talks a year, of which around 30 per cent were given by staff contributors. Keller's own role remained largely that of coordinator (this time unambiguously and officially): he himself produced no more than 10–15 per cent of the total output and his own appearances were not particularly frequent when compared with those of his colleagues. From Keller's point of view, 'the entire operation … worked frictionlessly, on the basis of diagonal harmony',[95] but by the middle of 1972 it appeared to Stephen Hearst that some music producers were finding the burden of talks production, added to their other duties, rather a strain. When Hearst told Keller this, and William Glock had added his opinion that Keller had 'employed a certain measure of persuasion when speaking to producers',[96] Keller, characteristically, 'decided to clarify the situation without any further delay,'[97] publicly and thoroughly. He approached all his colleagues directly, both in person and by way of a circular:

> Owing to the very fact of its being written – an unconventional step in this large and loveable, mumbling, murmuring, whispering place of ours: we are in the pub- and corridor-communication business – this memo will, unfortunately, seem dramatic. In substance, it is nothing of the kind: it is merely truth-finding … As you know, I always try to make sure that producers feel they have time for the operation in question, and that they are actively and unreservedly interested. I moreover remind them from time to time not to take on talks production unless they are absolutely sure that it will not result in overwork. The purpose of this memo is, simply, to find out whether I am mistaken, and to replace backstage ambiguity by straightforward communication and action.[98]

Keller also collected a series of supporting statements from different

---

93 Internal memorandum from Dodd to Keller, 7 November 1969 (BBC WAC R27/1084/1 Music Programmes: Talks: General, 1970–72).

94 Internal memorandum from Keller to Dodd, 25 November 1969 (BBC WAC ibid.).

95 Internal memorandum from Keller to Music Division producers, 2 June 1972 (BBC WAC ibid.).

96 Ibid.

97 Internal memorandum from Keller to Stephen Hearst, 31 May 1972 (BBC WAC ibid.).

98 Internal memorandum from Keller to Music Division producers, 2 June 1972 (BBC WAC ibid.).

producers, which he sent to Hearst. One of these was Elaine Padmore – 'Personally, I like doing talks' – a fairly recent appointment at the BBC, whom Keller had recruited for his talks-producing team soon after her arrival the year before, in terms which appear to justify his assertion that it was unfair to accuse him of coercing his colleagues into producing talks:

> When you have settled down, would you like to come and see me in order to discuss the possibility of your producing an occasional music talk? May I stress that such productions would not be an inevitable part of your duties: you should really only do them if you are keenly interested. On the other hand, you wouldn't have to be scared of this unknown area of activity: I would tell you how to do it all, would let you sit in on a talks production or two and, if there is time, help you with your first production myself.[99]

By the following summer, when the argument over producers' workloads was going on, Padmore was a regular member of Keller's talks team, producing a series of 15-minute talks under the title 'Composers on Criticism'. It was one of her productions in this series, an interval talk by Cornelius Cardew broadcast on 17 June 1972, which was the cause of one of the biggest controversies of Keller's BBC career.[100] It put an end to Keller's editorship of the daytime talks and, according to some of his colleagues, nearly cost him his job completely. Leo Black tells the story:

> There was a very unfortunate incident during an Aldeburgh Festival when Cornelius Cardew [had] been asked to do a piece – it was an avant-garde music festival and they wanted Cardew to come out with his line about Stockhausen is capitalism or fascism or whatever. And there was a passage in this talk about the British Army in Northern Ireland, and the producer had not actually thought that this was a problem, but had thought something else was a problem and had, in her mind with total correctness, referred the script to the editor, who was Hans. And he looked at this bit, and said, 'That's all right: I'll take responsibility for that,' and the producer had gone off and recorded the talk. The Director General at the time, Charles Curran, was in Aldeburgh at the concert, and when the interval came he went round to his car and turned on his car radio, expecting to hear

99 Internal memorandum from Keller to Padmore, 10 May 1971 (BBC WAC ibid.).

100 Although Padmore produced the talk, Cardew says that it was Keller himself who commissioned it (and, indeed, who was the organizer of the *Composers on Criticism* series): 'In 1972 Hans Keller of the BBC Music Section, knowing the history of my association with Cage, asked me to write an article in *The Listener* to prepare the public for some Cage performances planned for the summer. The result must have surprised him, but it seems also to have pleased him, for shortly afterwards he asked me for an introductory talk to a broadcast of Stockhausen's *Refrain* … I received a number of letters in response to the broadcast of "Stockhausen serves Imperialism", and the publication of the first half of this talk in *The Listener* provoked a storm in its correspondence columns … Punishments were also meted out inside the BBC on account of the Stockhausen broadcast which by mischance was heard by a high official of the Corporation' (Cardew, 1974, pp. 33–4; 54–5).

something suitably anodyne, in keeping with proceedings at the Aldeburgh Festival … and was appalled to hear Cornelius Cardew animadverting about the British Army in Northern Ireland. And Charles Curran was famous for his ability to go red in the face in a nano-second; he did precisely that, and when he got back to the office on Monday morning, there was a big blow-up. Hans argued that he had not been asked to vet the script; he had merely been asked to approve one particular page, which he had rightly determined was inoffensive. The producer said, 'I left the script with my editor and he didn't say there was anything wrong with it, so I'm in the clear.' And I think it was after that that … there seems to [have been] a feeling at the higher level that daytime talks were perhaps more trouble than they were worth.[101]

Stephen Hearst, then Radio 3's Controller, was in Germany when the storm broke:

> I found myself in Hamburg, negotiating a possible relay from the Hamburg Opera House. My wife phoned from home to say that Mr Newby, who was then Director of Programmes, had just phoned. Was I aware of a broadcast of the composer [Cornelius] Cardew about Stockhausen. I said, yes, I was aware of it. Who is the executive producer? I said, Hans Keller and the director was Elaine Padmore … It turned out that [in] a series of music talks which [Keller] was in charge of (and he believed enormously in music talks to break up the pattern), Cardew had started talking about Stockhausen, and in the middle suddenly launched into an attack on British policy in Northern Ireland: in the middle of this – absolutely nothing to do with Stockhausen! And the one chap who had listened to this was the Director-General, Charles Curran! So Curran gets on the phone and phones Newby, and Newby phones my wife and I am in Hamburg. And Keller was childish with this – he denied any responsibility because it was Elaine Padmore who'd actually recorded this. He was then hauled up in front of the Managing Director, together with the Controller of Music … This was considered so serious that it was immediately a matter for the Managing Director.[102]

Stephen Plaistow got the impression that Keller 'was very nearly sacked for that'[103] and Hearst agrees: 'It was touch and go – I mean, it was one of the worst things. If he'd been in television and this had happened, he would have been out, no question.' In a detailed diary of his office life which Keller kept for a fortnight a few weeks after this broadcast,[104] there are several references to two 'hostile' recorded interviews which he had just had with Howard Newby (then Director of Programmes, Radio) in the presence of William

101 Leo Black, oral communication, 4 August 1995.

102 Stephen Hearst, oral communication, 4 November 1996.

103 Stephen Plaistow, oral communication, 27 July 1995.

104 Keller had a habit of keeping a diary for a few days at a time. Several of these diary fragments survive in the CUL Keller Archive, and this one, which Keller kept from 5 to 21 August 1972, is one of the longest dealing with his day-to-day BBC work. This was also the time when Keller was arguing to keep two secretaries, so it may be that he kept the diary to give BBC managers an idea of the volume of work going through his office, and the long hours which he himself worked.

Glock: the official record of these interviews was at that time being passed back and forth between the three for correction and agreement, a process which Keller found 'a sterile, time-robbing, Kafka-like operation'.

The script of Cardew's talk is still preserved in the BBC's Written Archive Centre, and was reprinted as the title essay of Cardew's 1974 collection of writings, *Stockhausen Serves Imperialism*. Its ostensible subject is Stockhausen's *Refrain*, which formed the second half of the Aldeburgh Festival concert. Cardew begins by describing *Refrain* as 'a part of the cultural superstructure of the largest-scale system of human oppression and exploitation the world has ever known: imperialism'. After two pages on *Refrain* and the degeneracy of the current avant-garde movement in general, Cardew stops abruptly: 'Well, that's about all I wish to say about *Refrain*. To go into it in greater detail would simply invest the work with an importance that it doesn't have. No, my job is not to "sell" you *Refrain*. I see my job as raising the level of consciousness in regard to cultural affairs.' There then follows a four-page exposition of Marxist theory, necessary, Cardew explains, because 'in an imperialist country like Britain' Marxism is not likely to be taught in schools. The reference to Northern Ireland comes right at the end. It is very fleeting – 'If in the light of all this [*Refrain*] still retains any shred of attractiveness, compare it with other manifestations of imperialism today: the British army in Ireland, the mass of unemployed, for example. Here at least the brutal character of imperialism is evident' – but since it is set in the context of an exhortation to the listener to 'switch off and protect yourself from such ideas' one can well imagine that it proved the last straw for a Director-General already simmering from the general tone of the whole broadcast.

Reading this, it seems strange that the reaction to its broadcast could have taken Keller by surprise. However, his colleagues often comment on the way in which Keller, despite his constant involvement in and enjoyment of BBC politics, remained in many ways curiously naive and subject to some striking misjudgements in his dealings with the BBC's hierarchy. As Stephen Plaistow says,

> That was the kind of conflict that he often engendered. We thought it was a bit of a hoot, but it certainly led to some dicey moments, of which that was certainly one and Zak was the other one, yes. And both those incidents, I suppose, did show what one might call errors of judgement, which were a bit surprising.[105]

Another error of judgement, in the eyes of BBC management, was Keller's decision to record the psychiatrist Thomas Szasz advocating the legalization of all drugs.

---

105 Stephen Plaistow oral communication, 27 July 1995. For an account of the Zak affair, see pp. 122–25. Ironically enough, the person who took over coordination of daytime interval talks from Keller appears to have been Elaine Padmore (according to the minutes of the Music Programme Committee from early 1973, BBC WAC R27/1095/1).

> In a free society all drugs, regardless of their danger, should be legalized. I favor free trade in drugs for the same reasons the Founding Fathers favored free trade in ideas: as in an open society it is none of the government's business what idea a person puts into his head, so it is none of its business what drug a person puts into his body. In other words, just as we regard freedom of speech and religion as fundamental rights, so we should regard freedom of self-medication as also a fundamental right; and instead of mendaciously opposing or mindlessly promoting drugs, we should, paraphrasing Voltaire, make this maxim our rule: 'I disapprove of what you take, but I will defend to the death your right to take it!' … It is time indeed that we looked more closely not only at what harmful drugs and profit-hungry pushers do to us, but also at what harmful laws and power-hungry politicians do to us. In the history of mankind, many more people have been injured and killed by laws than by drugs, by politicians than by pushers. We ignore this lesson at our peril.[106]

This talk was suppressed by Stephen Hearst, much to Keller's disgust. (Keller later described Hearst himself as a 'drug pusher' for his published view that the BBC should aim 'to keep the viewer hooked'.[107])

Although Keller's relations with Stephen Hearst were generally stormy, they did occasionally find ground on which to meet. One long-running area of conflict between Hearst and the Music Department in which Keller's passion to communicate brought him eventually into fruitful collaboration with Hearst was the question of the use of technical language in music talks. The length and complexity of many music talks was the subject of frequent complaints from Hearst: 'I myself, who have listened to music with amateur passion for over 40 years … think you take too much for granted … It may be an arrogant thing to say, but I have been to three universities, have two academic qualifications, and believe that if I don't wholly grasp something then there isn't much of a general audience left who would.'[108] One of the many occasions which stirred up this issue was a series of programmes in which Keller produced Misha Donat introducing Haydn's Op. 50 quartets.

> Misha Donat, for example, a disciple of Hans, produced a series of programmes on Haydn's quartets … and he analysed the quartet to be played for twenty minutes. And I said there would be nobody left at the end of it! With all this musicology, I said, there are millions of people who don't understand what you're saying.[109]

'I think [Hans] may have encouraged me to expand,' remembers Donat, 'but I know they reached a stage where the introduction was longer than the

106 Thomas Szasz, 'Why All Anti-Drug Laws Should Be Repealed', 1 February 1974 (script preserved in CUL Keller Archive).

107 Hearst (1979); Keller, 'Stephen Hearst's BBC: An Insider's Reply to Hearst', unpublished article (CUL Keller Archive).

108 Memorandum from Hearst to Keller, 18 July 1972 (BBC WAC R27/1084 Music Programmes, Talks: General, 1971–72).

109 Stephen Hearst, oral communication, 4 November 1996.

music and at that stage Stephen Hearst took great exception to them.'[110] Although Donat's programmes drew large audiences (as Robert Ponsonby pointed out to Hearst[111]), and a very positive audience research report, some listeners did find the analytical introductions difficult: 'Misha Donat's introductions were occasionally considered too "technical" or simply too long – "one had to wait such a long time for the music".'[112] This report was followed by two months of memoranda flying back and forth between Hearst, Newby, Ponsonby, Keller, Peter Gould (Head of Music Programmes, Radio) and Robert Layton (Music Talks Producer). 'Here we are, once again launched on a delicious BBC battle by memo,' moaned Hearst. 'Generally the outcome of such exchanges is predictable: we carry on as before and secretaries are kept busy ... But I must continue to represent and fight for the general educated listener who, I believe, is frightened off by technical academic analysis.'[113] His frustration was all the greater because he had already raised the matter several times before, including at Radio 3 Committee, where he had used his senior producers to illustrate his point:

> C.R.3 [Hearst] ... asked the Editor, Pre-Classical Music whether he knew the meaning of 'ethological paradigm'. He did not. C.R.3 subsequently asked the Chief Producer, Science Programmes, whether he knew the meaning of 'Cantus Firmus'. Chief Producer, Science Programmes, did not know the meaning of 'Cantus Firmus'. C.R.3 concluded that here was one of the dilemmas of Radio 3 broadcasting: if the talks producers did not understand the language employed by music producers, and music producers equally could not comprehend what was said in our general talks, how many of the public could understand the output of both?[114]

Having illustrated the problem so graphically, Hearst proposed a public symposium on music talks, to be broadcast on the fiftieth anniversary of the first BBC music talk in 1922. Keller was most enthusiastic, suggesting 'the desirability of unscripted talks versus the rigid convention of scripted talks' as a possible subject for debate.[115] Although the symposium never happened, the BBC's internal debate on the subject produced at least one idea which did reach the air: the *Musical Glossary*. This was one of Hearst's suggestions for improving the comprehensibility of music talks – although, as he wryly points out, the fact that it was his idea did not endear it to the Music Department: 'I was the wrong man to have [this idea], because they would

110 Misha Donat, oral communication, 4 July 1995.

111 Memorandum from Ponsonby to Hearst, 13 May 1974 (BBC WAC R27/1054/1: Music Programmes, Talks Policy).

112 Audience Research report, 15 March 1974 (BBC WAC ibid.).

113 Memorandum from Hearst to Peter Gould, 2 April 1974 (BBC WAC ibid.).

114 Minutes of Radio 3 Committee, 14 February 1972 (quoted in Carpenter, 1996, p. 279; BBC file not yet deposited in WAC).

115 BBC WAC R27/1088/1: BBC Fiftieth Anniversary Musical Talks: Reflection.

immediately say, if he thinks it's a good idea, we mustn't do it!'[116] Keller, however, took up the suggestion with alacrity, as Leo Black describes:

> One of the criticisms of Radio 3 presentation – this was in the early Stephen Hearst days – was it was full of these technical terms that nobody understood. So Hans said, fine ... we will record two-minute pieces, one-minute pieces, which say what technical terms mean, and they will be broadcast in suitable gaps between programmes ... And this musical glossary was compiled, and these tiny little tapes were put in the cupboard and continuity announcers had the use of them ... I only ever did one, on canon, which I did think was actually rather good, rather funny, because I took it as a premiss [that] in speech you can't say the same thing ... at the same time, starting at a different point. But this is exactly what you can do in music. And to show that it couldn't be done, I got the studio manager to cut in the sentence over [itself], starting again a bit later: you got babble. And then I played a bit of the finale of the Cesar Franck Sonata, to show that you could in fact have the same thing going on twice, starting at different points, and in music it made perfect sense. Which pleased Hans, because one of his great arguments, as you well know, about music is that it doesn't conform to conceptual logic ... [But] Deryck Cooke was very irritated by this: he said, that's such a lousy canon ... which is quite true, actually: it is a lousy canon, though it's a jolly good tune. And that was all part of the atmosphere of the time.[117]

To Hearst's disappointment, however, the rest of the Music Department did not share Keller's enthusiasm for the project: 'The only chap who contributed to it was Hans, the others thought this was an unworthy thing to do.'[118] Leo Black agrees: 'Hans had problems getting people to do good, really illuminating glossary entries; therefore he did an awful lot of them himself, which added to the impression for a while that the airwaves were full of Hans Keller all the time.'[119] This was certainly the impression that Alexander Goehr, by this time no longer on the staff of the BBC, received when he switched on his radio in the early 1970s: 'It was an example of Hans' exhibitionism, which grew very tiresome around those years, when his voice started appearing every few minutes on the Third ... There were hundreds of them ... little four-minute jobs, or two-minute jobs ... whenever you put on the radio, there was Hans on about something or other!'[120] Not

---

116 Stephen Hearst, oral communication, 4 November 1996. In fact, the idea of the *Musical Glossary* was not entirely new, as a series called 'Music Dictionary' had been a part of Network Three's 'Study Session' from May 1965 until April 1967. This was a series of ten-minute talks by Roger North, produced by Peter Dodd, on subjects like 'Tonic and Dominant', 'Appoggiatura', 'Phrasing' and '12-note music'. The latter, which was broadcast on 23 July 1965, opens as follows: 'My job here is to explain what 12 note music *is*. And this hasn't got much to do with *enjoying* it. So if you don't like it now, I'm afraid you *still* won't like it when I've finished' (BBC WAC Script Library).

117 Leo Black, oral communication, 4 August 1995.

118 Stephen Hearst, oral communication, 4 November 1996.

119 Leo Black, oral communication, 4 August 1995.

120 Alexander Goehr, oral communication, 4 December 1996.

everyone found Keller's glossary entries irritating, however – indeed, one publisher wanted Keller to make them into a book:

> Following the Schubert Lieder recital yesterday afternoon I heard your stimulating gloss on perfect pitch. It reminded me of an idea that has occurred to me from time to time when hearing you speak in this way, namely that a publisher such as ourselves could successfully present a glossary of musical terms compiled by you.[121]

Nevertheless, it seems that the BBC's senior management began to feel that they were broadcasting too much Keller and, not for the last time, curbed his activities. Robert Simpson, for one, was outraged:

> Having just heard that you have banned my splendid colleague Hans Keller from broadcasting trails, I'm now letting you know that I'm banning myself from this activity until reason once more prevails.[122]

This was only one of several ways in which the BBC began to clip Keller's wings during the 1970s. It must be remembered, however, that this period was nevertheless his heyday as a radio speaker, since the BBC was now relaying many of the long analytical lectures which he gave at music festivals around the country, such as the famous four hours of lectures on Beethoven's String Quartet Op. 130 given at Leeds University in 1973, the centenary lectures on Schoenberg's quartets given at the Royal Northern College of Music in 1974, or 'Originality and Influence' at the 1971 Aldeburgh Festival and 'The String Quartet at its Greatest' at the Cheltenham Festival the same year. These lectures, all given without script, or even notes – 'I think it is an act of arrogance to address an audience without your having what you have to say fully inside you in the first place,' declared Keller[123] – and copiously illustrated by a live string quartet, are vivid in the memories of many who heard them and widely regarded as some of the best things Keller ever did. A few years later, after Ian McIntyre took over the Controllership of Radio 3 in 1978, such long lectures were no longer considered tenable,[124] but Stephen Hearst was all in favour: 'I listened to [them] absolutely spellbound!'[125]

Despite the increasing length of some of his own contributions, Keller had

---

121 Undated letter to Keller from Simon King of Fontana Paperbacks (CUL Keller Archive). There is no evidence that this project ever progressed any further.

122 Undated memorandum from Robert Simpson to the Controller, Radio 3 (CUL Keller Archive).

123 From an undated note preserved by Keller with the transcripts of his Schoenberg lectures.

124 McIntyre says he found the idea of broadcasting hour-long lectures on the radio 'preposterous' and he considered Keller to be an 'idiosyncratic and self-indulgent' speaker (oral communication, 15 May 1995).

125 Stephen Hearst, oral communication, 4 November 1996.

never lost sight of his 'musical short talks' idea, to which he often referred in discussions of other talks projects. The original series had ceased when Keller left the Music Talks Producer post and he had not subsequently been able to revive it, possibly due to a lack of enthusiasm on the part of Howard Newby, who, as Keller later complained, 'seemed prejudiced against them, perhaps because they did not quite fit into the Third Programme image of the late fifties or early sixties'.[126] In 1972, he took advantage of the previous year's change of Controllers to put the idea to Stephen Hearst:

> Between September 1959 and January 1960, I inaugurated a considerable number of so-called 'short talks', ranging between four and ten minutes, which proved highly successful with audiences, reaching appreciation indices (as they were then called) well in the eighties. My basic contention was that if a well-known, clear musical thinker has a point to make, he will often be able to get it across within a few minutes; to standardize the shortest talks space at twenty or fifteen minutes, I submitted, was unrealistic. From the planning point of view, too, the short talks proved extremely welcome, since they could be placed in odd spaces ... I suggest resurrecting the idea.[127]

Hearst agreed, and so *In Short: A Series of Short Talks with Long Thoughts Behind Them* became Keller's principal production project during his final years at the BBC. The range of speakers and subjects was wide, but the choice was still clearly Keller's: Benjamin Frankel asked 'Why Write Symphonies Today?', Hugh Wood spoke on musical conservatives and radicals, Alan Walker's subjects were 'Schopenhauer and Music' and 'Music and the Unconscious', and Lionel Salter's were 'Words about Music' and the nature of the music critic. Eric Warr asked 'Are Conductors Phoney?', Levon Chilingirian examined the Haydn Quartets from the point of view of a first violinist, Peter Cropper looked at risk-taking in performance and Susan Bradshaw at 'Chamber Music and its Orchestral Performances'. The series was most successful and ran at the rate of three or four talks a week (including fairly frequent repeats) until Keller's retirement. This time Keller produced them all himself and – the legalization of drugs apart – was largely left alone to do so by the BBC's management. Thus he returned, in his last talks productions, not only to his natural tendency towards aphorism, but also to the independence which he had so much appreciated in his early days as Music Talks Producer.

126 Memorandum from Keller to Stephen Hearst, 23 August 1972 (BBC WAC R27/1084, Music Programmes: Talks: General, 1971–72).

127 Ibid.

Chapter 5

Music and Management

Keller's BBC life was only a few months old when William Glock's reorganization of Music Division propelled him into the ranks of the Corporation's management. After this, as he put it, 'I was a manager all the way,'[1] successively in charge of Chamber Music and Recitals, Orchestral and Choral Music, Regional Symphony Orchestras and, for his last six years at the BBC, after Glock had retired, New Music. At first Keller was delighted by his promotion, but the 'initial flush of excitement' which he described feeling at 'now being in a position of musical "leadership"'[2] gradually gave way to a growing concern with the problems inherent in institutionalized artistic control. Although his preoccupation with what he called 'the myth of management' did not really emerge until half-way through his managerial life (after *Broadcasting in the Seventies*), it became from then on an increasingly dominant – and ultimately destructive – feature of his relationship with the BBC. Nevertheless, despite his frustration with the more commercial and pluralistic BBC of the 1970s, Keller continued to pour an enormous amount of his energy into it, maintaining to the last the crucial importance of broadcasting to music. His ongoing debate with his BBC bosses (which, after *Broadcasting in the Seventies*, took place to an increasing extent in public print) also served to clarify and publicize what one might call his philosophy of broadcasting.

In the spring of 1960, however, when Keller took up the newly-created post of Chief Assistant, Chamber Music and Recitals, he was still, as one of his colleagues of the time puts it, 'on a high with the new BBC'.[3] His deep knowledge of the repertoire made him an obvious choice for the post[4] and, given the traditional British suspicion of chamber music (usually regarded, according to Audience Research, as more esoteric and 'difficult' than orchestral music), there was much that needed to be done. Keller was responsible for the whole of the BBC's chamber music broadcasting which

1 *1975* (1977), p. 15.

2 Ibid., p. 20.

3 Alexander Goehr, oral communication, 28 November 1996.

4 Nevertheless, the post was advertised, and Keller applied and was interviewed for it formally. Writing to Glock beforehand, he suggested that his recent incidental music for *Izanagi und Izanami*, broadcast on Norddeutscher Rundfunk, might help his application: 'Since the score is essentially chamber music ... it strikes me that so far as the chamber-music interview is concerned, I have now proved my competence in the last possible dimension – all the more so since the players said the music was obviously "written by a colleague"' (letter from Keller to Glock, 6 February 1960, CUL Keller Archive).

was not taken from commercial gramophone records,[5] with the exception of the Invitation Concerts, which Glock planned himself – although even here Keller would doubtless have had substantial input into the planning process (the Mozart Quintets in the opening concert, for example, were probably his idea). Working under him, Keller had a team of producers dedicated to chamber music, one of whom was his own appointee, Leo Black. Black says he was a little surprised to find himself working for Keller, having assumed that his previous experience at Universal Edition (where he had worked on the orchestral catalogue) would have placed him more naturally in the BBC's Orchestral and Choral section:

> I had this feeling that I would be most at home in the orchestral group, and when I heard I was in chamber music group, I was a bit let down – but having had a ten-minute conversation with Hans on the first day, that feeling rapidly disseminated. He was pretty fabulous to work for; he was a very, very good boss, I think … He was very responsive to one's enthusiasms … He looked at things very hard, but most of the time he just took the view, 'I'm not here to throw my weight about: I'm here to facilitate things, to make sure things can happen.'[6]

And, it seems, it was relatively easy to make things happen in the BBC of that time: 'One was able, with the relatively short chain of command and the availability of studios, to hear someone, get very enthusiastic, have Bookings ring them up straight away and say, "Look, come and do something".'[7]

As in his talks policy, where he had asked contributors to speak on subjects which 'enhanced or disturbed their dreams',[8] Keller wanted his chamber music producers to act on their enthusiasms, to engage artists they believed in and promote repertoire they loved. To this end, he tried to change the BBC's audition system in favour of performers who aroused particularly strong feelings. BBC auditions at that time were judged by an anonymous panel of producers, who would vote on the merits of each candidate. In Keller's system, one strongly positive reaction was to outweigh any number of mildly negative ones, and such a candidate would be offered an experimental recording, to be broadcast if successful. 'The crucial factor,' explains Leo Black, who did several such recordings, 'was to have been the enthusiasm that had gone into its production – the feeling of *making a programme*.'[9] This, Keller hoped, would tap the potential spotted by the

---

5 Throughout Keller's time at the BBC, music programmes which were made up of gramophone recordings were the responsibility of a completely different department. Music Division had nothing to do with them, and coordination between the two departments was officially the responsibility of the network Controllers. Keller described this situation as an 'utter absurdity' (see 'Music on Radio and Television', *London Review of Books*, 7–20 August 1980).

6 Leo Black, oral communication, 4 August 1995.

7 Ibid.

8 'Musical "Short Talks"', *Radio Times*, 27 November 1959.

9 Leo Black, letter to the author, 7 August 1995.

positive panel member. Keller also challenged the anonymity of the auditions panels, in the same way that he had questioned the anonymity of Our Music Critic in *The Times* a few years earlier. As he himself described it,

> In the early Sixties ... I radically changed our audition system: anonymity was removed, as was the 'judging' situation; instead, there was artistic contact between us and the auditionees, problems of interpretation were discussed during the audition – which, in the end, never left a bad taste, because everything had happened *musically*, rather than in a regressive atmosphere which reduced the artist to a pre-artistic state, that of a student or pupil, of one who had been judged, although beyond the learning stage, judgement has nothing to do with art.[10]

Again, this was meant to be for the performers' benefit, but, as Leo Black remembers, Keller was unable ultimately to convince them that it would work:

> He strongly disapproved of the BBC's anonymous-audition system and refused to take part in it as it stood; he managed to get it agreed that members of the panel could if they so wished go into the studio and check their impressions 'live'. Ironically, it was the performers' organization, the Incorporated Society of Musicians, which asked that this be rescinded, since they felt the anonymity principle was all-important to ensure fairness.[11]

Eleanor Warren, a cellist who joined the BBC as a producer in 1964, has some sympathy with that view: 'The producers were allowed to go into the studio ... but I used to feel that it was rather unfair, because that would make them more nervous if they happened to know you, and often that was the case.'[12]

The experimental recordings, however, did become a regular part of the BBC's promotion of new artists, continuing (if sporadically) long after Keller had retired. Most of the early successful recordings were broadcast in a monthly series of Keller's devising called *The Rising Generation*, where they appeared alongside more orthodox audition passes. Keller's attitude to those of these young musicians whose performances he produced himself was very much that of coach to student. Indeed, according to Leo Black, this active coaching was a feature of all his chamber music production: 'Hans was a great one for telling people better, that the way they were doing it

10 Letter from Keller to Paul Hamburger and Leo Black, 20 February 1981 (CUL Keller Archive).

11 Leo Black, letter to the author, 7 August 1995. Keller himself recalled that he had not been sanguine about his new system's chances of success, even at the time: 'William is my witness when I say that I said to him, "It won't last – not because it won't succeed, but because it will: the common mind can't take this type of artistic success"' (letter from Keller to Paul Hamburger and Leo Black, 20 February 1981 (CUL Keller Archive).

12 Eleanor Warren, oral communication, 23 October 1996.

actually wasn't the truthful way of doing it … It was an unquenchable enthusiasm for the truth, the musical truth, as he perceived it.'[13] On one occasion when Black was with Keller in the studio, and Keller was producing a recital by Irmgard Seefried, 'I particularly remember him correcting her on something, which was a wrong note, or a rest missed out, or something, and she said, in German, "I'm most grateful to you." And the second time he did it, she wasn't at all grateful! … He was always a presence: he was never in the background doing nothing. He was not awed by anybody, I think … He treated everybody as an equal, including people who were supposed to be up there.'[14]

Leo Black has more memories than have his orchestral-producing colleagues of Keller as an active music producer. Although Keller's post was largely administrative and his productions were relatively few by the standards of a full-time producer, 'he certainly got into studios', says Black, who had many opportunities to observe his work there. This may be partly because Keller was more at home with chamber musicians than orchestras, but it is also true that he had more time for production at this time than later in his career: this period in charge of chamber music was the only part of Keller's BBC life in which he was not involved in talks production, his own appearances at the microphone in the early 1960s were also infrequent, in line with the (then) very stringent BBC policy on staff broadcasts, and he had not yet taken on his demanding European Broadcasting Union (EBU) role.

Keller did, however, make occasional forays into television during his chamber music days, with such success that it is perhaps surprising that he did not take this further. He first appeared on 11 February 1962, in conversation with Huw Wheldon, the presenter of the fortnightly late-night arts programme, *Monitor*.[15] The programme's subject was the accessibility or otherwise of modern music and it featured an argument about the melodic qualities of dodecaphonic music, during which Keller whistled the tone-row of Schoenberg's Variations for Orchestra, seeming, according to one enthusiastic reviewer, to be 'as lost in enjoyment of it as any old-age pensioner in a monastery garden'.[16] Keller's personality seems to have come

13 Leo Black, oral communication, 4 August 1995.

14 Ibid.

15 The programme went out at 22.05–22.50 and was entitled 'Do My Ears Deceive Me? An enquiry into the music of our day from Jazz to Schoenberg'. Also taking part were Aaron Copland, Michael Tippett, Deryck Cooke, Colin Davis and the London Symphony Orchestra.

16 Peter Black in an unidentified press-cutting preserved by Keller (CUL Keller Archive). Lionel Salter says that he remembers the programme because, to his surprise, Keller made an error in his whistling: 'They were talking about dodecaphony, and someone had said [this music had] no melodies in it. And Hans said, "Oh come, don't be silly, of course some of these tone rows are very melodious." And he said, "For example, this is the tone row of so-and-so," and then, to my utter astonishment, sang it wrong! Yes! Yes, actually got the tone-row wrong! I was absolutely flabbergasted' (oral communication, 10 January 1996).

over particularly vividly on screen and it was quickly apparent that he had made something of a hit with his audience.[17] 'Our programme on Sunday seems to have gone over like an absolute bomb,' Huw Wheldon told him afterwards. 'You seem to have made a great impression on everybody ("Who is this chap Keller?"). You certainly make an impression on me!'[18] The fan mail which Keller received from viewers was equally enthusiastic: 'Baby, you slayed them,' one of his female correspondents told him,[19] and, on a flight to Munich a couple of days later, Keller even received an appreciative note from the captain via an air hostess.[20]

On his next appearance on *Monitor*, defending Gershwin against Deryck Cooke, Keller apparently slayed them again, with Huw Wheldon noting that in the fan mail 'most of the nicer letters are from young (presumably) women!'[21] – to which Keller replied, 'Next time, don't forget to remind me to address myself to senile men with particular care.'[22] The *Sunday Times*'s reviewer judged it 'the most enjoyable *Monitor* of the season. A delightful dust-up concerning the greatness of Gershwin, championed by that singular and engaging character, Hans Keller.'[23] Keller sent some of the reaction to his television broadcasts to William Glock, telling him about 'certain observations I shall want to make to you regarding the re-organisation of TV music.'[24] Glock, however, did not seem to want to take up any of these ideas. 'Oddly enough, he didn't seem to be particularly interested in what was happening on television, which was, of course, becoming more and more important,' explains David Cox, Head of External Music Services and historian of the Proms; 'it's most odd: you'd think that Glock would have seen that there was a vast field in television.'[25] Lionel Salter, who was at that time in charge of television music, gives a similar picture: 'When I was Head of Music in television, I had absolutely no backing, no support whatever from Glock, and he left me badly in the lurch there.'[26] Glock was similarly uninterested when Keller tried to use the success of his television discussion to promote Gershwin on the Third Programme, seeking Glock's support

17 One who recorded his impressions of this programme was Geoffrey Wheatcroft (later literary editor of *The Spectator*), who found Keller (of whom he had not previously heard) 'hypnotically interesting, a thin, intense man in his forties with hooded eyes, beaky nose and moustache. He spoke with an audibly non-English intonation ... [but] had a formidable, even frightening command of the language which he used like a musical instrument, or like a weapon' (1989, pp. 77–8).

18 Letter from Wheldon to Keller, 13 February 1962 (CUL Keller Archive).

19 Letter to Keller from Christine McCausland, 11 February 1962 (CUL Keller Archive).

20 Keller preserved the note and circulated it on his return to William Glock and other colleagues (CUL Keller Archive).

21 Undated handwritten note from Wheldon to Keller (CUL Keller Archive).

22 Memorandum from Keller to Wheldon, 26 November 1962 (CUL Keller Archive).

23 Maurice Wiggin, *The Sunday Times*, 4 November 1962.

24 Annotation by Keller, dated 17 February 1962, on Wheldon's letter to him of 13 February 1962 (CUL Keller Archive).

25 David Cox, oral communication, 17 January 1996.

26 Lionel Salter, oral communication, 10 January 1996.

against a sceptical Howard Newby. 'While I had evidently convinced five million people,' Keller told him, 'I had yet failed to convince CTP [Controller Third Programme: Newby], who hadn't even been watching ... that the time had come for him to re-inspect his prejudices.' Keller wanted Glock's support because Newby had eventually promised that 'if I succeeded in persuading CMus [Controller Music: Glock] to include Gershwin in a Thursday Invitation Concert, he would consider further ventures.'[27]

Despite his success on television, the most famous broadcast which Keller made during his time in charge of chamber music was a ten-minute performance as an amateur percussionist during a chamber music concert conducted by Bruno Maderna broadcast on the Third Programme on 5 June 1961.[28] Keller's contribution, recorded separately from the concert, was a tape of himself and pianist Susan Bradshaw hitting about at random in a studio full of assorted instruments. The result was broadcast as the work of a little-known avant-garde composer called Piotr Zak. The fact that such nonsense could plausibly be inserted into the relay of a prestigious concert would, Keller hoped, demonstrate the parlous state of contemporary composition, by showing that random sound could be taken seriously as music.

The idea had apparently come to Keller during a conversation with Susan Bradshaw after the broadcast of another contemporary music concert. As she recalls:

> I can tell you how it started. It was a piece by Stockhausen, I think, and afterwards I was sitting in the control room with [Hans], and the attendants were moving the chairs in the studio, and they were scraping them across the floor. It just struck me that, actually, the noise of the attendants scraping the chairs across the floor might well have come from the same piece that we'd just heard. And Hans, instead of saying, 'Mm, yes,' or 'Don't be silly,' or something, he said, 'That's a wonderful idea!'[29]

Keller took the proposal to Newby: 'I ... went to the Controller of Third Programme and said I wanted to broadcast senseless noise in order to prove that, nowadays, we have reached a stage where even musicians can't decide whether something was music or not. He paused for 60 seconds, and then said, "Right, we'll do it.".'[30] 'I took a deep breath and said "yes",' says

27 Memorandum from Keller to Glock, 15 November 1962 (BBC WAC R27/1026, Music General: Music Programmes Policy).

28 The full programme of the concert was Petrassi: *Serenata* (1958), for flute, viola, double-bass, harpsichord and percussion; Webern: Six Songs Op. 14; Nono: *Polifonica-Monodia-Ritmica*, for flute, clarinet, bass-clarinet, horn, piano and percussion; Zak: *Mobile*, for tape and percussion; Mozart: Serenade in B flat, K. 361.

29 Susan Bradshaw, interviewed by Christopher Marshall for a portrait of Keller in the radio series *Reputations* (broadcast on Radio 3 on 2 October 1996).

30 Hans Keller, interviewed by Anton Weinberg in the summer of 1985 for the Channel 4 documentary *The Keller Instinct* (first broadcast on 23 February 1986). A transcript of the interview, by Mark Doran, is published in *Tempo*, 95 (January 1996), pp. 6–12.

Newby,[31] whose brief hesitation may have stemmed from a suspicion of what William Glock's reaction to the broadcast was likely to be. A note on the affair which Keller wrote 20 years later suggests that Glock and Newby were experiencing some differences of opinion at this time (possibly over Glock's contemporary music policy), and that Glock had already turned Zak down:

> Pjotr [*sic*] Zak ... would never have been allowed to be born in my mind if there hadn't been a chaotic conflict of directorial opinion at the time I submitted my invention. He slipped in behind the back of a boss whose No should have been final.[32]

Keller then collected together a large number of percussion instruments, 'everything he could possibly think of', says Susan Bradshaw, 'and he and I, with one producer, went in and started to try and see what would happen if we prevented ourselves thinking in terms of music and just hit randomly about.'[33] 'We produced, needless to add, utter nonsense',[34] said Keller, who nevertheless set to work on a serious presentation of their 'piece'. The press release which accompanied the broadcast reads as follows:

> Piotr Zak is one of the youngest and most controversial figures in contemporary music. He is of Polish extraction, and now lives in Germany. The strong influence of Kagel, Stockhausen and John Cage can be felt in his music, which he will not allow to be published, because he considers his scores as private instructions to the professional performer, which has certain renaissance parallels. 'Mobile' takes its name from the aerial sculptures of the American John Calder. It consists of an electronic tape, against which two percussion players play music written down, but giving scope for improvisation. The tape exploits the full range of the aural spectrum, controlled by strictly measurable quantities – frequency ratios, velocity graphs and decibel indexes ... The soloists CLAUDE TESSIER and ANTON SCHMIDT are coming to this country specially for the performance: they have already given the work in Europe.[35]

---

31 Howard Newby, interviewed by Humphrey Carpenter (quoted in Carpenter, 1996, p. 201).

32 'The Future of BBC Music: a Mystery', *Musical Times*, February 1982.

33 Susan Bradshaw, interviewed by Anton Weinberg for *The Keller Instinct*, Channel 4.

34 Hans Keller, interviewed by Anton Weinberg for *The Keller Instinct*, Channel 4.

35 CUL Keller Archive. Susan Bradshaw explained how they decided on the composer's name as follows: 'We sought around for some unlikely East-European name, and somebody – I don't know who – told us that Zak was like Smith in, I think, Czechoslovakia, and that we'd be fairly safe if we called our composer Zak, because it could be absolutely anybody' (interview for *The Keller Instinct*, Channel 4). Leo Black says, 'I heard from HK that it was a Polish barber, one of whose customers was Harry Croft-Jackson, Chief Assistant Music Progamme Organisation in Music Division, who came up with the name Piotr Zak when asked for the most typically Polish name. Keller had of necessity had to let Croft-Jackson in on the secret since the latter was in a position to "rule" on the admissibility of new works not suggested by the Controller himself' (letter to author, 1 February 2000).

The work was broadcast during the transmission of one of the flagship Invitation Concerts – a timing which probably increased the annoyance to William Glock, who had planned the original concert, but which also decreased the likelihood of Zak's genuineness being doubted. As Donald Mitchell pointed out later, 'When one thinks of the steps the BBC took to guarantee the "authenticity" of the hoax, it would have been astonishing indeed if any listener had heard the "Mobile" as anything else but a *bona fide* première.' This, for Mitchell – and for many others – made the whole experiment 'finally worthless. One cannot take seriously the findings of an experiment in which one set of participants has been subjected to influences that well-nigh determined the result.'[36]

Mitchell was one of two reviewers of the original broadcast whom Keller invited back to discuss the whole issue on air.[37] While he had been lucky enough to refer (unknowingly) to the piece's 'non-musical origins' in his original review, the other critic, Jeremy Noble of *The Times*, had unfortunately claimed to have grasped 'the music's broad outlines'. Although his review was as negative as Mitchell's, his evident effort to understand the piece and talk in terms of its structure was grist to Keller's mill. In the broadcast discussion, both critics held to Mitchell's point that they could not have done otherwise than to take the piece seriously, given its presentation, and, since they had not given it a favourable reception, they did not consider themselves to have been taken in. Keller's reiterated reply was that, whatever the presentation, such a meaningless collection of sounds could never have been mistaken for music in Mozart's time, and the experiment had therefore exposed the current crisis of language in modern music.

Most of Keller's BBC colleagues of the time agree that, although Piotr Zak is still well remembered today, 'it was the dampest of squibs at the time',[38] which required considerable effort from Keller to generate a scandal. Moreover, the serious point did not come across at all well, leaving some of the general public with the impression that Keller was dismissing all contemporary music – a result which Glock apparently viewed as a dreadful 'own goal'.[39] In this light, Keller's statement in the follow-up discussion with Mitchell and Noble that 'the audience research results I've seen … are completely indistinguishable from reactions to real works' can be seen as an indication not of the success of his experiment, but of the damage it might have done to the BBC's attempt to widen the audience for contemporary music. A letter to *The Telegraph* which appeared shortly after the follow-up discussion was unfortunately typical of many listeners' reactions: 'The

36 Donald Mitchell, 'Critics Were Not Deceived', letter to the editor, *The Daily Telegraph*, 18 August 1961, p. 10.

37 *The Strange Case of Piotr Zak* was broadcast on the Third Programme on 13 August 1961. A recording of the programme is preserved in the BBC Sound Archives (LP26787) and the script in BBC WAC.

38 Leo Black, oral communication, 4 August 1995.

39 Ibid.

revelation of the hoax itself contains another hoax. Mr Piotr Zak *does* exist. Under a variety of aliases he continues to contribute works to our broadcast programmes. He is a great friend of the BBC's Controller of Music, and lives in a private apartment in Broadcasting House.'[40]

Leo Black thinks that Piotr Zak caused real difficulties between Glock and Keller by exposing the fundamental difference between their approaches to modern music. 'I had the impression there was what the Greeks call a chiasmus crossing their paths,' he remembers, so that, despite their common endeavours on behalf of contemporary music, 'differences emerged, as they were bound to, differences of emphasis, differences of personality. The Piotr Zak incident, I think, was the thing that crystallized it.'[41] Most members of Music Division gradually became aware of the cooling of Glock and Keller's initially close working relationship – 'the quarrel was not disguised from colleagues', remembers Robert Layton[42] – but, for the most part, not until some years after Piotr Zak. The following year, Keller still appeared to be Glock's right-hand man when Glock transferred him to head the Orchestral and Choral section. As Keller described the move, 'he invited me, mildly pressed me, to clear up the orchestral area',[43] a picture which is confirmed by Leo Black's recollection:

> Glock felt that the Glock revolution was doing very nicely on the chamber music front: he'd got not merely *the* live wire in charge of it, but he'd also got a very good group of producers, newish producers, operating ... The orchestral music, for some reason, Glock felt was not moving along at quite his speed. Perhaps there were special problems associated with getting orchestras to play the sort of music he felt it his duty to get propagated ... He quite soon came to feel that Hans would get better results than Leonard Isaacs. So he swapped them over.[44]

Although, as Lionel Salter explains, 'there was a whole history in the BBC of swapping people around from job to job, sometimes for no apparent reason',[45] David Cox agrees with Black that Glock did have definite reasons for making this change. Cox says he got the impression that Isaacs had become the scapegoat for a 'disastrous' performance of Messiaen's *Turangalila Symphony*, which had been given by the BBC Symphony Orchestra to an almost empty Festival Hall, due to a problem with the publicity.[46] Whatever the reason, Isaacs evidently saw the move as a demotion, and left the BBC shortly afterwards. Keller, likewise, saw his move as a promotion, according to Alexander Goehr: 'He calculated it was the most powerful job. In that sense it was one of his rare banalities ... where

40 Letter to the editor from G.H. Bosworth, *The Daily Telegraph*, 12 August 1961, p. 6.
41 Leo Black, oral communication, 4 August 1995.
42 Robert Layton, oral communication, 11 November 1996.
43 *1975* (1977), p. 15.
44 Leo Black, oral communication, 4 August 1995.
45 Lionel Salter, oral communication, 10 January 1996.
46 David Cox, oral communication, 17 January 1996.

there's more money to spend, that's most important. And of course you spend more on orchestral music than you do on chamber music.'[47]

In the end, Keller had stayed in the chamber music post for less than two years, in contrast to the whole decade he was to spend in charge of orchestras. Alexander Goehr thinks it a shame that Keller's time as Chief Assistant Chamber Music and Recitals was so short, seeing it as

> the highpoint of his achievement, because he changed the whole representation of the performance of chamber music. He systematized it, and of course in that sense it was one of the occasions where he and William Glock were working hand in hand, because William also had very sophisticated views, especially about Haydn. And that was the best thing that the BBC did, or at least the most uncritical. I mean it was really very good indeed, because all these sort of basically dubious English string quartets were drummed into some sort of service, and the representation was good and it was interesting, and everybody learned [from] it, bec[ause] before that, unless you were, as Hans would say, a string player, one's knowledge of the repertoire was a bit on the sketchy side. I mean, suddenly you heard it all, and the presentation was terrific. He was a bit didactic and dogmatic, as he always was, and he said, this is good and that's not good, and this particular set of quartets is important, this one is not important, and so he would lay it out, as in the Haydn book and so on. And that affected the programming, so that you were able to test his views by hearing sets. I mean I don't think we knew that Haydn wrote his quartets in sets before that point, unless one had a special interest.[48]

Haydn was not the only beneficiary of Keller's chamber music programming, according to Goehr: 'Hans reinvented Mendelssohn; nobody had the least idea that Mendelssohn had written a string quartet – certainly no one played one … The idea of taking anything by Mendelssohn seriously [at that time] was entirely due to Hans.'[49]

Goehr, who now worked under Keller as part of the team of orchestral producers, thinks that Keller 'didn't feel at home' with orchestras in the way that he evidently did with chamber musicians: 'He didn't know how orchestras worked [and] he didn't understand the mentalities of orchestral musicians.'[50] This view finds some support in the long policy statement that Keller produced halfway through his period as Chief Assistant, Orchestral and Choral, the first section of which is concerned with the ways in which Keller felt his artistic policy was compromised by the practicalities of working with orchestras:

> The orchestral planner has to be more 'realistic', more accommodating, readier to make concessions to practical and indeed psychological circumstances, than the planner of chamber music … There is, artistically speaking, no orchestral

47 Alexander Goehr, oral communication, 28 November 1996.
48 Ibid.
49 Ibid.
50 Alexander Goehr, oral communication, 4 December 1996.

> repertoire, in the sense in which, say, a string quartet has a repertoire. There are works which the orchestra in question has played recently, and there are works which the conductor in question likes ... The reasons for which conductors include certain pieces in their orchestra's repertoire tend to be less exclusively musical than the motivating forces behind a string quartet's repertoire ... He has to adjust his preferences to the character of the orchestra (if any); and unless he is very fully established, he will also tend to adjust his musical preferences to what he considers desirable from the point of view of furthering his own career ...
>
> With certain well-definable exceptions, chamber music rehearsals are a private – and proportionately responsible – affair; orchestral rehearsals are not ... Orchestral rehearsals ... cost money and time. In present-day circumstances, the few leading orchestras we have ... tend to be fully engaged. Even where the money is available, therefore, they may not be able to cope with an ambitious programme at a given time, because rehearsal time is limited.
>
> The so-called large orchestra, which has a short span of life anyway, is gradually disintegrating even where composers retain it so far as sheer numbers of players are concerned – which now, however, tends to be used soloistically, or split up into smaller groups, with a proportionate increase in performing problems, both technical and musical ...
>
> Perhaps the greatest hurdle to be overcome in the planning of vital, and vitally performed orchestral programmes is the orchestral player's psychology. As everyone who has played in an orchestra knows, if he is strong enough to face the truth, orchestral playing is an unmusical occupation.[51]

The penultimate point, the disintegration of the symphony orchestra, was one which Keller made on numerous occasions, most notably in a famous debate at the Cheltenham Festival in 1970, in which he and Peter Maxwell Davies successfully proposed the motion 'That this House believes that the ultimate extinction of the symphony orchestra is inevitable'.[52] Keller's point

51 'Orchestral Music: Policy and Practice', 18 February 1965 (BBC WAC R27/1056, Music General: Orchestral and Symphonic Music Policy). The date on this document, added in an unidentified hand, is incorrect, as the document refers to the series *My Favourite Concertos* as having already begun: *My Favourite Concertos* did not reach the airwaves until January 1966. Also, the document refers to the planning of the 1967/68 inaugural EBU concert series as 'almost complete', but the Working Party in charge of the planning was not set up until the summer of 1965.

52 Opposing Keller and Maxwell Davies were Gerald McDonald (General Manager of the New Philharmonia Orchestra) and Professor Ivor Keys. Professor Alan Peacock, who had recently chaired an enquiry into orchestral resources in Britain, was in the chair. Extracts from the debate were published in *Composer*, no. 37 (Autumn 1970), pp. 1–9, which records that the motion was carried by 51 votes to 49. It also records that when the debate was repeated at a meeting of the Music Club of London the following September, the motion was lost by 16 votes. On 22 September the same year, the BBC held a studio discussion on the same subject between Gerald McDonald, Alexander Goehr, Norman Del Mar and Keller, chaired by John Amis. The debate was broadcast on Radio 4 on 8 December 1970, under the title 'The Death of the Symphony Orchestra'; recordings of it are held in both the BBC Sound Archive (LP33297) and the National Sound Archive (P588W).

was that, throughout musical history, 'the large band throws up the small band' – citing as examples the emergence of the string quartet from the orchestra, and the solo concerto from the concerto grosso – and that the artistic results of the small bands were unquestionably greater. The Romantic symphony orchestra, he argued, came into being only as a result of increasing chromaticism, which had 'urged music towards the point where it was absolutely necessary to blend sounds, especially the more difficult chords ... in a way which made them "beautiful", and more readily acceptable than they would have been had they been distributed amongst solo parts.' Nevertheless, 'as the symphony orchestra became larger than it had ever been before, that is to say in Mahler or in Schoenberg's *Gurrelieder*, you get the tendency [to split into solo instruments] again manifesting itself with a passionate urge ... determined amongst other things by the need for more counterpoint.'

Keller's statement of orchestral policy[53] set himself three basic aims: 'to reflect the country's concert life, both in the capital and in the provinces', 'to provide a fairly regular supply of the great masterpieces of the past' and, of course, to promote new music. In doing this, he was also concerned with the 'artistic shape' of individual programmes, and with the need, where possible, to combine new and old music in the same programme: 'Our age's crisis of musical comprehension will never be cured without the tangible relations between the present and the past being thrown into relief.'[54] With regard to new music, he continued to emphasize radio's distinct missionary role: 'substantial problematic music is radiogenic: while the radio listener doesn't get so enthusiastic as the concert-goer, he doesn't get so upset either when confronted with problems.' Even after he had abandoned new music in the concert hall, such a listener 'will yet turn on the radio: Audience Research supports this prognosis'.[55]

Active promotion of new repertoire, for Keller, entailed a necessary imbalance in the schedules:

> In order for programme-planning to be effective, it is desirable to draw attention to the more unusual aspects of the repertoire, past or present, not by sprinkling the contents of the relevant reservoir of recordings all over the place in equal distribution, but by working in waves. The recent Bruckner series created a far wider and more appreciative audience for Bruckner's symphonies than could have been achieved if Bruckner had merely taken his place within the context of a chronic total balance of programme content: to do everything means to do nothing.[56]

53 'Orchestral Music: Policy and Practice', 18 February 1965; but see note 51 above.

54 'Music on Radio', paper given to *Rencontres de Tenerife 1976*, an international conference on radio sponsored by the European Broadcasting Union, 16–20 March 1976 (EBU, 1977, p. 263).

55 'Orchestral Music: Policy and Practice', 18 February 1965; but see note 51 above.

56 Ibid.

Nowadays, such thematic programming is widely used, but then Keller's 'waves' were in marked contrast to what Robert Layton calls the 'more objective, civil-service kind of approach'[57] of the BBC in the 1950s, which Keller's predecessor, Leonard Isaacs, had continued. Alexander Goehr similarly describes the orchestral division under Isaacs as 'very well run in a sort of bureaucratic way. You made your proposals, and then there was a monthly meeting; Leonard sat there, you made eight proposals and two were taken.'[58] Keller, by contrast, allowed his producers a lot more freedom to act on their enthusiasms, and was prepared to devote considerable time and money to interesting ideas. This approach was probably more in harmony with that of William Glock, who, as Robert Layton remembers, also 'encouraged what he would call "creative imbalance"'.[59]

Keller was not above using popular ideas to make a musical point: he used the public's perennial interest in star performers, for example, to create the long-running series *My Favourite Concertos*, 'giving virtuosos the opportunity to play their two favourite concertos, and to explain, in the interval, why they are their favourites', and incidentally reviving 'a type of programme which used to be prevalent in less snobbish times and deserves revival … A doubly radiogenic purpose is here fulfilled: both the performer and the listener are offered something which they want and don't get in the concert hall, and the performance tends to become more spirited, because the performer is the sole programme builder.'[60] It was also an ideal opportunity to combine words and music – in which, of course, the listener would be hearing musicians themselves speak. Orchestral projects which Keller planned himself were frequently imaginative combinations of words and music: one particularly striking example was the extensive series of concerts with coordinated interval talks called *The Symphony* which was broadcast during the autumn of 1973. The programmes were a wide-ranging exploration of symphonism in all its forms: the opening concert, for example, featured performances of Britten's *Spring Symphony*, Stravinsky's *Symphonies of Wind Instruments* and Schoenberg's First Chamber Symphony, provoking in the interval a discussion by Denis Matthews of the meaning of the word 'symphony' in such contexts. Chamber music was combined with orchestral music throughout: for example, the programme in which Hugh Wood discussed 'Classical symphonism and its inherent elements of creative self-destruction' contained performances of Haydn's

57 Robert Layton, oral communication, 11 November 1996.

58 Alexander Goehr, oral communication, 28 November 1996.

59 Robert Layton, oral communication, 11 November 1996. According to Layton, Glock's periods of enthusiasm for certain performers and composers were very marked, and were often followed by complete neglect, something which those concerned naturally found very difficult to take. Layton also believes that Glock had similar waves of enthusiasm for individual producers, and therefore that the cooling of his relationship with Keller was simply the natural end of such a period of preference.

60 'Orchestral Music: Policy and Practice', 18 February 1965; but see note 51 above.

Quartet Op. 50 No. 6 and Mozart's Quintet K. 515, as well as Beethoven's *Eroica*. The combination of chamber music and orchestral music in the same programme – also a feature of his EBU programmes – was something which Keller considered a particularly valuable function of radio concert planning, since it 'opens up perspectives on the relationships between different types of creativity utterly concealed by normal concert life ... The development of symphonic thought can never be understood if one confines oneself to thinking about symphonies: the juxtaposition, in concert performance, of string quartets and symphonies belongs, purely artistically, to the most rewarding experiences.'[61]

There was one area of orchestral planning which, despite all the practical difficulties and expense, really did 'realise policy throughout', according to Keller. This was the International Concert Series of the European Broadcasting Union, which began in 1967. Keller described its purpose as follows:

> Realising that there were orchestral projects, especially when top stars were involved, that were far beyond our financial capacities and indeed any other radio station's, we persuaded the European Broadcasting Union to form a working party which would plan an annual international series consisting of outstanding public concerts in different European capitals; they would be relayed by all participant radio stations, who would pay a modest amount of money into an EBU kitty, with the result that we could jointly afford concerts which we couldn't have afforded singly ... The intention is to have at least one annual concert of modern music ... [and] to include an annual, or perhaps bi-annual concert with future rather than present stars – outstanding talents we hope to discover at international competitions and elsewhere.[62]

The idea of such a collaborative concert series had emerged at the EBU Music Sub-Committee's meeting in Geneva at the beginning of 1965, at which, according to Lionel Salter's report of the meeting,[63] the BBC was asked to coordinate the series. Since the report of the following meeting is not on file, it is not clear how the Corporation responded to this; by the time of Salter's next report, dated 14 June 1965, the planning of the series was already in the hands of an international working party, initially of three members (although it grew considerably larger in later years), chaired by Hans Keller.[64]

---

61 'Music on Radio', paper given to *Rencontres de Tenerife 1976* (see note 54 above).

62 'Orchestral Music: Policy and Practice', 18 February 1965; but see note 51 above.

63 Memorandum from Salter to Pelletier, 3 February 1965 (BBC WAC R27/730/1: Music General, European Broadcasting Union, File 1, 1963–65). Lionel Salter (then the BBC's Head of Opera) acted as the BBC's EBU music representative from November 1963.

64 According to Marriott, 'The group was fixed at three because it was thought that a very small number could work much more efficiently together, and also to save expense since it was expected that there would have to be many meetings and continual communication and consultation between the members. The broadcasting organisations of France,

Keller had previously had little involvement with the EBU – his name was not even mentioned during the BBC's internal discussions before Lionel Salter was appointed as its EBU music representative[65] – but, when he happened to be present during an EBU meeting at which the management of the concert series was being debated, he seized on the opportunity with alacrity, as Salter describes:

> The other thing about Hans, of course, was that he had to be the centre of everything! He had to be not merely the cynosure of all eyes, but he had to be the centre point of everything that was going on. In the EBU ... where he had originally just come in to talk on some particular subject, I forget what it was ... before you knew where you were, Hans had engineered himself into the centre point for the EBU concerts ... Everybody was so steamrollered, I think is the word, by his endless talk. And he was obviously very keen, and quite capable, and so there he was! And he then took over everything. But this was his way: he took over everything that he was allowed to.[66]

According to Salter, Keller was an 'authoritarian' chairman: 'He allowed them to speak, but he had his way in the end.'[67] Stephen Plaistow, who replaced Keller as chairman of the working party when Keller retired from the BBC, agrees with this picture: 'When I took over at the EBU, people said it's so nice you allow us to talk ... I was certainly made aware that there was a feeling that Keller had run this as his own private broadcasting service for too long.'[68] It is certainly true that a large number of the programmes bear Keller's personal stamp quite clearly, especially in later years, after the inauguration of the EBU's International String Quartet Series. Characteristically, chamber music was present in the programming right

---

Germany and Great Britain were chosen in the first place because they had large resources and perhaps more experience of organising large scale concerts' (letter from Marriott to R. Wangermee, Director General of Radiodiffusion-Télévision Belge (French Service), 11 January 1966, BBC WAC R27/730/2, Music General: European Broadcasting Union, File 2, 1966–67).

65 One of the reasons may have been that it was considered that 'An essential qualification ... is the ability to speak and understand French' (memorandum from Richard Marriott to Gerald Abraham, 29 October 1963, BBC WAC R27/730/1: Music General, European Broadcasting Union, File 1, 1963–65).

66 Lionel Salter, oral communication, 10 January 1996.

67 Ibid.

68 Stephen Plaistow, oral communication, 27 July 1995. Keller himself does not seem to have been much impressed with his colleagues in the early days of the Working Party: 'Everything went according to my plan; unfortunately it can't go any other way, because when I stop talking, nobody else says anything. The Working Party's function is now purely psychological: it has ceased to exist as a planning committee. Philippot, who probably is a good musician, is a silent passenger; as for Dr Baruch, he occasionally makes a practical remark, but isn't a *musician* at all. I did more hard Concert Season work in the course of unofficial conversations with various colleagues during the Berlioz meeting than in the entire Working Party session' (memorandum from Keller to ADR, 22 February 1968, private source).

from the start, although the series was primarily intended to broadcast expensive orchestral music.

If the practical problems involved in producing domestic orchestral programming had interfered with Keller's musical policy, one might have thought that the obstacles thrown up by such a large-scale international collaboration would prove insuperable. At the outset, as Lionel Salter reported to his BBC colleagues,

> There was considerable disagreement on this project, and a number of dissentient voices both in principle and in detail ... Holland is firmly against taking part on programmatic grounds; Switzerland fears repercussions with its own relations with soloists; Portugal and Israel are debarred from direct relay by virtue of the land lines situation; Denmark does not wish to enter; and even Norway, which had agreed, is slightly appalled at the thought of a two-hour concert, as well as having reservations about the programme content. Various objections were put forward to the details as drafted (which were intended as a basis for discussion); many thought the programmes too unadventurous, and there was considerable pressure for some more contemporary music in the scheme; doubts were expressed whether Klemperer would still be active in two years time in order to undertake a big work like the Mahler. The thought of three eminent Russian soloists arriving together was viewed with scepticism; and others questioned the role of major orchestras purely for accompanimental purposes. The whole matter was referred back to the Keller working party.[69]

Keller's handling of such problems, however, was apparently superb. Unlike Glock, he was considered by all his colleagues to be an excellent administrator. The question of the inclusion of modern music remained a vexed one, nevertheless. The programmes did become a little more contemporary, but cautiously so. Keller was very aware that 'the idea of a contemporary concert within this series will always receive a certain degree of opposition, and unless we justify it by the palpably exceptional character of each of these concerts, it may not survive.'[70] One person who was keen that the concerts should not be too contemporary was Richard Marriott, who, according to Salter, asked at the outset that 'these concerts should be rather of first class performances of the current repertoire.'[71] Indeed, in 1967,

69 Memorandum from Salter to Marriott, 14 June 1965 (BBC WAC R27/730/1: Music General, European Broadcasting Union, File 1, 1963–65). The 'three Russians' were Oistrakh, Rostropovich and Richter, who were to perform the Beethoven Triple Concerto and, in a chamber concert two weeks later, Schubert and Mendelssohn Piano Trios. Fairly early in the planning, Richter was replaced by Gilels, but otherwise all appeared to be well until four months before the concert date, when Keller reported to Newby that both concerts had 'disintegrated' and were urgently being replaced (memorandum from Keller to Newby, 25 October 1967, BBC WAC R27/730/2, Music General: European Broadcasting Union, File 2, 1966–67). As feared, Klemperer also did not appear.

70 Memorandum from Keller to the members of the working party, 13 December 1966 (BBC WAC ibid.).

71 Memorandum from Salter to Rooney Pelletier, 3 February 1965 (BBC WAC R27/730/1: Music General, European Broadcasting Union, File 1, 1963–65).

according to a note from Keller to Glock, Marriott tried to get Keller's working party to drop a performance of Schoenberg's *Jacob's Ladder* from the plans for the second EBU series.[72] Nevertheless, the performance eventually took place in London, as a BBC production – despite the fact that William Glock was privately not all that keen on it either (according to Alexander Goehr, who produced the programme):

> We organized a performance of *Jacob's Ladder*, and I was even sent to Los Angeles to get Mrs Schoenberg to come ... But William didn't turn up, characteristically – he did one of his many diplomatic 'flu's, and then sent a message to Mrs Schoenberg, would she sit in his box. And she said, that's the least I can do for you![73]

In 1967 it was proposed that the EBU should promote a separate series of contemporary concerts, which would 'remove the presently-felt necessity to include a sizeable element of "difficult" music in the Concert Season [concerts] themselves and might thus render these more generally "popular".'[74] This idea did not materialize, but, in 1975, Keller did launch a separate specialist series of concerts: the International String Quartet Series. Originally designed to run for two seasons only (during which, according to Keller's opening programme note, it would 'throw spotlights on the development of the string quartet – not chronologically, but in terms of what one might call related peaks'[75]), it ran until Keller's retirement in 1979. The quartet who opened this inaugural season, with an all-Haydn programme on 29 September 1975, was the Chilingirian Quartet, winner of the EBU's first International String Quartet Competition which had taken place in Stockholm the year before (they were, incidentally, students of Keller). Both the International String Quartet Series and the competition were evidently Keller's initiative, as the rules of the competition make clear. Amongst its stated aims is the intention 'to make this musical competition more musical than competitive', to which end, 'in an attempt to attain the highest possible degree of musical realism, there will be no pre-determined prizes'. The list of repertoire from which candidates had to choose, though not entirely Kellerian, is very largely so, with appropriate emphasis given to the classical masterpieces. In the further interests of 'musical realism', competing quartets did not just concentrate on public performance: the second round of the competition, for example, consisted of study sessions on the Haydn quartets:

72 Note to Glock on a memorandum to Keller from the General Manager, Radio Enterprises, 25 April 1967 (BBC WAC R27/730/2, Music General: European Broadcasting Union, File 2, 1966–67).

73 Alexander Goehr, oral communication, 28 November 1996.

74 From the minutes of an EBU Bureau Meeting quoted by Richard Marriott in a memorandum to Lionel Salter, 17 July 1967 (BBC WAC ibid.).

75 CUL Keller Archive. Keller wrote extensive programme notes for all the EBU String Quartet Series concerts.

> To work at, show *musical – i.e. not technical* – knowledge of one of the 45 masterpieces of Haydn contained in List 3 … The working period of each such session will be 45 minutes and the piece will be chosen by the jury, which will give the quartets at least one hour's notice of it, the purpose of this study session being twofold: to establish the ensemble's basic literacy as well as its understanding of the essential improvisatory nature of all characteristic string-quartet playing.[76]

One can imagine that such sessions could become very like one of Keller's 'coaching' BBC auditions or chamber music productions.

'Those were good years for Keller, when he started all that' [the EBU concerts], remembers Stephen Plaistow. 'He had good friends, and people saw what a force for good he was … In the early days of international music co-operation, he did some marvellous stuff.'[77] Indeed, the start of the EBU concerts in 1967–68 was the culmination of Keller's very happy and successful first decade with the BBC. His influence had grown steadily, from those first intoxicating days as Music Talks Producer, through his 'clearing up' of first chamber music and then orchestral music planning, his brief control of the fledgling Music Programme in 1965, followed by his increasingly prominent role in its talks, to his successful inauguration, planning and execution of Europe-wide concerts. Within Yalding House itself, his presence was felt in almost everything that Music Division did. 'His views were pervasive,' says Stephen Plaistow. 'Even if they were often irritating and you didn't agree, they were always there as something you had to consider – and he showed what could be done.'[78] Lionel Salter agrees:

> His best qualities were the incessant flow of ideas, as well as of conversation and of memos; his determination – call it wilfulness if you like, hotheadedness sometimes; the very stimulating atmosphere in which one found oneself if one was ever in any kind of discussion with him; his clarity of mind and his ability to think on his feet; and he exercised an extraordinary magnetic influence, on younger people in particular: he used to have little coteries, you know, which used to gather round him at the pub round the corner, the Stag's Head.[79]

In 1969, however, Keller's life at the BBC changed dramatically. As he himself described the change in an article written on the occasion of his retirement, 'My first decade at the BBC was paradise, while my second would have been hell if I hadn't been I … The turning point was "Broadcasting in the Seventies" and the so-called staff rebellion against this

76 From the rules for the 1978 String Quartet Competition in Helsinki (CUL Keller Archive).

77 Stephen Plaistow, oral communication, 27 July 1995.

78 Ibid.

79 Lionel Salter, oral communication, 10 January 1996. The Stag's Head was the 1970s pub, however: during the 1960s Music Division used to patronize the Horse and Groom in Great Portland Street.

document, a public protest which I initiated.'[80] As has been seen in Chapter 4, *Broadcasting in the Seventies* was not the first time the BBC had reviewed its radio policy, nor was it the first retrenchment. The storm which it provoked, however, was unprecedented, and it remains one of the most controversial documents the BBC has ever produced. Keller himself dubbed it 'a major exhibit in the evidence of the decline of the West'.[81]

Broadcasting in the Seventies and the way in which it undermined Keller's relationship with the BBC will be the subject of the following chapter. It is enough, for the present, to say that nothing was quite the same again. As has been pointed out already, its effects were compounded for Keller by the replacement of three senior figures he admired with three he did not. Nevertheless, the change in his attitude towards the BBC at this point and the strength of his feelings about what he evidently considered to be a betrayal is startling. The BBC had abandoned principles of fundamental importance and was therefore to bear responsibility for the difficulties which followed. 'I was fascinated by your describing me as a dissenting personality,' he wrote to the newly appointed Managing Director, Radio, Aubrey Singer, in 1979. 'I'd win a handsome bet if you accepted it – to find me a single example of Kellerian dissent in the BBC between 1959 and 1969. Did I change personality at the turn of the decade, or did we?'[82] Indeed, all the evidence is that Keller would have won his bet: the sort of 'Kellerian dissent' that so infuriated the management of the 1970s – 'there he was ... putting a spoke into the wheels all the time,' complains Stephen Hearst[83] – is conspicuous by its absence in the files of the 1960s.

Nevertheless, from the very start of Keller's BBC life, his interest in matters beyond the specific responsibilities of his own post was abundantly evident. He was quick to praise, criticize and comment on almost everything the BBC was – or ought to have been – doing. Never content to wait for scheduled meetings, his opinions would fly round the BBC in a torrent of incisively written, and often very witty memoranda, with multiple copies to all who cared to express an interest. 'He was a compulsive writer,' says Lionel Salter:

> I expect you've heard from other people how in the BBC he would write endless memos – thousands of them! – usually written on the backs of discarded programme sheets. And these would go round to everybody – hand-written always, and on a variety of subjects – and they were an absolutely unstoppable flow. They were very, very stimulating, and, of course, Hans himself was immensely stimulating. However much one disagreed with him, he was a wonderfully fluent instigator of ideas.[84]

---

80 'Fare Better, BBC', *Spectator*, 20 June 1979.

81 Review of *A Seamless Robe* by Charles Curran, *The Spectator*, 15 September 1979, pp. 18–20.

82 Letter from Keller to Singer, 5 January 1979 (CUL Keller Archive).

83 Stephen Hearst, oral communication, 4 November 1996.

84 Lionel Salter, oral communication, 10 January 1996.

'Oh yes, he wanted to do all kinds of things, he wanted a finger in lots of pies,' agrees David Cox. 'Not everybody wanted him to be in the middle of everything, but that was certainly what he was aiming at.'[85] During the 1970s, the 'unstoppable flow' became increasingly irritating to the BBC's management, especially as Keller's subject-matter became less specifically musical, and his tone more self-righteous. Stephen Hearst, who took over from Howard Newby as Controller of Radio 3 in 1971, found the task of dealing with correspondence from Keller no light burden: 'The mere cost of the secretarial effort [caused by] Hans would have gone into thousands of pounds, because the memos had to be answered, and they were addressed with copies to everybody, and he'd pronounce on everything!'[86] Says Stephen Plaistow, '[Hans] didn't always recognise that he wasn't getting anywhere by doing this great flurry of memoranda, sending notes to everybody ... He made the assumption that he was the musical conscience of the department, if not the BBC. And it could be irritating, and it could also be counter-productive.'[87] 'I am not responsible to you and do not owe you an explanation for my planning,' Stephen Hearst once wrote to Keller in a moment of frustration, 'and must ask you in future not to consider yourself the sole musical conscience of the BBC.'[88]

There is, as Leo Black expresses it, and all Keller's colleagues confirm, 'no shadow of a doubt' that Keller was sidelined by the BBC in later years – although 'he was very active on the sidelines, because he was very active wherever he was'.[89] His move in February 1971 from Chief Assistant, Orchestral and Choral, to Chief Assistant, Regional Symphony Orchestras, is seen by some as an example of this, although it may have been little more than a retitling of his position, shifting its emphasis, since the Regional post was new and his old job seems at this point to have disappeared.[90] Keller approached his new task with characteristic enthusiasm, starting with a

85 David Cox, oral communication, 17 January 1996.

86 Stephen Hearst, oral communication, 4 November 1996. Indeed, in 1973, during the row over whether Keller should continue to have two secretaries (see below, note 110), it was actually recommended that 'C[hief] A[ssistant] N[ew] M[usic] should drastically reduce the volume of correspondence he generates' (from 'a recent administrative document' quoted by Keller in a memorandum to Peter Gould, 6 September 1973, CUL Keller Archive).

87 Stephen Plaistow, oral communication, 27 July 1995.

88 Undated and unsigned extract from a memorandum from Hearst to Keller, preserved by Pauline Beesley. The occasion of this outburst had been Keller's response to Hearst's scheduling of *Parsifal* for Good Friday: 'How can one let Easter pass without a Matthew Passion? There we go discussing, in shallowness, the respective claims of audiences and of the art of music as such – but on one of the few occasions when the two wholly coincide, we don't do anything about it. If I were not I, I would be speechless.'

89 Leo Black, oral communication, 4 August 1995.

90 A letter from Keller to Jock Beesley of 24 February 1972 makes clear that Keller's new post was part of the wholesale reorganization of Music Division which followed the amalgamation of the Third Programme and the Music Programme (private source). Leo Black, in a biographical note published in the programme of the Keller memorial concert

'comprehensive review of all orchestral repertoire, both of BBC orchestras and outside', which he undertook in conjunction with the Regional heads of music and their producers.[91] This became a major project to eliminate duplication of the music broadcast by the different orchestras, enlarge the regional orchestras' repertoire, promote their involvement in new music, and explore the possibilities of special concert series for each orchestra, in order, ultimately, to foster their distinct musical characters.

While this was going on, however, Music Division was also engaged in a protracted discussion of its procedures governing the broadcast of new music, specifically the way in which it handled the flood of unsolicited scores which it continually received. Traditionally, such scores were reviewed by the Panel – a committee of distinguished musicians who acted as outside readers for the BBC – whose recommendations were then passed to the BBC's New Music Committee for consideration. Accepted works were not then guaranteed a broadcast, however, as there was no specific mechanism in place to ensure that producers placed them in programmes. The resulting backlog was a source of continual complaint from composers and in the summer of 1971 Leo Black, recently appointed Chief Producer, was asked to become 'a central reference point for these works ... forward[ing] details to interested producers'.[92] This arrangement was not sufficient to iron out the problems in the existing system – a system which Black himself has described as 'a dog's dinner'[93] and which Keller thought 'indescribable'[94] – which continued to be a subject of much debate.

It was Keller himself who first suggested the eventual solution:

> CARSO [Chief Assistant Regional Symphony Orchestras – Keller] recommended the abolition of New Music Committee and said that consideration of reports by one senior member of staff would be more economical. No dissenting view was expressed, and HMPR [Head of Music Programmes, Radio – Gould] agreed to minute his intervention.[95]

---

held on 6 October 1986 at the Wigmore Hall, confirms this: 'The 1970 reorganisation included the reinstatement of a post, Head of Music Programmes, which went to a close colleague and friend, slightly younger but with many more years of service. [This was Peter Gould, who was previously Chief Assistant, Chamber Music and Recitals, after Leonard Isaacs left the BBC.] The orchestral brief in Hans Keller's work then became concentrated on liaison with the out-of-London BBC orchestras.'

91 See the minutes of the Music Programme Meeting held on 6 May 1971 (BBC WAC R27/1095/1, Music Programme Meeting Minutes, 1971–74).

92 Minutes of the Music Programme Meeting held on 19 July 1971 (BBC WAC ibid.).

93 Leo Black, oral communication, 4 August 1995.

94 Memorandum from Keller to Peter Gould, 26 June 1973 (BBC WAC R27/1030/1, New Music, General, 1970–83).

95 Minutes of the Music Programme Meeting held on 21 October 1971 (BBC WAC ibid.). Keller had been urging the abolition of New Music Committee for some time, including during meetings of New Music Committee itself (see minutes of the meeting held on 8 June 1970, BBC WAC R27/1091/1, New Music Committee Minutes 1970–73), emphasizing afterwards (in a correction to the minutes) that 'at no stage, did I suggest,

Whether or not Keller had himself in mind for the post is not clear, but initially, when New Music Committee was eventually disbanded in January 1973, Leo Black retained his coordinating role 'with help from CARSO, HMPR and others'.[96] This arrangement lasted for just over two months before it became obvious to all concerned that the job really ought to be Keller's alone, as Leo Black describes:

> Hans was around, enormously enthusiastic about new music, friend of many composers (in principle friend of all composers with any talent), very glad to find a field in which he could pull things together, run things efficiently, and he took it on. He took on the Panel, the communicating [of] decisions, the trying to get pieces promoted, either by BBC orchestras or by producers. I had quite enough to do: I was supposed to be enlarging the foreign tape output, I [was] still doing some production, [so] I was very glad not to have to handle [new music] as well. It was an eminently sensible decision, and, as far as I'm aware, he did it very well.[97]

Keller did indeed do it very well, earning the lasting gratitude of composers, who, through the Composers' Guild, awarded him the Guild's Special Award for Services to British Music on his retirement from the BBC. One of his first priorities, he announced, was to abolish both the backlog of scores awaiting broadcast and the lengthy waiting period for consideration of new material by the Panel, which he described as 'the basic, chronic source of friction between the composing world and us'.[98] Another was to reform the membership of the Panel, excluding all critics: 'Previously we had plenty of critics on our panels and, for better or worse, but very probably for better, I have decided that their reports are not sufficiently dependable for the profession of music criticism to be included amongst the professions from which I choose people for our score-reading panels.'[99] Another – and, so far as individual composers were concerned, particularly significant – innovation was to take personal responsibility for explaining Panel decisions: 'I am trying my best to replace cold standard replies by individual letters,' he announced during his early days in the post. 'I propose to take over all replies to composers: even when they are unhappy they can then write directly to the man responsible – and one possible source of friction or

---

imply, or admit that New Music Committee was anything but absolutely useless' (memorandum from Keller to Glock, 24 July 1970, BBC WAC R27/1030/1, Music General: New Music, General, 1970–83).

96 Minutes of the last meeting of New Music Committee, 30 January 1973 (BBC WAC R27/1091/1, New Music Committee Minutes 1970–73).

97 Leo Black, oral communication, 4 August 1995.

98 Memorandum from Keller to Peter Gould, 18 February 1974 (BBC WAC ibid.).

99 'New Music: Radio's Responsibility', *Composer*, Summer 1976. This article was written as a response to an interview with Robert Ponsonby published in *Composer* the previous summer. Ponsonby had not sanctioned Keller's article and, when it appeared, regretted his original interview: 'Oh, that was a disaster! ... I walked into [it] with my eyes shut' (oral communication, 14 July 1995).

irritation will have been removed.'[100] This meant, as Keller later explained to Derek Bourgeois, Chairman of the Composers' Guild, that he 'guaranteed that every composer who wanted to know the specific reasons for the rejection of a work of his would get them'.[101] Stephen Plaistow, who took over as Chief Assistant, New Music, when Keller retired, stresses how much this meant to composers:

> It wasn't just the Voice of the BBC that sent rejection slips to composers... I mean, Hans Keller – whom everybody had heard of in the music business – you actually got a letter from him: things must have been very different! And he was a great letter-writer – written or dictated, he could write them as fast as he could talk, almost. That was a very good side of him, and was an example of how he could communicate very effectively ... He was a very good man in that new music job ... and I remember when I took over, I was very glad to have inherited that good sense that he showed in dealing with a huge range of composers, the majority of whom were not terribly talented, were not terribly gifted, but had to be dealt with fairly and honestly by a representative of a large organization.[102]

Keller's responsibility for explaining Panel decisions was also meant to ensure that the decisions themselves were fully justifiable. Where there was any doubt, he made sure that it was the composer who got the benefit: 'I based our entire New Music Policy,' he later remembered, 'on the widest possible benefit of the doubt in the composer's favour.'[103]

As he had since his early days in the BBC – and, perhaps, true to his fundamental belief in the value of mixed programming – Keller continued to treat new music as an integrated part of general music broadcasting, rather than a specialized activity. This was in contrast to the approach of some of his colleagues, who saw more of a future in devoting particular parts of the schedule to modern music. Stephen Plaistow, for example, had long been the producer of such a specialist programme, *Music in Our Time*, of which, he says, Keller made his disapproval very evident:

> Hans was very critical of *Music in Our Time* and would have nothing to do with it, and gave me no support at all, because he thought it was a ghetto and thought that this was not the way to programme new music.[104]

---

100 Memorandum from Keller to SAMS, 8 May 1973 (BBC WAC ibid.).

101 Letter from Keller to Bourgeois, 30 November 1982 (CUL Keller Archive).

102 Stephen Plaistow, oral communication, 27 July 1995. Ironically, during the long-running later dispute over the amount of correspondence generated (and thus secretarial time used) in Keller's office (see below, note 110), it was recommended that 'the use of [a] standard letter for New Music rejections should be readopted and individual letters written only where there are special reasons for doing so' – a recommendation which Keller considered 'a continuing process of de-humanization' (from 'a recent administrative document' quoted by Keller in a memorandum to Peter Gould, 6 September 1973, CUL Keller Archive).

103 Letter from Keller to Leo Black, 17 November 1983 (CUL Keller Archive).

104 Stephen Plaistow, oral communication, 27 July 1995.

Keller's attitude was not only a product of his commitment to mixed programming, but also, of course, of his Schoenbergian view of new music as a continuing development of the old, a view with which Robert Ponsonby, who took over from William Glock as Controller, Music, at around the same time that Keller assumed the New Music post, did not concur: 'I don't think he had much instinctive sympathy for contemporary music which was not in some sense traditional … [but] I happen to believe that contemporary music has to find its own new format.'[105] For this reason, Ponsonby considers that the selection of Keller for the New Music job was 'a surprising appointment' and he has little recollection of Keller's work in the post: 'I'm actually rather puzzled to recall that he held it for so long, because I have the sensation that from fairly early on I was working with Stephen Plaistow … I certainly did not work closely with Hans over contemporary music.'[106]

Indeed, according to Keller, he and Ponsonby did not work closely at all: 'It is my submission that, throughout the period upon which Robert Ponsonby has reported, he has not been in touch with my work,' complained Keller some years later to Jock Beesley of the BBC's Personnel Department.[107] Keller was complaining about a comment in his annual report – although how he came to hear of it is a mystery, for he famously declined to take part in the annual reporting system and refused to read anything written on him. This did not stop him taking issue with what was allegedly said, an inconsistency which Beesley lost no time in pointing out to him:

> C[ontroller] Mus[ic] has a right to report on his staff. I would have thought that you would have considered it both courteous and indeed advisable to have read what he has written before advancing this argument. The argument itself, if developed, would in any case be weakened by not knowing the substance of the criticism. The normal way to substantiate your case is again in the context of challenging your report … The Corporation's procedures give adequate protection to staff and the fact that you or anyone else disagree with the annual reporting procedure, does not entitle them to special treatment … You must handle this case according to the normal usage or drop the matter.[108]

---

105 Robert Ponsonby, oral communication, 14 July 1995.

106 Ibid.

107 Letter from Keller to Beesley, 2 August 1976 (CUL Keller Archive). Beesley was Assistant Head of the Radio Personnel Department at the time. He and Keller had a long and interesting correspondence throughout the rest of Keller's years at the BBC and beyond.

108 Letter from Beesley to Keller, 11 August 1976 (CUL Keller Archive). Keller's personnel file at the BBC, which would contain the rest of this correspondence, remains closed until the year 2035, so the detail of his complaint is not known. However, there is a copy of his annual report from 1974 in CUL, which was preserved by Keller attached to the 1976 correspondence with Beesley, so it is conceivable that, among other things, he was objecting to the mild criticism of his EBU work which this contains. The criticism is in Robert Ponsonby's section of the report, and Howard Newby, in the Director of Programme, Radio's 'endorsement' section, appears specifically to disagree with it. Ponsonby wrote: 'A man of the strength of character of

Keller considered the reporting system 'both useless and harmful' and as having 'a degrading effect on reporter and reportee alike',[109] especially since it only operated in one direction, a situation which he sought to remedy, at least in his department, by asking his staff to write reports on him. These were forwarded, unseen by Keller, to the Personnel Department, who would then, in their turn, refuse to place them on his file.

Keller's attitude to the BBC's reporting system is a good illustration of the way in which he reacted to the BBC's administrative procedures in general. Constitutionally unable (as he would have put it) to go along with any system with which he was not in full agreement, he did not simply ignore or withdraw from it: his protests were always very evident, self-conscious, and carefully thought out. Aware all the time of the particular system's requirements and implications, his attacks have a curious – rather legalistic – appropriateness. In the case of the annual reporting procedure, for example, he withdrew only from that side of it which was not a formal requirement of his post, by refusing to read reports written on him. He fulfilled his obligation to write reports meticulously, but neutralized their 'regressive' effect by matching his reports on staff with their reports on him. And when a long-running dispute over the staffing of Keller's office left him temporarily without any secretarial assistance, Keller simply took to working at home.[110] Keller's passion for the law, of course, was of long standing – 'You ought to run our legal department,' one of his publishers told him in

---

Hans Keller does not shape himself easily to bureaucratic practice and it is therefore a matter of mutual credit to him and to the BBC that cohabitation has continued – not without some turbulence, it is true, but entirely fruitfully. The post of Chief Assistant, New Music, is an arduous one – and of vital importance. Hans Keller has filled it to admiration. That relations with composers and music publishers are exceptionally good (or so I believe) is substantially due to him. He has successfully continued the production of *In Short*, has produced an important series of programmes on Haydn's Op. 50 and contributed memorably to the Schoenberg celebrations. His work for the EBU has been under some rigorous self-scrutiny but his contribution to EBU meetings remains memorable, if occasionally eccentric.' Newby added, 'It should be noted that Mr Keller declines to take part in the annual reporting system, so presumably these remarks will not be seen by him. In my personal experience he is a very good representative of the BBC at EBU meetings and his work for the International Concert season is widely appreciated.' If this report figured in Keller's complaint, it was not the main substance of it, however. In a letter of 2 August 1976, Keller also takes issue with a remark made by the then Director of Programmes, Radio, Douglas Muggeridge, who 'told me that I had "an adverse effect on Music Division" ... Ever since, I have said that Douglas should substantiate or withdraw his damaging remark.' He was told by Beesley in his letter of 11 August that the remark was 'based on your last annual report', presumably that of 1975, of which no copy is available.

109 Unpublished letter from Keller to the editor of *Ariel*, 15 July 1975 (CUL Keller Archive).

110 'In order not to have my time wasted in a secretary-less office,' Keller announced to Peter Gould (then Head of Music Programmes, Radio), 'I shall work at home in office hours, though I shall be at the office outside office hours … For the rest, I shall only be here if I am required, or if I require somebody. At home, I shall constantly be available

1954 after a long-running book contract negotiation[111] – and no point was too small for his attention: 'He would argue passionately, for months sometimes, about trivialities,' says Lionel Salter.[112] It was not in Keller's nature to let an argument drop, either, and all his memoranda required an answer, as Stephen Plaistow remembers: '[you] felt obliged to respond, because if you didn't respond, you would soon get a reminder!'[113] There were times, as most of those who worked closely with him attest, when the unremitting pressure from Keller was simply too much: 'My head is dizzy with your letters and cards of criticism and rebuke,' one of his later editors told him.[114]

On 11 March 1974, exactly five years before his retirement,[115] Keller made a symbolic withdrawal from the 'organisational illusions, myths, and vapid conventions'[116] of the BBC in a letter sent to Robert Ponsonby which was afterwards, 'without my taking any initiative in the matter',[117] published in *Ariel*.[118]

> I have given prolonged and serious thought to this matter, and have decided to give myself a birthday present: for the next five years, I shall resist all symptoms of organisational illusions with their resultant disrespect for the individual, and shall not accept that any end sanctifies means which involve hurting human beings. This note, a personal one from man to man, not a memo from title to title,

---

on the telephone, prepared to appear at the office within 10'–15'' (letter from Keller to Peter Gould, 23 September 1974, private source). Since 1972, Keller had been fighting to retain two secretaries – or, in fact, one secretary and one EBU assistant. Since he was then the only person below Controller level to have two secretaries, his office was seen as a potential area for economies, as Stephen Hearst explains: 'It was one of those economy measures. You've got to bear in mind also that some of these struggles become very much fiercer if the money is short. And until about 1970 the licence was sufficient ... By 1973 inflation had gone to 28% ... and suddenly there was a shortfall. And ever since there's been less and less' (oral communication, 4 November 1996). The unresolved dispute meant that posts in Keller's office were not advertised when they fell vacant, leading to the 'secretary-less office' of 1974.

111 Letter from André Deutsch to Keller, 17 March 1954 (CUL Keller Archive). The book in question was *Criticism: A Musician's Manifesto*, for which Keller was under contract to André Deutsch from 1954 until 1960, when he returned their advance and indefinitely postponed the project. *Criticism*, which he eventually wrote 20 years later, has no actual relation to this earlier work, despite sharing some of its concerns.

112 Lionel Salter, oral communication, 10 January 1996.

113 Stephen Plaistow, oral communication, 27 July 1995.

114 Letter from Karl Miller, editor of the *London Review of Books*, 12 January 1981 (CUL Keller Archive).

115 The contract of employment for BBC personnel in established posts usually stipulated retirement on the holder's sixtieth birthday.

116 Letter from Keller to Robert Ponsonby, 11 March 1974 (CUL Keller Archive).

117 Unpublished letter from Keller to the editor of *Ariel*, 15 July 1975 (CUL Keller Archive).

118 'My birthday gift: away with all these rituals', *Ariel*, 66 (3 April 1974), p. 8.

> is a clear preview of the way in which I propose to communicate with people. It will be a natural, real way, without mythological adjuncts, without organisational rituals.
>
> Mine will not be a campaign, but simply a mode of professional life, which will refuse to accept a basic distinction between the demands of professional and private conduct. Nor will it be a struggle – or, if you wish to call it a struggle, it will be a struggle without an opponent, a struggle for people, not against them ...
>
> Let me hasten to add that I am not only concerned with the dignity of the individual within our Corporation, but, of course, also with one's respect for outside individuals: the way in which I deal with composers, and about which Peter [Gould] knows more, is the first indication of the new approach towards humanisation ...[119]

'He was doing that anyway,' says Ponsonby. 'It was an elaborate statement of an attitude which I think had been his throughout his life, probably. I mean, he wasn't a Corporation man, Hans.'[120] Following the publication of the letter in *Ariel*, Keller began writing a monthly column for *Broadcast*, the journal of the Association of Broadcasting Staff, in which, under the heading 'Collective Fantasies', he argued that 'the very concept of management, as we use it, is an illusion: management does not exist ... One by one, *sine ira et studio*, without anger or fervour, I shall analyse our collective fantasies; one way or another, they affect all our organisations and institutions, all organised group life – unions, of course, included.'[121]

While writing his column for *Broadcast*, Keller kept up a lively correspondence with a number of people on 'the Myth of Management', as he called it, and discussion of their opinions formed part of his subject. Although the *Broadcast* column ended prematurely, Keller continued the theme in the preface to his book *1975 (1984 minus 9)*: 'I have been a manager, I have been managed, and I have proved consistently unmanageable,' he announced proudly, continuing that, as 'one of the two or three people I have been in touch with throughout organisational life who haven't been maimed by it', he was ideally placed to know what management was all about:

> I have come to the long-considered, long-delayed conclusion that it's all about nothing – that 'management' and 'control' don't exist. They do, of course, exist as illusions shared by the 'controller' and the controlled ... Management, to be sure, is a game played to perfection, a ritual enacted with ever-renewed fervour, by managers and the managed alike. The psychological reasons are obvious.

---

119 Letter from Keller to Ponsonby, 11 March 1974 (CUL Keller Archive).

120 Robert Ponsonby, oral communication, 14 July 1995.

121 'Collective Fantasies', *Broadcast*, May/June 1974, p. 7. The column ran until January 1975, when it was terminated, in mid-argument, after the National Executive Committee decided that it would no longer pay contributors who were also members of the Association, and that articles of a general nature, in which class they included Keller's, were to be excluded. See letter from Alan Jones, editor of *Broadcast* to Keller, 14 January 1975 (CUL Keller Archive).

> Under the regressive influence of group life, which was recognised by thinkers about human behaviour long before Freud came in and showed how it happened, the double urge develops to be the parent one would have liked to be as a child, and to return to childhood more straightforwardly and whole-mindedly, henceforth assured of parental protection.[122]

The manager and the managed, Keller concluded, 'have both forgotten the importance of being human – one in his search for power, the other in his search for the next best thing (since power, by sheer accident, happened to elude him), which is a father to hand his conscience to, with compliments.'[123]

The roots of all this in Keller's work on group psychology in the 1940s – and before that, in his experiences in Vienna – are obvious. Keller was also continuing here his long tradition of 'treachery' to his profession, now styling himself as an 'anti-manager' in the same way in which he had become an 'anti-critic' 20 years before: 'I am an experienced traitor: as an anti-critic critic, anti-word writer on music, anti-teacher teacher, and perhaps even anti-radio radio man, I have learned to help many a struggle by fighting it'.[124] The hesitancy with which Keller here describes himself as 'anti-radio' is noteworthy. Keller was deeply committed to radio, to the unique opportunities which he felt it offered to musicians, and even in the midst of a stern critique of the 'phoney professionalism' of some of his colleagues, he still held that 'the musician who entrenches himself upon an anti-radio position is ... as much of a phoney as his pet adversary, the professional broadcaster'.[125] The dangers of broadcasting, unlike those of criticism or teaching, were not so much inherent in the activity itself, but in the way in which it operated in the group context – in 'managed' or 'professional' radio. Keller's main quarrel with the 'phoney professionals' of broadcasting was the way in which they lost sight of the purpose of broadcasting in their attempt to elevate the craft of radio to the status of an art in itself:

> Broadcasting is a craft, not an art. There is only one conceivable distinguishing characteristic of an art, and that is a specific system of communication ... through which new truths are conveyed which could not possibly be conveyed to anything like the same extent, by means of any other system. The phoney broadcasting professional, because he has no truths inside him anyhow, because he is the second-hander *par excellence* and knows it, debases the concept of art in an unsuccessful attempt to elevate the craft of broadcasting.[126]

Stephen Hearst in particular was infuriated by this:

---

122 *1975* (1977), pp. 17–19.

123 Ibid., p. 14.

124 'Schoenberg: The Future of Symphonic Thought', *Perspectives of New Music*, Fall–Winter (1974).

125 EBU (1977), p. 263.

126 *Criticism* (1987), p. 47.

> Hans had preached that this was a phoney profession, which totally went against my grain! There *was* such a thing as a radio producer: when you think of what Douglas Cleverdon achieved with Dylan Thomas, and then to say that there isn't such a thing as radio production![127]

Hearst was one of those who felt that Keller's presence on the BBC's permanent staff was becoming counter-productive: 'I thought he ought to have been used as a consultant, but never on the staff. [But] there he was, on the staff, actually putting a spoke into the wheels all the time.'[128] Hearst was by no means alone in this view, as Stephen Plaistow remembers:

> Certainly, in the later years, my impression was there were an awful lot of people who, merely at the mention of Hans' name, would throw their eyes upwards and think, 'Oh my God, he's at it again!' ... I don't want to sound too dark or depressed about things, but there is a feeling that he dug quite a pit for himself, really, in the BBC, and some of the best work of his later years was certainly not appreciated, because he was this man who'd been a nuisance for a long time and, well, now his wings had been clipped ... It surprised me that the man who played political games so often ... should often have come out of it not greatly advantaged.[129]

Keller himself came to feel that 'if I had been unknown, the BBC would now have tried its best to get rid of me'.[130] As it was, he still thought he had been subjected to 'a chronic, albeit civilized, witch-hunt' ever since *Broadcasting in the Seventies*[131] and Eleanor Warren (who headed the Music Department for two years in the mid-1970s) confirms that there were some in high positions at the Corporation who would have been very glad to see him go:

> It was very tricky towards the end of my time in the BBC with Hans, because I had tremendous admiration for his knowledge and all his gifts, which were extraordinary. But he was difficult, very difficult, and I was being urged by management ... always they said, 'you know, it's up to you, you can throw him

---

127 Stephen Hearst, oral communication, 4 November 1996. Douglas Cleverdon was a renowned Features and Drama producer at the BBC for 30 years, until his retirement in 1969. He was responsible, among other notable projects, for commissioning and producing Dylan Thomas's *Under Milk Wood*.

128 Stephen Hearst, oral communication, 4 November 1996. An example of one such spoke was Keller's describing the new phone-in programme *Your Concert Choice* as 'a disgrace' in a memorandum to Robert Ponsonby. Hearst, who was famously irascible, exploded at this, telling Ian Trethowan (Managing Director Radio) and Howard Newby, 'I regard this conduct by a senior official ... as wholly unprofessional. We cannot go on with Keller as if he were an unimportant gadfly' (memorandum from Hearst to Trethowan and Newby, 12 April 1973; quoted in Carpenter, 1996, p. 289).

129 Stephen Plaistow, oral communication, 27 July 1995.

130 'Fare Better, BBC', *The Spectator*, 30 June 1979.

131 Undated letter from Keller to Jock Beesley, probably written in April 1979 (CUL Keller Archive).

> out: we'd love it'. And I said no, I can't, I won't ... It was a very FBI type of atmosphere.[132]

Keller's impatience with various aspects of the BBC's bureaucracy had often been evident during the 1960s. Most famous was his eloquent comment on the hours he was required to spend at meetings: as William Glock remembers, 'Hans had the somewhat infuriating habit of sitting exactly opposite me as chairman at staff meetings in Yalding House and concentrating, it seemed, only on clearing his correspondence for the morning.'[133] While Keller could never have been described an easy colleague, he maintained, nevertheless, 'there was no personal friction between me and the establishment'[134] during that time; nor was 'the establishment' part of his thinking. Keller's expressed concern with both phoney professionalism and the evils of management dates only from after *Broadcasting in the Seventies*, when he felt that the phonies were gaining the upper hand, while his own work was being deliberately sidelined and frustrated by BBC managers. While this has led some to suspect the sour grapes of thwarted ambition behind his campaign, it is not clear to what extent Keller ever harboured ambitions to rise further up the BBC's management ladder. Misha Donat, for example – a close colleague in the 1970s – thinks not: 'I don't think he had ambitions to climb the hierarchy. No, I would have said that he never wanted to be the head of the department, or anything like that.'[135] Donat did not join the BBC until 1972 and, while he is probably right that Keller was not interested in more senior positions by then, those who worked with Keller earlier have a different view.

> I thoroughly applaud the business of kicking upwards rather than downwards ... but in the case of Hans, part of this was sour grapes because he wasn't allowed to take any more senior positions. The upper management – I'm not talking about Glock, but people above him – were very suspicious of Hans ... But, for example,

132 Eleanor Warren, oral communication, 23 October 1996. As a cellist, Eleanor Warren had been something of a protegée of Keller's in the early 1960s, and joined the BBC in 1964. In 1975 she was promoted above Keller, to Head of Music Programmes, Radio, a move which she describes as 'very embarrassing'. She was unhappy in the post and left after two years.

133 See Glock in Wintle (1986), p. 379. Robert Ponsonby also remembers this: 'He used to bring his in tray! I made the same mistake: I used to have departmental meetings once a week, or once a fortnight, or whatever, and we had a very long table in a very long, narrow room, and I sat at one end of it, and Hans always sat at the other end of it and challenged me!' Unnerved by this, Ponsonby decided to sit in the middle of the long side, whereupon Keller moved to the middle of the opposite long side (Robert Ponsonby, oral communication, 14 July 1995). Eventually, according to David Cox, 'Hans at one point refused to go to any more of Ponsonby's Controller's meetings, because they were in such disagreement over practically everything' (oral communication, 17 January 1996).

134 'Fare Better, BBC', *Spectator*, 20 June 1979.

135 Misha Donat, oral communication, 4 July 1995.

> when Gerald Abraham left [in 1967] and I was appointed to take his place [as Assistant Controller of Music], Hans was initially very chagrined, because he had wanted to take that job over, and I think that he felt that Glock had let him down on this. But in fact we very, very quickly came to amicable terms, and we respected each other. But all his ambitions to rise higher in the BBC would not have been acceptable to the then management ... He was regarded as a hot-head.[136]

> He wouldn't have been averse [to] it: if somebody had offered him the Controller job, I'm pretty sure he would have taken it – Controller of Music – oh yes, I'm sure. But I don't think it would have worked, because I think his views would have got people's backs up in the BBC. He would never have been able to work with other Controllers and with the DG and people like that. I don't think it would have worked. He was very much an individual, who would be very positive amongst other people who were open to discussion, you know, and he was felt to be a positive influence among a lot of people with different views.[137]

> He never got one of those jobs, because the management never trusted him. You see, he would write to the newspapers about how awful the management were, so of course they didn't trust him, although he was one of the most honest people possible – I mean, he was embarrassingly honest at times ... I think probably he would have loved the job as Controller.[138]

Keller finally left the BBC at the normal retiring age of 60. Given his unhappiness with many aspects of the Corporation by then, several of his former colleagues have wondered why he did not leave earlier. Even when his final retirement date arrived, he didn't seem to want to leave then either, but continued to come to work in his old office, almost daily, for some months. Stephen Plaistow, who was taking over both Keller's New Music and EBU posts, remembers this:

> I think I can remember [his] words – very characteristic – Hans said, 'People shouldn't expect that my retirement means that I have suddenly lost all my interest in music broadcasting, and I shall continue it.' And he expected to come in to his office, although he hadn't got a job. He came in, and did do so for quite a long while, until ... in the end he had to be put out like the cat. Very painful.[139]

---

136 Lionel Salter, oral communication, 10 January 1996. Salter's own ambitions were also disappointed, by his own account: 'I was very upset, because when I had been appointed Assistant Controller, it had been agreed that I would be considered as Controller when William left. William was extended by three years, so didn't leave until the age of 63, whereupon they told me that they thought I was too old to take over, which was breaking their promise to me.'

137 David Cox, oral communication, 17 January 1996.

138 Eleanor Warren, oral communication, 23 October 1996.

139 Stephen Plaistow, oral communication, 27 July 1995.

On his retirement, Keller was presented with a small book in which all those who had worked with him had written their farewell messages.[140] True to his anti-collectivist principles, he wrote and thanked every one of them individually, sending them not just a formal note, but a thoughtful reply to what they had written. To the BBC's management he wrote an open farewell – or rather 'Fare Better' – which was published in *The Spectator* shortly after his retirement.[141] 'My valediction to the BBC is not what some of my ex-bosses expect – an aggressive, "rebellious", personal, indeed idiosyncratic list of complaints and accusations,' he began – although the autobiographical and dissident elements in it are not insubstantial. The article ends, however, with Keller's view of what cultural broadcasting should be:

> Culturally, the most essential demands are the future's, which the BBC is in a position to make present: the Third Programme here shines as factual proof. On the cultural (i.e. Radio 3 and Radio 4) level, there is something wrong with every programme which, instead of provoking thought, fully satisfies – as thought-killing background. It needs courage to desist from alleviating, druglike, what T.S. Eliot called 'the growing terror of nothing to think about' and, instead, to provoke thoughts unforeseen, unsuspected by the potential thinker – thoughts which inevitably produce equally unforeseen demands. Without Third Programmes, ours and Europe's, the 20th-century classics would still be odd-minds-out. But before an odd mind becomes a classic, your most outstanding programme might well have to be content with 49,999 listeners, which is an audience too small to be recorded – and, therefore, from a thoughtless, anxiety-ridden, 'professional' point of view, virtually identical with nil. The BBC rightly prides itself on not being commercial; the trouble is that again and again, it plans as if it were.

140 Radio 3 announcer Tom Crowe wrote: 'What will become of us without our Prince of "demonology"? I shall miss you because, across the havoc of organisation, I felt you to be an ally in the underworld of the individual. I console myself with the thought that perhaps you have bestowed on us some of your intellectual and moral energy, your astringent wit, your refusal to compromise. Be assiduous in your haunting, lest our conscience fall asleep.' Leo Black suggested: 'Do force yourself, for half an hour once a year, to loaf – just so as to complete your insight into human behaviour!'

141 'Fare Better, BBC', *The Spectator*, 20 June 1979.

Chapter 6

Dissent

As he himself pointed out to Aubrey Singer in 1979, Keller became a BBC dissenter only after the publication of *Broadcasting in the Seventies*. The famous letter to *The Times*, which he instigated and 134 producers signed, was the first time he had broken his BBC contract in publishing unauthorized views about broadcasting. It was also the first time that he had really turned his attention to some of the wider issues of broadcasting, and it sparked off his interest in that illusory and dangerous concept 'management'. It was the major turning point in Keller's relationship with the BBC, when both he and the Corporation redefined themselves in, fundamentally, incompatible ways. This chapter therefore examines *Broadcasting in the Seventies* in detail – the BBC's document, its reception and Keller's 'rebellion' against it.

Broadcasting in the Seventies was the product of research and debate even more extensive than that which had produced the Marriott Report 12 years earlier. Richard Marriott himself chaired the Working Group on the Future of Radio from the end of 1967, before handing over to a full-time Policy Study Group, headed by the Controller of Radio 4, Gerard Mansell, a year later. From the Spring of 1968, the management consultants McKinsey and Company were also involved in examining the BBC's administrative structure and use of resources, and consultations with the BBC's various Advisory Councils took place throughout the review process. All this work was carried out as confidentially as possible and there was no discussion with production staff. Three months were set aside after publication to enable 'public discussion' to influence the plans before the new schedules were actually drawn up, but since BBC staff were forbidden by the terms of their contracts to discuss broadcasting in public, even this possibility of contributing to the process was limited.

Brian Trowell, at that time in charge of opera on radio, has vividly recalled the panicky atmosphere engendered among producers by the secrecy of the review process:

> BBC management ... were unnecessarily secretive, and the grapevine, of course, fairly shook with intimations of disaster. They seem to have taken no one into their confidence below the rank of Controller ... [and] the confidentiality of the proceedings must have imposed a great strain on the Controllers. No doubt they felt guilty about keeping secrets from their own senior staff. In some cases there was an almost complete rift in communication at this level of management. In Music Division the normally fairly regular Direction Meetings of senior staff were postponed or left to a deputy to chair, and eventually they were cancelled

> for months at a time. The quarterly London meetings of the Heads of Regional Music were also cancelled; in July 1969 the Regional Heads united to send in a perfectly reasonable memorandum pointing out that there were things they needed to know and requesting an opportunity to discuss their growing problems in regard to the rumours and the increasing restiveness of their own staffs and orchestras … Fears multiplied in geometrical progression; the rumours flew like hail – all surprisingly accurate, as it turned out later; the worried producers set up a nation-wide internal news service to keep track of them. Disquieting scraps of information were let drop. I recall Sir William Glock saying to a group of us, quite early on, completely out of the blue, 'Well, I think we've saved the Symphony Orchestra' – and he meant the BBC Symphony.[1]

Keller, together with some of the other senior staff who were to become leaders of the later staff protest, were already voicing their concern. During the period when the Policy Study Group was meeting in private, they tried, unsuccessfully, to discuss their worries with its Chairman, Gerard Mansell. As Asa Briggs reports, 'Three senior members of Radio, Lord Archie Gordon, Talks and Documentaries; Hallam Tennyson, Drama; and Hans Keller, Music, asked to see Mansell formally. They were among Mansell's close colleagues, but when he saw them he listened and raised no questions and made no comments of his own.'[2]

Inevitably, all this ferment within the BBC reached the press, which naturally did not wait for the scheduled three months of public discussion before beginning the debate on the BBC's future. *Broadcasting in the Seventies* was not published until July 1969, but speculation about the BBC's plans began to appear in newspapers and journals months beforehand, and the future of the Third Programme was a frequent question. The *Guardian*, for example, published a series of articles during March and April entitled 'Radio in the Seventies', the fourth and last of which dealt with Radio Three, the Third Programme and the Music Programme. This accused the Third of being at times 'mesmerised by minute minorities into producing such specialised programmes that only a handful

---

1 Trowell (1972), p. 35–6. This article was a reprint of a lecture given to the Royal Musical Association in April 1972. A BBC talk by Trowell on the same subject was recorded by Keller, but its broadcast was cancelled after the RMA lecture brought Trowell's views to the attention of BBC management. Stephen Hearst, newly arrived as Controller of Radio 3, wrote to Keller on 14 April, 'I am surprised by your enthusiasm for, and championship of, Brian Trowell's talk. It seems to me that it is entirely Dr Trowell's business what he wants to say in public outside the BBC about its policies but when he proposes to talk about the same policies on our network it would have been fairer to give those who are attacked either personally or by implication suitable advance warning so that a really high-level discussion could have been arranged … As it was the BBC found itself in a guillotine situation. What was advertised in the Radio Times was rather different in emphasis and content from what eventually emerged in the paper … When you consider, further, that Sir William Glock, who was deeply implicated, was not consulted, I find it really hard to understand how as a member of staff you could give your whole-hearted backing to this operation' (CUL Keller Archive).

2 Note from Mansell to Briggs, 12 June 1993 (quoted in Briggs, 1995, p. 748n.).

of postgraduates working on PhD theses could possibly have been interested'.[3]

At the beginning of April 1969, the BBC's new Director-General, Charles Curran, made a move to quieten the speculation with his first formal statement on the future of radio. Reported next day in *The Times* under the heading 'Third Programme is safe at present, BBC chief says', he is quoted as saying that 'dropping the Third would be quite contrary to the policy of the BBC, which is to provide a comprehensive service'.[4] This statement may have had the effect of diverting some of the closure fears from the Third to the Music Programme, which became the subject of a concerted campaign for its survival launched by *The Sunday Times* at the beginning of June. Included in its 8 June issue, however, among a series of detailed articles, interviews and letters from listeners, was a long interview with Curran in which he discussed the cost of minority programming and the BBC's role as musical patron. This time, the threat to the Third Programme, the BBC's house orchestras – and live music broadcasting in general – was clear:

> The BBC has traditionally taken the position that it has a responsibility to the cultural life of the country. I do not think it has ever faced head on the question of whether it has a greater cultural duty to the country than that which it necessarily has to carry in relation to broadcasting ... When the BBC's patronage of music was conceived of as a proper duty, modes of recording in the studio – that is, apart from the gramophone studio – were inadequate. Even the normal recording studio was seriously limited in what it could do. We are now in an age when recording of high quality is commonplace. Must broadcasting maintain the live orchestras whose performances can be recorded, whose performances in many cases are already on records? ... The cost of Radio 1 is less than half that of the Third Programme as it is at the moment. But the Music Programme during the day-time costs per hour about the same as Radio 1, so it does not follow simply that minority programmes are more expensive. Some are, certainly; but it is perfectly possible to have a change in programme mix and yet not move away from the concept of minority programming.[5]

When *Broadcasting in the Seventies* was finally published on 10 July 1969, it was a disappointingly slim document of only 13 pages, giving little evidence of the extensive research behind it. The Board of Management had instructed Ian Trethowan,[6] the author of the final draft, to present the proposals as concisely as possible, but it later came to feel that this brevity had been a mistake. Reviewing the reception which the document received in the early weeks after publication, the Board concluded that 'part of the

3 Terry Boston (MP and former radio producer), 'Lending an ear to minorities', *The Guardian*, 11 April 1969.

4 *The Times*, 2 April 1969. Terry Boston's *Guardian* article, however, quotes the same statement as assuring the future of Radio Three, rather than the Third Programme.

5 *The Sunday Times*, 8 June 1969.

6 Ian Trethowan was then Managing Director (Radio) designate, and later Director-General.

trouble had been that "Broadcasting in the Seventies" had necessarily been too summary a document to reflect the extent of the thought that had gone into the BBC's proposals', which resulted in 'basically a lack of confidence in the BBC which could not be overcome until critics were reassured by seeing the new proposals in operation'.[7]

Broadcasting in the Seventies opens with a statement of the problems currently facing the BBC, the most fundamental of which was that the existing structure of network and regional radio had long been out-grown. Reorganization was therefore desirable in itself, even had present financial difficulties not made it necessary:

> The last few years have seen significant changes in BBC radio. It has moved into new areas – the Music Programme, Radio One, local radio. These changes, however, have been grafted piecemeal on to a tree planted in an earlier age of broadcasting.

Added to this, television had caused huge changes to the pattern of radio listening. The radio had lost its central place in the home and was now seen 'less as a medium for family entertainment, more as a continuous supplier of music and entertainment' (p. 2). The new radio audience, it was suggested, now expected planning to be based not on the traditional principle of mixed programming, but on 'the specialised network, offering a continuous stream of one particular type of programme, meeting one particular interest' (p. 3). *Broadcasting in the Seventies* also announced that the existing English regions would be reorganized, and that the Corporation was seeking to 'develop local radio as a major element in the BBC's services' (p. 6) by a proposal for 40 new local stations – a proposal which had already been put forward to the Postmaster General.

Such a venture could not be financed without cuts elsewhere, however. *Broadcasting in the Seventies* therefore reconsidered the BBC's role as music patron and announced that it could no longer afford to maintain several of its house orchestras, namely the Scottish Symphony, the Northern Dance, the London Studio Players and the Training Orchestra, together with the BBC Chorus. As Charles Curran went on to say at the press conference following publication, 'Since one of the criticisms which is most frequently levelled at the BBC is that it tries to do too much … I don't think it's unreasonable that we should suggest that the function of musical patronage should be carried out by somebody else.'[8]

While insisting that the BBC was 'not abandoning programmes for minorities', *Broadcasting in the Seventies* asked 'whether this function is best fulfilled within a single enclave. There is a good deal of evidence that

7 Minutes of the Board of Management, 8 September 1969 (BBC WAC R2/22/4, Board of Management Minutes, July–September 1969).

8 *Broadcasting in the Seventies* Press Conference, 10 July 1969 (BBC WAC R78/576/2: *Broadcasting in the Seventies*: Distribution and Public Discussion).

some listeners are deterred by the label "The Third". Programmes originated on the Third invariably attract bigger audiences when repeated on Radio Four' (p. 4). The majority of Third Programme talks, for example, were currently achieving audiences of less than 50,000 (the minimum number which the BBC deemed to be 'measurable'), and it was noted that the element of Third Programme output which did most frequently achieve a 'measurable' audience was music. *Broadcasting in the Seventies* announced, therefore, that the title 'Third Programme' should be dropped and that Radio Three should increase its hours of music broadcasting, causing much of its speech output to be cut or moved to Radio Four. Despite an acknowledgement that 'few aspects of British broadcasting have aroused more passion than the Third Programme' (p. 4), *Broadcasting in the Seventies* did not appear to take such feelings very seriously for, when its Conclusion summed up the losses and gains produced by the new proposals, the demise of the Third received only an oblique reference: 'a few may regret a shift in emphasis in Radio Three in the evening' (p. 13).

From the initial reaction of the press, it would seem at first as though the regrets were indeed few. The coverage of the BBC's plans was massive, but the Third Programme's disappearance was scarcely mentioned. The central issue in the minds of the leader-writers was whether the BBC's duty as public servant was to be comprehensive or to concentrate on those areas of broadcasting which could not be supported commercially – in other words, whether it was right that the BBC should be disbanding orchestras in order to fund Radio One and local stations. There would be no difficulty finding willing commercial 'patrons' for popular music, and many newspapers were of the opinion that the BBC should step aside from Radio One, conserving its precious revenue for the threatened orchestras. 'On one assumption, and one only, the BBC's plans make sense. It is that the Corporation's business in the field is to provide a complete and comprehensive national service,' was the opinion of the *Daily Telegraph*. 'Yet the plain fact remains that almost all the necessary economies which the Corporation is now making fall on those types of broadcasting which alone are really suitable for a public body financed by taxation.'[9] The suspicion that the BBC was putting the preservation of its monopoly above the quality of its broadcasting was strengthened by the perception that the disbanded orchestras were direct casualties of the BBC's foray into local broadcasting, a move which was widely considered to be an unnecessary and politically-inspired extension of the service. To *The Times*, the Corporation's motives were far from those of the pure public servant: 'Faced with the Tory proposals for a network of commercial radio stations, and with the probability of a Tory Government within a couple of years, they have obviously concluded that it is necessary to get in first.'[10] To the *New Statesman* the move appeared to be 'a panic

9 Leader, *The Daily Telegraph*, 11 July 1969.
10 Leader, *The Times*, 11 July 1969.

lurch into strategies and surgeries, dictated by a highly visible managerial and accountant logic, dancing to the tune of those unseen musicians, the politicians and commercial interests'.[11]

The BBC was caught between the view that its public funding was only justifiable because of its role as artistic patron and educator, and the wish to be true to its original vision of a unifying Voice of the Nation, which must cater for majorities as well as minorities in order to warrant the imposition of a universal licence fee. The Corporation's sensitivity to the implications of its funding was emphasized by its feeling unable at this point to ask the Government for an increase in the licence fee (then one of the lowest in Europe) and its refusal to contemplate alternative means of income, such as a specific Government grant (which might limit its independence), or the acceptance of advertising. In *Broadcasting in the Seventies*, the BBC eventually opted for comprehensiveness, but at a price which many considered laid the Corporation open to the charge of wanting to preserve its monopoly at any cost, particularly as the need for local stations, or indeed the public demand for them, was far from being convincingly demonstrated, as Frank Gillard was happy to admit: 'I don't think we've made a claim that there's a big demand for local radio. I don't see how you can expect a big demand for something of which most people in this country have no concept and no experience. But it's our business as professional broadcasters, and has been all the way down the ages, to spot the ways in which our service can develop and become of improved value to the listener.'[12]

The BBC's argument that 'in a television age' radio listening was becoming increasingly determined by time rather than content, which meant that generic broadcasting was inevitable, was accepted by many commentators. This assumption about the increasingly casual nature of radio listening also crept into the arguments of many who supported mixed programming, when they asserted the value of listeners being proselytized by accident, by finding themselves listening unintentionally to something new. As Yehudi Menuhin put it, 'the whole point of a catholicity of choice within the same channel [is that] it can break down prejudices in both directions.'[13]

To Keller, whose picture of 'sharply and meaningfully contrasting programmes which, throwing each other into relief, invite the clearest possible choice'[14] was rather different, it was the fault of the BBC itself if its audience was treating what it offered less carefully, for the desire to be comprehensive was dangerous:

> Public Service Broadcasting is a euphemism for over-stimulation, as are all the duties which the mass-communicator is supposed to have in order to make all the

11 Hall (1969).

12 Transcript of *Broadcasting in the Seventies* press conference, 10 July 1969 (BBC WAC ibid.).

13 *The Sunday Times*, 8 June 1969.

14 'Broadcasting in the 'Eighties', *The Spectator*, 10 July 1976.

> things available which the public is supposed to want. If the mass-communicator has one demonstrable duty, it is Thou Shalt Not Over-Stimulate And Prevent Independent Thought. At our present stage, there is simply no danger of under-stimulation.[15]

The scheduled three months of public discussion continued the debate furiously, and at all stages it was evident how seriously the BBC was taking the task of presenting its point of view. As well as special briefings held for MPs, for the TUC General Council and for members of staff both in London and the regions, there were discussions and interviews on radio and television, debates in both Houses of Parliament, and umpteen letters to the newspapers (particularly *The Times*) – in all of which BBC executives of the highest rank participated.

In September 1969 a formidable alliance of opposition to the BBC's plans was created when John Donat founded the Campaign for Better Broadcasting. From the outset it was expertly managed and there is no doubt that the BBC's Board of Management took its threat extremely seriously – indeed, the first Board meeting to discuss 'the CBB' resolved that 'the BBC should not risk making enemies at the level of those who supported the campaign'.[16] As well as securing a high level of VIP support,[17] the CBB proved itself extremely adept in managing its publicity – even to the level of parodying the BBC's logo on its letterhead and operating from an address in Portland Place. Significantly, it also managed to articulate with extraordinary accuracy the disaffection amongst the BBC's own production staff.

To launch its action, the Campaign published *Crisis in Broadcasting*, a short but well-presented and perceptive pamphlet. Among its first accusations was the interesting suggestion that the brevity of *Broadcasting in the Seventies* had been a deliberate attempt to cloud the real issues, that the specific details given about money and the cuts to BBC orchestras had successfully 'created a press-trap [which] could not have been more elegantly baited', deflecting press and public alike from 'the death of mixed programming, the demolition of the concept of the Third Programme [and] drastic cuts in the spoken word at length and in depth':

> It is a policy mesmerised by head-counting but apparently indifferent to what goes into the heads or how long it stays there. It absolutely fails to distinguish between minorities in the true sense (which in BBC terms include farmers,

---

15 Quoted in *The Keller Instinct*, Channel 4, 23 February 1986.

16 Minutes of the Board of Management, 8 September 1969 (BBC WAC R2/22/4, Board of Management, Minutes, July–September 1969).

17 The signatories to its initial circular were Professor Max Beloff, Sir Adrian Boult, James Cameron, Professor G.M. Carstairs, Sir Tyrone Guthrie, Dr J.C. Kendrew, Frank Kermode, George Melly, Dr Jonathan Miller, Henry Moore, Sir Roland Penrose and Peter Shepheard. Gerard Mansell later claimed that one of these persons had told him, 'When you're asked to support something about better broadcasting, it's rather like being asked if you're against sin. You can't really say no' (*Ariel*, 1 December 1969).

> motorists, gardeners and nature lovers) and relatively small, but general, audiences. It has abandoned the notion of broadcasting policy directed from within with cultural and intellectual purpose (it was inner-directed broadcasting that fostered public taste for serious music) and replaced it with a policy directed from without, by trying to understand and assess 'public demand'.[18]

This was a document which Keller and those who shared his views must have greeted with delight. Keller himself immediately sent his copy to William Glock to read. There was one paragraph at the end, moreover, which must have been particularly heartening. This doubted the genuineness of the 'public discussion' in view of the secrecy within the BBC which withheld all the detailed information on its plans, and concluded thus: 'There has been a monumental psychological error within the BBC in presenting these proposals without prior consultation at production level.'

It could be said that another 'monumental psychological error' was then made by the Corporation's being seen to be over-hasty in closing its period of public discussion without really conceding any of the points of criticism. At a Board meeting held on 15 September (only a week after that at which the Campaign for Better Broadcasting was first mentioned, and with a month of the scheduled public discussion period still to run), the Director-General, Charles Curran, was already saying that 'he was concerned that there should not be a lengthy suspension of action on the proposals, which had been approved by the Board, whilst the various consultations were completed'.[19] It was this attitude that convinced dissenting production staff that they must start a concerted campaign, and by the time Curran made his promulgation to staff on 16 October that the Board had decided to go ahead with developments on the general lines of *Broadcasting in the Seventies*, and that the period of public discussion was now closed, Keller and his colleagues had already acted, sending to Managing Director (Radio) Frank Gillard on 3 October a protest memorandum signed by 154 producers, to which were subsequently added another 25 signatures.

Stephen Plaistow remembers the start of the rebellion: 'There was a great deal of resentment about what was going on ... and you retained the impression that the Board of Management didn't give a fig for what its staff thought: they were just determined to push this thing through.'[20] 'The sense of outrage was so widely felt,' agrees Robert Layton, 'and feelings ran very high indeed.'[21] According to Brian Trowell, 'the internal pressures built up until we all seemed to be sitting inside a Krakatoa'.[22] Nevertheless, such feelings needed to be actively coordinated to make an effective protest, and

18 CBB (1969).

19 Minutes of the Board of Management, 15 September 1969 (BBC WAC R2/22/4, Board of Management, Minutes, July–September 1969).

20 Stephen Plaistow, oral communication, 27 July 1995.

21 Robert Layton, oral communication, 11 November 1996.

22 Trowell (1972), p. 36.

a group of six leaders quickly emerged. As Leo Black recalls, they campaigned vigorously, with 'a vast amount of talking to people in the canteen, in their offices, in the pub … The sheer enthusiasm and toughness of the minds that were going into it spurred [on] those who might have been a little more inclined to compromise.'[23] Of the six leaders, three were from Music Division – 'yes, we musicians were the first to kick,' noted Keller,[24] who was joined by Deryck Cooke (at that time Senior Assistant, Music Information) and Robert Simpson (then Assistant, Music Programmes). The three non-musicians were Lord Archie Gordon (Programme Editor, Arts, Science and Documentaries), Hallam Tennyson (Assistant Head of Drama) and – particularly significant – Leslie Stokes, who with George Barnes and Etienne Amyot had formed the original triumvirate which ran the Third Programme in its opening years.

Keller's campaign was not the only concerted staff protest. At around the same time, one of Tennyson's colleagues in the Drama Department, R.D. Smith, together with the Association of Broadcasting Staff's London branch secretary, T.R. Jennings, took action through the union. An ABS meeting called in October to oppose *Broadcasting in the Seventies* carried unanimously the motion 'This meeting denies absolutely that proper discussion with staff, unions and the public has taken place and demands that implementation of the plans contained in *Broadcasting in the Seventies* be halted forthwith until a public enquiry has taken place'. Robert Layton was involved in the ABS campaign, but he nevertheless considers it to have been less successful than that initiated by Keller. He describes Keller's group of six as 'sort of self-appointed, but thank goodness they did appoint themselves and fight this: they were more effective, I think, than the resistance that was channelled through the ABS'.[25] Keller later claimed that 'every culture-conscious staff member who was not a coward joined – and believe me, there were quite a few cowards around.'[26] Keller probably included his Controllers, William Glock and Howard Newby, among the 'cowards', since, characteristically, he would not see that their position within the BBC's hierarchy would cause them legitimate difficulties. Although he sent Glock the CBB's pamphlet, he could have had little hope of a reaction, as Glock was famously unpolitical.[27] With Newby, however, he seems to have tried harder, and Milein Cosman well remembers the day on

23 Leo Black, oral communication, 4 August 1995.

24 'From the Third Programme to Radio 3', *Music and Musicians*, December 1984.

25 Robert Layton, oral communication, 11 November 1996.

26 'From the Third Programme to Radio 3', *Music and Musicians*, December 1984.

27 'William really wasn't interested in preserving the Third Programme as such,' says Robert Layton, who also remembers Glock's reaction to the 1957 cuts: 'Glock came round and he was very cool and remote, I thought, and he said, "Well, I'm not concerned if the Third Programme is cut down; it's become so inferior. The quality of the performances aren't as good, and it's no longer as adventurous as it was." He betrayed no sense of concern' (oral communication, 11 November 1996).

which Keller came home after a huge argument with Newby, whom he had apparently accused of cowardice.[28] By all accounts, Newby had a fatalistic view of the matter: 'In the middle of the row over the so-miscalled "rebellion" against "Broadcasting in the Seventies",' wrote Keller in later years, 'Howard took me aside: "Hans, our civilization is going down and we'd better go with it."'[29] Robert Layton's recollection gives the same picture: 'I remember Howard Newby on Great Portland Street station saying to me … "The whole of society is going downhill and the BBC will have to go with it."'[30] Keller was not alone in his disappointment with his Controllers: 'There was a general feeling that if Howard [Newby], Martin Esslin [Head of Drama] and William Glock had threatened to resign,' explains Robert Layton, 'the original Third Programme structure would have been saved.'[31]

After Charles Curran had announced the implementation of *Broadcasting in the Seventies* on 16 October, Keller and his five co-leaders sought a meeting with the BBC's management to urge delay. Having canvassed again the views of their 179 supporters, they wrote to Ian Trethowan (author of *Broadcasting in the Seventies*, and Frank Gillard's designated successor as Managing Director, Radio) on 20 November. Trethowan passed the memorandum to Curran, who agreed to meet the Six, stressing the while the importance of getting them to agree on publication 'or they will certainly leak!'[32]

Curran also agreed at this time to meet the Association of Broadcasting Staff protesters. Indeed, BBC management at this stage showed no lack of willingness to talk to dissenting staff, although the area open to discussion was strictly limited, as is shown by a report of a short meeting between Curran and Jennings preparatory to Curran's receiving the ABS delegation. When asked whether he would agree to postpone the implementation of *Broadcasting in the Seventies*, 'he said he could not agree to that and has made it clear that unless we go ahead now, we shall have no basis on which to plan programmes next April. While the debate on the networks must be over for practical reasons, the debate on content would never be over and could go on permanently. DG [Director-General] proposes to say this again to any meeting he attends.'[33]

While the BBC Governors and management felt enough disquiet at continuing protests both within and without the Corporation to launch a

---

28 Milein Cosman, oral communication.

29 Letter from Keller to Ian McIntyre, Christine Hardwick and Ernest Warburton, undated, but probably one of the series of letters to BBC colleagues which Keller wrote immediately after his retirement in March 1979.

30 Robert Layton, oral communication, 11 November 1996.

31 Ibid.

32 Memorandum from Curran to Trethowan, 10 November 1969 (private source).

33 Memorandum from the Director-General's Secretary to the Director of Administration, 21 November 1969 (private source).

renewed publicity counter-offensive in December, starting with a special edition of its staff magazine *Ariel*, it was nevertheless clear that they were determined not be moved:

> The Chairman [Lord Hill] said that some of the BBC's staff as well as outside critics thought it possible that the BBC might have been shaken by the criticisms; it was therefore important to make it plain now that the BBC was going forward.[34]

It is not very surprising, therefore, that the protesters were not satisfied with the meetings which followed. Keller's group had their first meeting with BBC management on 26 November,[35] and, from the minutes which they circulated afterwards to their supporters, it is clear how little they felt their objections had been understood: 'Throughout the discussion, Frank Gillard, Ian Trethowan and Gerry Mansell summarized the contents of the special issue of *Ariel*; no agreement was reached about what seems to us a fundamental principle of radio – the importance one should attach to quality of listening.'[36]

Keller's next meeting – this time with Curran present – took place on 11 December, and is dismissed in a single sentence in the memorandum subsequently circulated to the protesters by the Six: 'It lasted about 1½ hours and covered the same ground.' However, a few small concessions had been won, most notably an increase of two hours per week in the proposed speech content of Radio 3. Keller and his fellow leaders concluded, therefore, that 'our campaign has not been fruitless' and took the opportunity to consult their colleagues once again, in a meeting held on 22 December, before pressing on on the basis that 'we six signatories feel disquiet at the premises on which *Broadcasting in the Seventies* appears to be based. We have heard no support for the network changes from anybody, apart from the Chairman, the Director-General, Frank Gillard, Ian Trethowan, Gerry Mansell and Tony Whitby. Programme staff remain virtually unanimous in opposing them.'[37]

---

34 Minutes of the meeting of the Board of Governors held on 20 November 1969 (BBC WAC R1/1/45–46, Board of Governors, Minutes, 1969).

35 The management was represented on this occasion by Frank Gillard (Managing Director, Radio), Ian Trethowan (Managing Director, Radio, designate), Gerard Mansell (now Controller Programmes, Radio, and Chair of the Policy Study Group), Howard Newby (Controller, Radio 3) and Anthony Whitby (Controller, Radio 4).

36 Memorandum from the Six to the rest of the protesting staff, 15 December 1969. The Six had submitted draft minutes to Ian Trethowan after the meeting, and the final version which was circulated consisted of their original text interspersed with Trethowan's comments and corrections. His reply to the sentence quoted above was, 'no doubt … [this] expresses your view, but clearly it does not express ours, because we believe that our plans will improve the quality of listening, particularly on Radio Four' (private source).

37 Memorandum from the Six to the rest of the protesting staff, 15 December 1969 (private source).

The BBC's management clearly hoped that these meetings, together with their slight concession on the issue of speech on Radio 3, would go some way towards defusing the situation. As Anthony Whitby[38] told Trethowan, Mansell and Newby, when drafting a letter for Lord Hill to send to the ABS delegation, 'I have tried to make the draft conciliatory in tone because my estimate, and I think the Chairman's too, is that these people want to get off the hook and should be helped to do so. They need something that can be interpreted as a concession.'[39] Before his 11 December meeting with Keller's group, Charles Curran was also 'hoping that it might be possible to reassure them – and help them off their hook – by offering a concession like more talk on Radio 3 at the weekend.'[40]

This hope was a forlorn one, and all that the management managed to achieve by these strategies was to delay the moment when their dissenting staff went to the press. Curran was very anxious about 'the link between some members of staff and the criticism advanced by the Campaign for Better Broadcasting',[41] and Keller's group had already threatened to publish a letter which they had written to Trethowan after the BBC's plans had been debated – and much criticized – in Parliament:

> We have now reached the stage where 'Broadcasting in the Seventies' is without staff support and, aside from the political issue of commercial versus local radio, without support in the House of Commons. In the circumstances, we should like an answer to this simple question: what is the ethical justification for going ahead with the implementation of 'Broadcasting in the Seventies'? As you know, we have, throughout, been most anxious to keep our opposition strictly constitutional. In view of what we have now said, however, it seems to us that the time has come to bring the public in on what, after all, is its own problem: with your permission, we propose to release this letter to the press.[42]

Permission was of course refused, but the public discussion was in any case not short of contributors. Another influential group entered the debate on 18 December when the entire High Table of King's College, Cambridge, wrote to *The Listener* in support of a letter in an earlier issue from Alan

38 Whitby succeeded Gerard Mansell as Controller of Radio 4 at the beginning of 1970, when Mansell became Director of Programmes, Radio.

39 Memorandum from Whitby to Trethowan, Mansell and Newby, 28 November 1969, asking for their comments on his draft. The letter which was actually sent to Smith was not quite as conciliatory as the draft: for instance, one omission from the final version, which appears in the draft, was 'if it will help to bridge the gap I am ready to concede that we could have done more to carry with us the people who produce the programmes' (private source).

40 Minutes of the Board of Management meeting held on 8 December 1969 (BBC WAC R2/22/5, Board of Management, Minutes, October–December 1969).

41 Minutes of the meeting of the Board of Management held on 8 December 1969 (BBC WAC ibid.).

42 Letter from the Six to Trethowan, 4 December 1969 (private source).

Bennett, who queried the genuineness of the BBC's claim to have taken account of public discussion in its implementation of *Broadcasting in the Seventies*: 'Surely comment on the publication of the report does not constitute discussion. Discussion involves exchange and adjustment and there's been very little of that. It is as if Hitler had claimed the annexation of Austria as the product of public discussion by virtue of the comment it had aroused in the newspapers.'[43] A month later, the King's dons transferred their protest to the letters column of *The Times*, to be followed there by a series of multi-signature protest letters from prominent figures in the Arts and Universities. The letters pages of *The Times* were carefully watched and frequently debated by the BBC's Board of Management, whose members also contributed several long explanatory letters of their own. Curran himself made arrangements to dine at King's on 22 February, in order to try to defuse that protest informally.

Finally, on Saturday 14 February, the day on which the press reported the BBC's final confirmation of the abolition of the Third Programme, Keller and 133 fellow members of the BBC's London radio programme staff also wrote to *The Times*. This time, they did not announce their intentions to the management beforehand, nor did they ask for permission to publish their letter. They were therefore in clear breach of the BBC's regulations on public statements by staff, which forbade a member of staff to publish anything or speak in public on any matter connected with broadcasting without the BBC's prior permission.

The final straw for the protesters had been the publication in *The Listener* on 13 January of the BBC's new programme plans for radio, announcing the detail of the implementation of *Broadcasting in the Seventies*, followed by Curran's refusal to allow the Six a meeting with the Board of Governors. Much to the management's relief, the newspaper coverage of the new schedules had been mild, leading Curran to consider this press conference to have been 'a turning-point in the discussion of "Broadcasting in the Seventies", because it had directed people's attention to the actual programmes … The press coverage generally had been quite favourable … [and] the Campaign for Better Broadcasting had obtained little publicity for their statements after the press conference.'[44] In confident mood, therefore, Curran refused Keller and his colleagues' request to see the Chairman, Lord Hill, and the Board of Governors, in a letter of 23 January. As he later told the Board of Management, 'the dissentient group's views were well-known to the Board, which had seen their earlier written representations and DG's report of his meeting with them, before reaching its decision on the implementation of the new plans. If he had acceded to their request for a meeting with the Governors it would have meant calling

43 Alan Bennett, letter to *The Listener*, 4 December 1969.

44 Minutes of the meeting of the Board of Management held on 19 January 1970 (BBC WAC R2/23/1, Board of Management, Minutes, January–March 1970).

in question the whole basis of the policy for radio evolved over the last year.'[45]

The protesters thus felt that they had no option but to publish their opinions. As their letter began, 'Your distinguished correspondents who oppose the new plans for radio have mentioned BBC radio programme staff's agreement with their views. Members of BBC management have ignored this point in their replies, and a request for six delegates of London programme staff to see the Board of Governors was refused. We feel, therefore, that we have a duty to the public which must override the BBC ruling that members of staff should not communicate directly with the press: the public should know the nature and extent of our opposition to the management's policy.'[46] In another letter sent to *The Times* ten years later, Leslie Stokes recalled that day:

> I am proud that ten years ago, when I was Assistant to the Controller of the Third Programme, which was then threatened with demise, I had the honour to be associated with my colleagues Hans Keller, Dr Robert Simpson, Lord Archie Gordon (now Lord Aberdeen), Hallam Tennyson, and the late Deryck Cooke, in the instigation and organisation of a movement of staff who disapproved the plans for *Broadcasting in the Seventies*. Our action resulted, Sir, in your publishing in January [sic] 1970 a letter from over 130 members of BBC staff, in which we expressed our misgivings. Our letter had been prepared in surreptitious haste and I found later that many other colleagues, in London and the Regions, were disappointed, even resentful, that they had not been invited to add their signatures. On the afternoon when I was in Printing House Square, delivering the letter, another of the group of six instigators was called into the office of one of our 'superiors', who had caught wind of it, and asked to put a stop to it. It was too late.[47]

The protesters' letter naturally attracted considerable press interest and was covered on the front page of *The Times* on the day of its publication. It was followed by much speculation in the rest of the press as to the likely reaction from the BBC, and the possible fate of the 134 signatories. The letters pages were filled with letters of support – 'May a former BBC servant express his cordial support of the courageous letter in your columns today signed by 134 members of the BBC programme staff?' wrote Sir Adrian

---

45 Minutes of the Board of Management meeting held on 16 February 1970, BBC WAC ibid.

46 Letter to the editor, *The Times*, 14 February 1970. See overleaf for a facsimile of the full text.

47 Unpublished letter to the editor, *The Times*, 16 August [1980]. Leslie Stokes was writing in the wake of Robert Simpson's resignation from the BBC and in response to a letter from Keller published in *The Times* on 15 August. 'It seems that the time comes every ten years when BBC producers and other members of staff are driven to dispraise infamous men they find among their Chairmen, Governors, Directors, Controllers, Uncles Tom Cobbleigh and all,' remarked Stokes, who concluded that 'The time has come, Sir, for them to write another letter to you' (CUL Keller Archive).

Letters to the Editor

POLICY ON RADIO BROADCASTS: OPPOSITION FROM STAFF

From 134 members of London radio programme staff

Sir,—Your distinguished correspondents who oppose the new plans for radio have mentioned B.B.C. radio programme staff's agreement with their views. Members of B.B.C. management have ignored this point in their replies, and a request for six delegates of London programme staff to see the Board of Governors was refused. We feel, therefore, that we have a duty to the public which must override the B.B.C. ruling that members of staff should not communicate directly with the press: the public should know the nature and extent of our opposition to the management's policy.

What we object to is the abandonment of creative, mixed planning in favour of a schematic division into categories on all four programmes; and, above all, the refusal to devote a large, well-defined area of broadcasting time to a service of the arts and sciences.

Practically all serious music broadcasts will be diverted into Radio 3, and Radio 4 will become an all-speech service, save for one concert on Sunday night, with an excessive proportion of newsy magazines. The Third Programme, the outstanding creative achievement of B.B.C. radio, will be abolished, and no project of comparable vision will take its place; the substitute will be a truncated allowance of plays and other speech programmes among the predominant music on Radio 3 in the evenings.

We feel we can confidently anticipate public repudiation of the consequences of the policies imposed upon us. Our hope for the future, as professional providers of radio entertainment, information, and education, must now lie in the public's support for our view that we can work best to serve listeners by the eventual development of creative, mixed planning. For the immediate future, we are determined to provide programmes worthy of the responsibility of the B.B.C. as a leader of the nation's culture, so far as this is possible in the difficult circumstances created by B.B.C. management.

Yours faithfully,

Drama

William Ash, Archie Campbell, Susanna Capon, Douglas Cleverdon, Betty Davies, David Davis, Margaret Etall, H. B. Fortuin, Graham Gauld, Martin Jenkins, Gerry Jones, Charles Lefeaux, Ronald Mason, Nesta Pain, Marie Parotte, John Powell, Raymond Raikes, R. D. Smith, Hallam Tennyson, Terence Tiller, Colin Tucker, John Tydeman, Guy Vaesen, Keith Williams, Norman Wright

Talks Group

Jack Amos, George Angell, Patricia Brent, Archie Clow, Leonie Cohn, Elizabeth Cole, Robert Cradock, A. T. Derville, Jocelyn Ferguson, Doreen Forsyth, Philip French, Michael Gilliam, Archie Gordon, Rosemary Hart, Patrick Harvey, Neil Hepburn, Thena Heshel, Anne Howells, Laurie John, R. E. Keen, Wyn Knowles, Mollie Lee, George MacBeth, Archie MacPhee, Michael Mason, Brigid Maxwell, Lorna Moore, Michell Raper, Jocelyn Ryder-Smith, Jack Singleton, Daniel Snowman, Edith Temple Roberts

Gramophone Programmes

Jeremy Barlow, Clive Bennett, Christine Hardwick, Arthur Johnson, Derek Lewis, Hilary Pym, Veronica Slater

School Broadcasting

T. K. Butcher, Elizabeth Ornbo, Rita Udall, Jenyth Worsley, Richard Wortley

Music Programmes

David R. Allen, Leo Black, Robert Bowman, J. W. Burnett, M. A. Cockburn, Deryck Cooke, Helen Cooke, David Cox, Harry Croft-Jackson, Martin Dalby, John Davies, Anthony Friese-Greene, Allan Giles, Diana Gordon, Freda Grove, Michael Hall, Louis Halsey, James Hamilton, Michael Howard, Alan Jefferson, Hans Keller, Barry S. Knight, Basil Lam, Robert Layton, D. G. Martin, John Meloy, Alan G. Melville, Alan Owen, Anthony Philpott, Stephen Plaistow, Michael Pope, William Relton, C. B. Samuelson, Robert Simpson, Brian Trowell, Alan Walker, Gareth Walters, Eleanor Warren

Planning and Presentation

Robin Boyle, Thomas Crowe, Jon Curle, Pat Doody, Victor Hallam, Robin Holmes, Patricia Hughes, Peter Latham, Angela Moss, Cormac Rigby, Leslie Stokes, John Webster

Radio Production Services

A. H. Catlin, Josette Charles, Helen A. Fry, David Greenwood, Denys Gueroult, Reginald Kennedy, P. H. W. Norris, L. Pitt, A. R. Reid, Madeau Stewart, M. Wise

Staff Training

Elwyn Evans, Peter Fettes

Further Education

Clare Falkner, Helen Rapp

Broadcasting House, W.1, Feb. 13.

Figure 1 Letter to the Editor, *The Times*, 14 February 1970

Boult[48]) – and advice to BBC management – 'An enlightened statement from the BBC could, at this moment, radically change a dangerous and deteriorating situation,' wrote Marius Goring.[49]

Throughout the dispute, the BBC had foreseen the possibility of public action by its employees and had prepared to take a firm stand: 'DG ... wished to make it clear that if they used their position inside the BBC to conduct a public campaign against management they would have to consider whether they wished to stay or go.'[50] The Board of Management discussed their response at length in a meeting the following Monday (16 February), and were divided between the need to be conciliatory, to 'aim at occupying the middle ground of the dispute by pointing out to staff that management's views were as sincerely held as it acknowledged their own to be', and the desire to be seen to be in control of the situation, since their reply to staff would obviously be published and it was therefore 'important for it to be seen to be as firm a one as the staff concerned undoubtedly expected it to be'.[51] Having rejected as impractical the idea of individually interviewing all 134 signatories, the BBC decided that Ian Trethowan would see only their leaders 'to warn them of the consequences of backstairs intrigue' and write to all the others, 'recognising the respectable motives of the staff concerned and then develop[ing] the point about their contractual obligations to the BBC'.[52] Keller remembered that interview clearly:

> 'If this were the Gas Board,' he made a show of containing himself in my presence, 'you'd be sacked tomorrow'. 'Sack me then, I don't want any favours' was my amiable reply. He didn't. Why not? The reader shouldn't find the real answer difficult.[53]

The BBC's response was considered by many of the protesting producers and some sections of the press to be surprisingly mild, but it is difficult to see how more stringent action could have been taken, given the numbers of staff involved, without jeopardizing the very new schedules which the BBC was trying so hard to put into practice. On 17 February more multi-signature staff letters appeared in the pages of *The Times*: from producers at the Bristol and Birmingham regional centres ('our colleagues in London have exactly expressed the bitterness and disillusionment with which they confront the BBC management's plans for radio, and we support them') and from the

---

48 Letter to the editor, *The Times*, 16 February 1970.

49 Letter to the editor, *The Times*, 16 February 1970.

50 Minutes of the Board of Management meeting held on 8 December 1969 (BBC WAC R2/1/45, Board of Management, Minutes, 1969). Ian Trethowan added that it was his belief that some of the protesters would in fact be prepared to resign over the issue.

51 Minutes of the Board of Management meeting held on 16 February 1970, BBC WAC R2/23/1, Board of Management, Minutes, January–March 1970.

52 Trethowan wrote the following day – 'a very nice, palliative letter from a very shrewd guy', as Leo Black remembers it (oral communication, 4 August 1995).

53 'From the Third Programme to Radio 3', *Music and Musicians*, December 1984.

Manchester branch of the ABS ('We believe there are some fundamental errors in the proposed basic structure [for the new schedules] – a basic structure which BBC management has never been willing to discuss or modify'). The response from Patrick Beech (Controller, English Regions) to these dissenters was even milder than Ian Trethowan's:

> When I first learnt the new proposals last summer, my reaction and arguments were much as yours are now. But when I had an opportunity to study them in depth, I became convinced that they represented the best possible deal for the regions in the light of all the relevant circumstances … I am sorry I haven't yet persuaded you to share my convictions. And I know there are problems … [but] there are enormous opportunities ahead. Let us seize them, and make them work for the good of regional broadcasting.[54]

Despite the drama of this public protest, it was becoming clear to both sides that this was the beginning of the end. The start of the new schedules was barely a month away, and it was not really possible to believe that the BBC, after such a long struggle, would give way at this late stage. Ian Trethowan had pointed out to the protesters that 'in your letter to *The Times* you tacitly assumed that the changes will go ahead as planned',[55] an inference that was not really disputed, as is illustrated by the reported views of one of the dissident producers: 'We all work a long way ahead and many of us have been preparing plans for programmes in the first quarter, from April to June, under the new schedules. But we felt we had to put on record the nature and extent of staff objection to the plans.'[56]

The discussion in the letters columns of *The Times* lasted a little longer, with the BBC wheeling out some of its biggest guns thus far: former Director-General Sir Hugh Greene ('I am ashamed of the members of staff, many of them my friends, who have signed the recent letters to *The Times*'[57]), 11 BBC Governors ('Final responsibility rests with us and we have every confidence in the Director-General and his staff in carrying out the reorganisation within the high traditions of the BBC'[58]), and the longest letter yet (preceded by negotiations for space with *The Times*' editor) from Charles Curran,[59] who also took the precaution of consulting Lord Reith beforehand to check that he would not be entering the debate. On the other side, the protesting staff received new support from the heads of Oxford colleges[60] and from the chairman of the 1960 Home Office Committee on Broadcasting,

54 Letter from Patrick Beech to protesting staff, 18 February 1970 (private source).

55 Letter from Ian Trethowan to protesting staff, 17 February 1970 (private source).

56 As reported in *The Times* of 19 February 1970.

57 Letter to the editor, *The Times*, 20 February 1970. Sir Hugh's letter was also given headline billing on the newpaper's front page.

58 Letter to the editor, *The Times*, 21 February 1970. This was also reported on the front page.

59 The letter was published on 23 February 1970.

60 Letter to the editor, *The Times*, 20 February 1970.

Lord Pilkington, who entered the fray on the eve of 26 February's broadcasting debate in the Lords. One suggestion from both Lord Pilkington and the Provost of King's College, Cambridge,[61] was that the BBC should retain the title Third Programme 'as a working basis for co-operation and a token of good faith from the BBC management',[62] an argument which only revealed the extent to which all real debate was now closed.

'It was a blow against the management of the BBC, in no uncertain terms, and nothing was quite the same again,' says Stephen Plaistow.[63] Robert Ponsonby agrees that the 'horrible wounds' created by the *Broadcasting in the Seventies* row were deep and long-lasting; three years later, when he took over as Controller of Music from William Glock, they were still very much in evidence:

> I arrived after *Broadcasting in the Seventies* and I couldn't believe what bad feeling had been created inside the BBC by the rebels. I can remember walking down a corridor in my first few months with Ian Trethowan, and people walking ahead and Ian [pointing them out,] saying, 'Gould – he didn't sign the letter; Keller did.' ... The pain and poison lasted a very long time.[64]

Nevertheless, for most of the dissenting producers, the fire of protest began to die down as they started work on the new schedules. 'I think the waves died away, in most people's minds, very quickly,' says Leo Black. 'They stayed much more turbulent in the minds, obviously, of people who'd given such a lot of themselves trying to get it [the protest] to happen. I mean Hans, Hallam Tennyson, Deryck Cooke, Bob Simpson ...'[65]

Indeed, the Six remained together, became known as 'the Group', and began to take on a new role as an unofficial watchdog for the new schedules. This seems to have continued, quite vigorously, for some time. Keller's 1972 and 1973 office diary fragments, for example, refer several times to their activities:

> *Th[ursday] Aug[ust] 17 [1972]* ... p.m. Meeting with members of Music Dep[artment] about The Group's draft schedule for a new Radio 3 (the Group members present being those from Yalding – Simpson, Cooke and myself). Chief criticism: too trendy. Robert Layton to put his criticisms on paper. Simpson, Cooke and I to write to those staff who were not present, with copies of schedule, inviting them to annotate it critically and add a summary of their reactions ...
>
> *Mon[day] Aug[ust] 21 [1972]* ... p.m. R[adio] 3 Committee Meeting re and with Audience Research. My suggestion to go into *quality of listening* accepted: I shall

61 Letter to the editor, *The Times*, 24 February 1970.
62 Lord Pilkington, as reported on *The Times*' front page, 25 February 1970.
63 Stephen Plaistow, oral communication, 27 July 1995.
64 Robert Ponsonby, oral communication, 14 July 1995.
65 Leo Black, oral communication, 4 August 1995.

> call a Group meeting and we'll devise a questionnaire for Audience Research. R[adio] 3 meeting very lively and basic – owing, I think, to my interventions …[66]

Robert Layton remembers the Group: 'That would have been the Six: they were still together. This was resented by the management, who thought that these were self-appointed and a little bit making a certain amount of propaganda for themselves, as well as mischief for the management … It went on for quite some while.'[67] If this was indeed the management's opinion, it was hardly fair to the Group, who do appear to have been very constructive and practical in their criticism. Rather than simply commenting on the plans of others, the Group was responsible for planning initiatives of its own, some of which did reach the airwaves. For example, the 'Group's *Women's Lib* weekend' referred to in Keller's 1973 diary fragment bore fruit in the Women's Day broadcast on 30 September that year, which Keller coordinated.[68]

In 1975, the Group raised the question of mixed *versus* generic programming again during the investigation of the BBC by the Committee on the Future of Broadcasting chaired by Lord Annan. Their initial submission begins by examining the practical problems of generic broadcasting – arguing that at least one more wavelength and 'a massive campaign of cross-trailing' were necessary to enable it to operate satisfactorily, 'even if this were desirable' – and ends with a statement of their vision for Radio 3:

> Radio 3, freed from the incubus of being 'the music programme' can then become what those who work for it (whether from Music, Talks or Drama Departments) have always wished it to be, an all-round Arts and Sciences Programme. It would include coverage of world drama (more important than ever in our present economic climate when the classics may be too expensive for both the stage and TV), the projection of our poetic heritage, lesser-known musical classics and operas as well as the commissioning of new work of every kind. More time should be devoted to the concepts and ideas underlying the political and social issues of our time, as well as to an intelligent assessment of such contemporary phenomena as the pop scene. The present policy of weekends or evenings devoted to specific themes should be expanded. At present with its limited speech allocation there is simply not enough time for Radio 3 to make the intellectual impact it deserves.[69]

---

66 CUL Keller Archive.

67 Robert Layton, oral communication, 11 November 1996.

68 See 'About 30 September on Radio 3, Which Will Be a Day by and about Women', *Listener*, **90**/2322 (27 September 1973), pp. 428–9.

69 Memorandum from the Group to the Secretary of the Committee on the Future of Broadcasting, 22 April 1975 (CUL Keller Archive). This memorandum shows the Group's personnel to have expanded beyond the original Six leaders: the signatories here are Keller, Deryck Cooke and Hallam Tennyson from the Six, plus George MacBeth, John Tydeman, Leonie Cohn and Susanna Capon (all of whom had been part of the original *Broadcasting in the Seventies* protest, and signed the letter to *The Times*). These

The Committee evidently found their arguments impressive, for its final report notes that, despite the widespread opposition which generic broadcasting was still inspiring (including that of bodies such as the Society of Authors and the Arts Council), 'the strongest criticism of generic programming came from a group of BBC Radio producers'.[70] The Group appears to have been in confident mood, declaring that 'the concept of generic radio introduced in "Broadcasting in the Seventies" has failed'. They were not alone in this view, and indeed the Annan Committee found it to be 'also the view of the present management of BBC Radio. The Chairman and Director-General told us that the re-shaping had been less of a change than the protesters feared.' Leo Black agrees that, in the mid-1970s, it looked as though they had been overly pessimistic: 'I think the decline in the intellectual level either began or got much more serious long after [*Broadcasting in the Seventies*]. I put it a good ten years later.'[71] Even as much as ten years later, however, Keller was still reasonably optimistic about the prospects for mixed programming, writing to Peter Gould that '*Broadcasting in the Seventies* is dying a fairly rapid and, characteristically, discreet death'.[72] Much of his optimism at this point was due to the attitude towards the spoken word on Radio 3 of its new Controller, Ian McIntyre, who took over from Stephen Hearst in 1978. In a newspaper article published shortly after Keller's retirement, McIntyre is quoted as saying, 'Over the years, and certainly since about 1970, Radio 3 in the public mind has come to be regarded as the music channel. I now have the approval of the Board of Management and the Board of Governors for trying to make it a rather more mixed channel.'[73]

Keller himself appears to have had several meetings with the Annan Committee,[74] and among the other issues which he discussed with them was that clause in the BBC staff contract which he and the other protesting

---

seven people also took their protest, in June 1975, over Stephen Hearst's head to Howard Newby (then Director of Programmes, Radio). The BBC files of this period are closed, but an account of this episode is found in Carpenter (1996), pp. 295–6. The Group's complaint was that the restriction on speech programmes diminished the cultural impact of the network as a whole, to which, apparently, 'Newby's response was: "Show us the excellence that would drive us to increase the speech output." He told them that as Controller of the Third and Radio 3 he had been conscious "from about 1964 onwards" of "diminishing vitality" in speech broadcasts.' Stephen Hearst's own view seems to have been even more pessimistic: 'The great days of the Third Programme were before television.'

70 Home Office (1977), para. 8.12, p. 83.

71 Leo Black, oral communication, 4 August 1995.

72 Letter from Keller to Peter Gould, 20 April 1979 (CUL Keller Archive).

73 Paul Ferris, 'Rocking the Boat at Radio 3', *The Observer*, Sunday 1 July 1979.

74 A letter which Noel Annan wrote to Keller some years later refers to 'our talks with you during the time when we were taking evidence' and discusses one of the ideas which Keller 'inspired' – 'a plan to have once a month a day devoted to the discussion of one serious theme' (letter from Annan to Keller, 31 March 1978, CUL Keller Archive).

producers had broken in their famous letter to *The Times*. The Annan Committee's report upheld his view:

> We were disturbed at the extent of the restrictions which the BBC in particular find it necessary to impose upon their staff. For example, we were surprised to find that the BBC did not allow their staff to publish anything or speak in public about broadcasting generally, without seeking the BBC's permission. We consider this an unnecessary restriction which in law would most likely be held against public policy ... The BBC should thoroughly overhaul their regulations and restore rights to individuals which they should never have been asked to surrender.[75]

Encouraged by this support, Keller published several articles on broadcasting during the rest of his time at the BBC, despite the fact that the Corporation did not take Annan's advice to change its regulations. He seems to have sought the BBC's permission for these activities, at least at first, although an administrative error meant that the Preface to *1975 (1984 minus 9)* was published amid official disapproval.[76] In 1978, a year before his retirement, he published a very definitely unapproved open letter to Ian Trethowan (now Director-General of the BBC) on the very subject of this contractual restriction:

> Dear Ian: On 3 March, Brian Trowell, King Edward Professor of Music at King's College, London, published an extended letter in *The Times*, under the title, 'Music on Radio 3'. In it, he criticised the running of Radio 3 and beyond it, our 'philosophy of management' and our 'hierarchical structure'. Inevitably, Dr Trowell's observations are being widely and passionately discussed, both in and outside the BBC ... and, right or wrong, I wish to be able to discuss them in public.[77]

Trethowan did not reply – as Keller pointed out in print the following year[78] – and disciplinary action, once again contemplated, did not materialize. Keller was shortly to retire and, it seems, the management had long realized how well he thrived on opposition.

Keller never really left the BBC in his short 'retirement': it was too important to him. As he wrote in 1979, 'We have arrived at a critical stage in the development, or the envelopment, of the broadcasting of a living art, and I shall feel as involved, as actively involved from the outside as I have been

---

75 Home Office (1977), para. 28.8, p. 436.

76 A memorandum of 21 February 1977 from Keller to Jock Beesley of the BBC's personnel department explains that he never received the BBC's refusal to publish. The BBC was evidently considering disciplinary action over the matter, but, as Keller told Beesley, 'I face the future with perfect equanimity. My conscience towards the licence-payer, which is stringent, does not invite me to be upset' (CUL Keller Archive).

77 'Open Letter to Ian Trethowan', *The Spectator*, **240**/7812 (25 March 1978), p. 27.

78 'Fare Better, BBC', *The Spectator*, 30 June 1979.

involved within.'[79] He continued to write about broadcasting, both in public – in his radio reviews in *The Listener* and in his occasional articles on radio for other publications; and in private – in the many long letters he wrote to his former colleagues. From these writings, Keller's broadcasting credo – crystallized by *Broadcasting in the Seventies* and essentially unaltered since – can perhaps be taken. Fundamental to it was his continued belief in the importance of radio to music. 'Radio plays a central role in the patronage and development of music,' he wrote when reminding Radio 3's Controller of his duty to new music.[80] The other arts 'would survive without radio's help, however uncomfortably. *Music would not*: it's as simple as that.'

What the BBC was now failing to do – crucially, according to Keller – was to place any value on the quality of listening, as opposed to the quantity of listeners. As a public service broadcaster, it was – to Keller – almost incomprehensibly sensitive to commercial and competitive pressures in its planning: 'The BBC rightly prides itself on not being commercial; the trouble is that again and again, it plans as if it were.'[81] Comparing the World Service with the less high-minded domestic networks in 1980, he concluded that the difference was 'one of kind, not merely of degree. The normal mass medium must needs think of its customers; the World Service has no customers, does not sell its wares. It is the difference, fundamentally, between selling something to somebody, and giving one's best friend a present.'[82]

Instead of relying on audience figures, wrote Keller, broadcasters should 'measure success in terms of the listener's increased independence, not (like a pathological teacher) in terms of increased dependence'.[83] He warned that 'music as a drug is the gravest danger associated with broadcasting',[84] a drug which generic broadcasting was designed to promote. Television, Keller noted, was less susceptible to this danger, and its planning was, in any case, still based on the principle of mixed programming:

> Paradoxically, though, television seems more conscious of the need for meaning – for the incidental reason that television music cannot, as easily, be used as a drug: the television producer has to invite his viewer to pay attention where the radio producer might merely invite his deaf listener to have the radio on while he drives or does his income tax.[85]

Keller often concentrated in his writings on the things which radio could do which were not possible in the concert hall, and he considered it the duty

79 Letter from Keller to Ian McIntyre, 5 March 1979 (CUL Keller Archive).
80 Ibid.
81 'Fare Better, BBC', *The Spectator*, 20 June 1979.
82 'An Untainted Mass Medium', *The Spectator*, 20 December 1980.
83 'Broadcasting: in the 'Eighties', *The Spectator*, 10 July 1976.
84 'Music on Radio and Television', *London Review of Books*, 7–20 August 1980.
85 Ibid.

of the broadcaster to do these things. The ability to create 'meaningful contrasts' of style, period and texture was radio's alone and, although he had long looked for the amalgamation of Music Division with Gramophone Department to maximize this possibility, he considered live studio broadcasting to be crucial nevertheless; its current decline, he wrote, 'is a catastrophe'.[86] He deplored the BBC's increasing reliance on recordings, and its confusion between 'live' and 'public' broadcasting: 'For "broadcasts of live musical performance" read "relays" ... "Live" now merely means "public", even though "public" doesn't always mean "live".'[87]

> Musically ... it's a matter of live and death: there is no substitute for a genuinely continuous, intrinsically unrepeatable interpretation; it is the performer's sustained improvisatory act that is the tail-end of composition.[88]

'What's more,' he reminded his readers, 'to record music out of living existence costs a lot of your money.'[89] He remained sceptical of the BBC's motives whenever it was claimed that an undesirable policy was being driven by a shortage of cash: 'In a complex organisation whose allocation of money can be subjected to infinite variations, the financial excuse can easily be shown to be so much gas.'[90] Keller frequently pointed out inappropriate wasting of resources at the Corporation – the salaries of the too many chiefs being one – as well as absurdities in the BBC's administrative structure. On one occasion, however, he conceded that such irrationalities may have their advantages: 'It is only in chaotic circumstances that extreme minority ideas get a chance.'[91]

'Work of importance which, for some reason or other, has not reached the public, or unusual and unappreciated performing talent – that's the area on which radio ought to concentrate,'[92] according to Keller, and not 'countless ... relays' – particularly of opera, which he considered not particularly radiogenic in any case:

> Now, would it be unrealistic to say that in the entire history of opera, we can't find more than about 20 musical masterpieces of the stature of Sunday's *Rheingold*? The others stand or fall by the stage, and on radio they fall rather heavily whenever the music lets up.[93]

As for generic broadcasting, Keller's optimism at the time of his retirement, based on the new Controller, Ian McInytre's initial statements,

86 Ibid.
87 'Public Service Plus', *The Listener*, 18 September 1980.
88 Ibid.
89 'Whose Airtime?', *The Listener*, 4 December 1980.
90 'Music on Radio and Television', *London Review of Books*, 7–20 August 1980.
91 'The Future of BBC Music: a Mystery', *Musical Times*, February 1982.
92 'From the Third Programme to Radio 3', *Music and Musicians*, December 1984.
93 'Whose Airtime?', *The Listener*, 4 December 1980.

had faded by the time he recounted the *Broadcasting in the Seventies* story in 1984: 'After all these years, we can assert, with hurtful pride, that things have gone exactly as we predicted.'[94] Particularly upsetting was the decline of music talks, now almost confined to *Music Weekly*. Keller's own first BBC post, Music Talks Producer, no longer existed – 'can there be more conclusive evidence of Radio 3's attitude to music talks?'[95] Even more personally distressing to Keller was Radio 3's refusal, in 1980, to broadcast any further functional analyses. He described this as 'one of the few major shocks of [my] life',[96] only slightly alleviated by the subsequent commission he received from BBC2 for a functional analysis for television.[97] The story of functional analysis, he felt, 'shows the BBC at its most creative and, subsequently, at its most sterile.'[98] Although Keller insisted that he was not simply looking back to a golden age (pointing out what he saw as the Third Programme's 'snobbishness' for example), the new Radio 3's deadening attention to audience figures and public demand stood in increasingly stark contrast to the extraordinary creative impact made by the Third:

> The historic part which the Third Programme can now be shown to have played in the development of our culture was due to its acceptance of a criterion which, nowadays, we ignore – its heedfulness of potential audiences, not only of actual ones. Time was when an appointment with a broadcast was an overriding priority; that time has simply gone.[99]

* * *

'I devoted so much of my time to radio because, in my opinion, radio plays an enormous role in the musical life of a country.'[100] Thus, a few months before he died, Keller answered the criticism, often expressed, that he gave too much to the BBC. There are many opinions about what Keller should have done as a broadcaster: he should have remained a producer, he should have stayed with chamber music, he should have left the BBC earlier, he should never have joined the staff at all. It is generally felt, however, that the battle with the BBC's management in which Keller became locked after *Broadcasting in the Seventies* absorbed far too much of his creative energy, perhaps preventing the appearance of the long-promised exposition of his theory of music. But, to Keller, radio mattered deeply, and his life at the BBC

94 'From the Third Programme to Radio 3', *Music and Musicians*, December 1984.
95 Ibid.
96 Letter from Keller to Ian McIntyre, 18 November 1980 (CUL Keller Archive).
97 In the event, this analysis was never completed or broadcast.
98 'From the Third Programme to Radio 3', *Music and Musicians*, December 1984.
99 Letter from Keller to Ian McIntyre, 5 March 1979 (CUL Keller Archive).
100 Hans Keller, interviewed by Anton Weinberg in the summer of 1985 for the Channel 4 documentary *The Keller Instinct*, first broadcast 23 February 1986. A transcript of the interview, by Mark Doran, appeared in *Tempo*, 95 (January 1996), pp. 6–12.

was an integral part of his working out of the practical implications of his view of music and its meaning.

If Keller truly believed that, in our age, radio is of such crucial importance to music that music would not survive without it,[101] he could do no other than to pour his formidable creative energy into it. His promise to William Glock that 'I shall put my whole mind and heart into the BBC job'[102] remained as true at the end of his BBC life as at its beginning. So when broadcasting fashions changed, reflecting (and possibly accelerating) a wider cultural decline, he could not simply acquiesce in Richard Marriott's view that 'radio has lost its compulsiveness' any more than he could agree with Robert Ponsonby's opinion that 'contemporary music has to find its own new format'. In both cases it was the obstacle they placed in the path of meaningful communication that he found unsupportable.

Keller's life at the BBC was a gradual and remarkably consistent working out of truths originally perceived long before, a process which broadened and clarified his thought, and immeasurably widened his influence. Within the Corporation, however, this influence was in decline well before he left its staff and today's BBC – espousing as it does values which are so far from Keller's own – bears little imprint of his extraordinary presence.

---

101 As he said in a letter to Ian McIntyre, 5 March 1979 (CUL Keller Archive).

102 Letter from Keller to Glock, 1 September 1959 (CUL Keller Archive).

Bibliographical Note

As with any work dealing with such recent history, a wealth of primary source material abounds. The secondary material on the BBC and broadcasting in general is likewise extensive, although the proportion of it which relates specifically to the Third Programme and Radio 3 is relatively small. Keller himself, as is well known, was a prolific writer who, in his published writings and private correspondence, documented his own life and theories to no small extent. As yet, however, he has inspired little secondary material. This book therefore relies principally on primary material, much of which has not been examined before.

There are two major archival sources: the BBC Written Archive Centre at Caversham, Reading (BBC WAC) and the Hans Keller Archive at Cambridge University Library (CUL Keller Archive). The BBC Written Archive Centre currently holds papers dating from the BBC's founding until the 1970s. More recent papers are held in the BBC's Records and Programme Information Centre, which is not open to outside researchers. The Written Archive Centre allows outside researchers access up to a certain date, which is updated periodically, but unpredictably – 1962 when research for this book was begun; now 1974. Every file consulted is also subject to the BBC's own vetting procedure, and any material deemed to be still sensitive is removed. For example, most files dealing with *Broadcasting in the Seventies* remain closed. In addition, the personnel files of individual members of staff are kept confidential until 50 years after their death. The Written Archive Centre also holds an extensive library of scripts and transcripts of individual programmes. Actual recordings, where they exist, are held in the BBC's Sound Archive at Broadcasting House. This is not generally open to outside researchers, but there has been some limited access for the purposes of this book. Most of Keller's own broadcasts of which recordings survive, however, are also held in the National Sound Archive, where they are freely available to researchers.

In 1996 Keller's private papers were given to Cambridge University Library by his widow, Milein Cosman Keller, and the Hans Keller Archive was established. This is still in the process of being sorted and catalogued, but a substantial proportion is now available to researchers. It is a very large archive, since Keller did generally keep copies of his many writings, and much of his correspondence. Copies of his letters, however, tend to date from two periods only: the early period (1946–60), when he was typing his own correspondence (according to Milein Cosman, the onset of motor neurone disease – then unidentified – in the early 1960s put an end to Keller's typing, as well as his skiing and viola-playing); and his last years (1980–85), when

Julian Hogg acted as his amanuensis. The archive therefore includes relatively little of his personal correspondence dating from his time at the BBC. There is, however, a certain amount of internal BBC correspondence of which Keller evidently kept copies at home: his first three months on the staff at the BBC, for example, are well documented. He also preserved scripts or transcripts of most of his own broadcasts (many of which, although BBC-made transcripts, are no longer in the Written Archive Centre). This collection, together with his many programme notes for BBC and EBU concerts, was meticulously sorted by his BBC secretary, Pauline Beesley, in 1974, before she left Keller's office for a post elsewhere in the Corporation.

Secondary sources which have been particularly useful are as follows: Asa Briggs' monumental *History of Broadcasting in the United Kingdom* provided much invaluable background information, especially since the fifth volume, covering most of Keller's period, was published in 1995. I am also indebted to two histories of the Third Programme: Kate Whitehead's *The Third Programme: A Literary History*, which appeared in 1989, and Humphrey Carpenter's *The Envy of the World: Fifty Years of the BBC Third Programme and Radio 3, 1946–1996*, which was published to mark the Third's fiftieth anniversary. David Cox's 1980 history of the Proms and Nicholas Kenyon's 1981 history of the BBC Symphony Orchestra have also proved extremely helpful. All these books, with the exception of Whitehead's, are official BBC histories and, as such, have benefited from access to files at the Written Archive Centre and the Records and Programme Information Centre which are closed to external researchers. They can therefore provide much information which would otherwise be unavailable.

Contemporary publications by the BBC, to which Keller frequently contributed, are an important primary source: reading through the *Radio Times*, *The Listener*, *BBC Yearbooks* and, in the earlier period, the *BBC Quarterly* does much to give a sense of the time. Of incalculable significance in this regard, however, have been the interviews which Keller's former BBC colleagues have been kind enough to grant. Many were happy to be interviewed at length and allowed the interviews to be recorded, they provided a wealth of detail which could not have come from any other source, they explained confusing documents, corrected misinterpretations, and lent correspondence and recordings from their own archives. More important still was the insight they provided into the whole atmosphere of the BBC and Keller's place within it; their words have given this history a colour and life without which it would be much the poorer.

Select Bibliography

ARCHIVAL SOURCES

Cambridge University Library Hans Keller Archive

Extensive reference has been made throughout this book to the archive of Keller's papers now held in Cambridge University Library, and I am most grateful to the Library's Syndics for permission to publish from their holdings. Unfortunately, since cataloguing of this archive is still in progress and files are not yet numbered, it is not yet possible to give clear indication of the location in the archive of documents referred to here. Documents are therefore identified in footnotes only by their date and title.

BBC Written Archive Centre

Internal BBC files consulted are listed below. Internal documentation from the period January 1975 onwards is not currently available to external researchers, so post-1974 papers contained in any of the files given here have not been seen.

Board of Governors

R1/1/45-46 Minutes, 1969

Board of Management

R2/22/1-5 Minutes, 1969
R2/23/1-5 Minutes, 1970

Audience Research Files: Programme Reports

R9/6/69 'The Unity of Contrasting Themes', 7 September 1957
R9/6/75 'The Unity of Contrasting Themes' (2), 2 March 1958
R9/6/84 'The Unity of Contrasting Themes' (3), 7 December 1958
R9/6/89 'The Unity of Contrasting Themes' (4), 6 May 1959
R9/6/99 'Functional Analysis', 11 March 1960
R9/6/123 'Functional Analysis', 4 March 1962
R9/6/159 'Music All Day', 21 March 1965
R9/6/167 'Portrait of Schoenberg', 6 November 1965

R9/6/260	'Schoenberg's First Quartet', 1 September 1974
R9/6/265	'Beethoven Op.130' (1), 27 July 1975
	'Beethoven Op.130' (3), 10 August 1975
	'Beethoven Op.130' (4), 17 August 1975

Music Department Files

R27/236	'Music Magazine', 1941–54
R27/500/1-7	Third Programme, 1945–57
R27/730/1-3	European Broadcasting Union, 1963–68
R27/779	Music Department Meetings, 1955–62
R27/780	Music Direction Meetings, 1963–68
R27/782	Mozart Bicentenary, 1956
R27/808	'Momente' (Stockhausen), 1969–70
R27/816	'Music Magazine', 1955–70
R27/818/1-4	Music Programme, 1960–71
R27/819	Music Programme Meeting Minutes, 1962–65
R27/855/1-5	Third Programme Meetings, 1959–70
R27/871	Routine Music Division, 1955–69
R27/876/1-2	Radio 3 Music Meeting Minutes, 1970–72
R27/990	Music General A–AM
R27/1014	Music General A–Z
R27/1026	Music Programmes Policy, 1962–74
R27/1029	Radio 3 General, 1970–74
R27/1030	New Music General, 1970–74
R27/1039	Music In Our Time
R27/1053	Music Programmes: Talks General, 1973–74
R27/1054	Music Programmes: Talks Policy, 1962–74
R27/1056	Orchestral and Symphonic Music Policy, 1965–73
R27/1061	Composers' Guild of Great Britain, 1965–74
R27/1084	Music Programmes: Talks General, 1970–72
R27/1088	BBC 50th Anniversary – Music Talks: Reflections
R27/1091	New Music Committee Minutes, 1970–73
R27/1092	Music Producers' Meeting Minutes, 1971–73
R27/1095	Music Programme Meeting Minutes, 1971–74

Policy Files

R34/420	Home Services Policy, 1944–47
R34/442/3	Home Services Policy, 1957–65
R34/578/1-2	Post-War Planning: General and Numbered Documents, 1941–44
R34/580	Post-War Planning: Programmes, 1944–45
R34/951/1-2	Working Party on Sound Broadcasting: AHS's papers, 1956–57

R34/1020/1-3	Future of Sound Broadcasting in the Domestic Services: Programme Planning, January 1957
R34/1021	The Future of Sound Broadcasting in the Domestic Services: Report, 1957
R34/1022/1-6	The Future of Sound Broadcasting in the Domestic Services: Working Party, 1956–57
R34/1034/1-2	Music Programme: 1960–76
R34/1035	Programmes: Network Three, 1957–60
R34/1184	Pilkington Committee of Enquiry, 1960–62
R34/1333	International Broadcasting Arrangements: Music – Serious: General and Miscellaneous, 1965–69
R34/1454	Presentation: Music, 1964–71
R34/1553	Third Network, 1960–63
R34/1555	Third Programme Committee, 1957–63
R34/1540	Sound Broadcasting Programme Committee, 1963–64
R34/1541	Sound Broadcasting Reorganisation: Working Party Report, 1957
R34/1581/1-3	Policy Study Group: Progress Reviews, 1969
R34/1582	Policy Study Group: Radio News and Current Affairs: 1969
R78/576/2	*Broadcasting in the Seventies*: Distribution and Public Discussion

Talks Files

R51/889/1	Music and Music Intervals, 1955–64
R51/997/1-4	Third Programme Minutes, 1955–60
R51/1184/1	Concert Interval Talks, 1965–71

Contributors', Artists' and Composers' Files

Aeolian String Quartet
Boulez, Pierre
Bradshaw, Susan
Britten, Benjamin
Cooke, Deryck
Curzon, Clifford
Dartington String Quartet
Dorati, Antal
Frankl, Benjamin
Gerhard, Roberto
Keller, Hans
King, Thea
Kokoschka, Oskar
Leibowitz, René
Mitchell, Donald
Pears, Peter
Rostal, Max
Schmidt, Franz
Schoenberg, Arnold
Schoenberg, Gertrud
Seiber, Mátyás
Swarowsky, Hans
Tippett, Michael
Walton, William
Wellesz, Egon

Oral Evidence and Private Archives

I am very grateful to the following friends and colleagues of Hans Keller who generously gave interviews and lent private papers and recordings.

Interviews

Pauline Beesley
Leo Black
Milein Cosman
David Cox
Misha Donat
Alexander Goehr
Paul Hamburger
Stephen Hearst
Julian Hogg
Robert Layton
Ian McIntyre
Christopher Nupen
Stephen Plaistow
Robert Ponsonby
Lionel Salter
Graham Sheffield
Gordon Stewart
Eleanor Warren

Private Papers and Recordings

Pauline Beesley
Leo Black
Susan Bradshaw
Milein Cosman
Julian Hogg
Robert Layton
Keith Lovell
Donald Mitchell
Alan Walker
Christopher Wintle
Hugh Wood

PUBLISHED WORKS BY HANS KELLER

A full bibliography of Keller's publications, compiled by Renée Atcherson and Celia Duffy, appeared in *Music Analysis*, **5**/2–3 (July–October 1986) and is therefore not repeated here. Below is a list of the publications referred to in this book, including some early publications which were omitted from the *Music Analysis* bibliography.

Books

[1946] 1995 *Three Psychoanalytic Notes on* Peter Grimes, edited by C. Wintle, London: Institute of Advanced Musical Studies, King's College, London.
1947 *The Need for Competent Film Music Criticism*, London: British Film Institute.
1981 edited with Donald Mitchell, *Music Survey 1949–52*, London: Faber.
1952 edited with Donald Mitchell, *Benjamin Britten: a Commentary on His Works from a Group of Specialists*, London: Rockliff.

1977 *1975 (1984 minus 9)*, London: Dobson; reissued in 1986 as *Music, Closed Societies and Football*, London: Toccata.
1987 *Criticism*, edited by Julian Hogg, London: Faber and Faber.
1994 *Essays on Music*, edited by C. Wintle, Cambridge: Cambridge University Press.

Articles

1941
'Schonend, weil in Kuerze', *Zeitspiegel*, **43** (25 October), p. 10.

1945
'On Maturity', *The Psychologist*, **13**/151 (July), p. 5; German translation published as 'Reife', *Die Weltwoche*, 27 December 1946.
'Don Juan Again', *Kite* [December], p. 16.

1946
'Male Psychology', *British Journal of Medical Psychology*, **20**, pp. 284–8; reprinted in *World Psychology*, **2**/7 (July 1947).

1947
'Benjamin Britten's Second Quartet', *Tempo*, 3 (March), pp. 6–8.
'A Note on Film Music', *Tribune*, 13 June, pp. 21–2.
'What IS Maturity?', *The Psychologist*, **15**/176 (August), p. 17.
'On Maturity …', *The Psychologist*, **15**/177 (September), p. 18.
'Maturity', *The Psychologist*, **15**/178 (October), p. 31.
'On Maturity', *The Psychologist*, **15**/179 (November), p. 27.
'Mozart and Boccherini', *Music Review*, **8**/4 (November), pp. 241–7.

1948
'Britten and Mozart', *Music and Letters*, **19**/1 (January), pp. 17–30.
'The Psychology of Film Music', *World Psychology*, **3**/3 (March), pp. 23–6.

1949
'Film Music – The Question of Quotation', *Music Survey*, **2**/1, pp. 25–7.
'Kyla Greenbaum and the Psychology of the Modern Artist', *Music Review*, **10**/4 (November), pp. 297–9.

1950
'Resistances to Britten's Music: Their Psychology', *Music Survey*, **2**/4 (Spring), pp. 227–36.

1951
'Schoenberg and the Men of the Press', *Music Survey*, **3**/3 (Spring), pp. 160–68.
'Schoenberg: *A Survivor from Warsaw*', *Music Survey*, **3**/4 (June), pp. 277–80.
'Obituary: Arnold Schoenberg', *Music Survey*, **4**/1 (October), p. 312–17.

1952

'The BBC's Victory over Schoenberg', *The Music Review*, **13**/2 (May), 130–32.

'Bedside Editorial for the BBC', *Music Survey,* **4**/3 (June), pp. 448–9.

'Unpublished Schoenberg Letters', *Music Survey*, **4**/3 (June), pp. 449–71.

1954

'National Frontiers in Music', *Tempo*, 33 (Autumn), pp. 23–30.

1955

'The Audibility of Serial Technique', *Monthly Musical Record*, **85**/971 (November), pp. 231–4.

'Strict Serial Technique in Classical Music', *Tempo*, **37** (September), 12–24.

1956

'The *Entführung*'s "Vaudeville"', *The Music Review*, **17**/4 (November), pp. 304–13.

'K. 503: The Unity of Contrasting Themes and Movements', *The Music Review*, **17**/1 (February), pp. 48–58; **17**/2 (May), pp. 120–29.

'Key Characteristics', *Tempo*, **40** (Summer), pp. 5–16; reprinted in A. Gishford (ed.) (1963), *Tribute to Benjamin Britten on His Fiftieth Birthday*, London: Faber and Faber, pp. 111–23.

'A Slip of Mozart's: Its Analytic Significance', *Tempo*, **42** (Winter 1956–57), pp. 12–15.

'The Chamber Music', in H.C. Robbins Landon and D. Mitchell (eds), *The Mozart Companion*, London: Rockliff, pp. 90–137.

1957

'Elgar the Progressive', *The Music Review*, **18**/4 (November), pp. 294–9.

'Functional Analysis: Its Pure Application', *The Music Review*, **18**/3 (August), pp. 202–6.

'The Musical Analysis of Music', *The Listener*, **58**/1483 (29 August), p. 326.

'Rhythm: Gershwin and Stravinsky', *The Score*, **20** (June), pp. 19–31, 73.

'Wordless Analysis', *London Musical Events*, **12** (December), pp. 26–7.

1958

'Functional Analysis', *Musical Opinion*, **82** (December), p. 157.

'Functional Analysis', *Jewish Quarterly*, **5**/3 (Winter), p. 26.

'The Home-Coming of Musical Analysis', *Musical Times*, **99**/1510 (December), pp. 657–8.

'Knowing Things Backwards', *Tempo*, **46** (Winter), pp. 14–20.

'Let the Music Speak', *Radio Times* (28 February).

'Wordless Functional Analysis No. 1', *The Score*, **22** (February), pp. 56–64.

'Funktionsanalyse – eine neue Analyse der Musik', *Basler Nachrichten,* **52**/26 (29 June – Sunday Supplement).

'Wordless Analysis: the First Year', *The Music Review*, **19**/3 (August), pp. 192–200.

1959

'Hans Keller on His Wordless Functional Analysis', *London Musical Events*, **14** (May), pp. 16–17.

'Musical "Short Talks"', *Radio Times* (27 November), p. 9.

'A New Critical Language', *The Chesterian*, 34 (Summer), pp. 8–15.

'Television Music', *Musical Opinion*, 82 (January), p. 247; 82 (February), p. 319; 82 (March), p. 389; 82 (April), p. 463; 82 (May), p. 539; 82 (June), pp. 597, 599; 82 (July), p. 677; 82 (August), pp. 735, 737; 82 (September), p. 807.

'The New in Review', *The Music Review*, **20**/2 (May), p. 158.

1960

'Wordless Functional Analysis: the Second Year and Beyond', *The Music Review*, **21**/1 (February), pp. 73–6; **21**/3 (August), pp. 237–9.

1962

'Zak on Stockhausen', *Musical Times*, **103**/1433 (July), pp. 484–5.

1963

'Conductorless *Eroica*', *Radio Times* (4 April), p. 41.

'How Great is Britten? or Why I am Right', *Music and Musicians*, 12 (November), pp. 12–13.

1964

'What Happens in *Erwartung*?', *The Listener*, **72**/1846 (13 August), p. 250.

1965

'Schoenberg the Man', *Radio Times* (4 November), p. 10.

1966

'My Favourite Concertos', *Radio Times* (27 January), p. 18.

'Are Records Musical?', *Audio Record Review* (March).

1967

'Gershwin on the Third', *The Listener*, **77**/1986 (20 April), p. 536.

'The European Broadcasting Union', *The Listener*, **78**/2022 (28 December), p. 856.

1969

'Problems in Writing about Music', *Times Literary Supplement* (10 September), pp. 1149–50.

'Gershwin's Songs on the Third', *The Listener*, **82**/2126 (25 December), p. 901.

1970

'Truth and Music', *Music and Musicians* (April), pp. 21–3, 74.

'Beethoven's String Quartets', *The Listener*, **83**/2148 (28 May), pp. 728–30.

'Frankel and the Symphony', *Musical Times*, **111**/1644 (February), pp. 144–7.

'The Greatest Mind Ever?', *The Listener*, **84**/2176 (10 December), p. 822.
'Towards a Theory of Music', *The Listener*, **83**/2150 (11 June), p. 795–6.

1971

'Closer Towards a Theory of Music', *The Listener*, **85**/2186 (18 February), pp. 218–19.
'Music and Psychopathology', *History of Medicine*, **3**/2 (Summer), pp. 3–7.

1972

'Why This Piece is about *Billy Budd*', *The Listener*, **88**/2270 (28 September), p. 419.

1973

'Benjamin Britten and the Role of Suffering' [interview], *Frontier*, **16**/4 (Winter), pp. 235–9.
'European Concerts', *The Listener*, **90**/2327 (1 November), p. 606.

1974

'Schoenberg: the Future of Symphonic Thought', *Perspectives of New Music*, **13**/1 (Fall–Winter), pp. 3–20.

1976

'Broadcasting: in the 'Eighties', *The Spectator*, **237**/7724 (10 July), p. 29.
'New Music: Radio's Responsibility', *Composer*, 28 (Summer), p. 41–3.
'Phoney Professions', *The Spectator*, **237**/7734 (18 September), p. 32.

1977

'Description, Analysis and Criticism: A Differential Diagnosis', *Soundings*, 6, pp. 108–20.

1978

'Broadcasting: Open Letter to Ian Trethowan', *The Spectator*, **240**/7812 (25 March), p. 27.
'Wordless Analysis', *The Spectator*, **241**/7844 (4 November), pp. 23–4.

1979

'Fare Better, BBC', *The Spectator* (30 June), pp. 29–30.

1980

'Do It Now', *Listener*, **103**/2665 (12 June), p. 776.
'Music on Radio and Television', *London Review of Books*, **2**/15 (7–20 August), pp. 7–8.
'Radio's Task', *The Listener*, **103**/2666 (19 June), p. 808.
'Public Service Plus', *The Listener*, **104**/2679 (18 September), p. 380.
'Ghetto or Elite', *The Listener*, **104**/2680 (25 September), p. 416.
'Neglected Classics,' *The Listener*, **104**/2689 (27 November), pp. 735–6.
'An Untainted Mass Medium', *The Spectator*, **245**/7954–5 (20 December), pp. 35–6.
'Whose Airtime?', *The Listener*, **104**/2690 (4 December), p. 768.

1981
'Behind Our Backs', *The Listener*, **105**/2713 (21 May), pp. 686–7.
'Schoenberg's Return to Tonality', *Journal of the Arnold Schoenberg Institute*, **5**/1 (June), pp. 2–21.
'National Institutions', *London Review of Books*, **3**/19 (15 October–4 November), pp. 22–4.

1982
'The Future of BBC Music, A Mystery', *Musical Times*, **123**/1668 (February), pp. 108–9.
'Epi/Prologue: Criticism and Analysis', *Music Analysis*, **1**/1 (March), pp. 9–31.

1983
Review of *Vindications: Essays on Romantic Music* by Deryck Cooke, *Music Analysis*, **2**/2 (July), pp. 227–31.

1984
'From the Third Programme to Radio 3', *Music and Musicians* (December), p. 15.

SECONDARY SOURCES

Amyot, E. (1946), 'Covering Two Musical Worlds', *Radio Times*, 27 September, p. 17.
Barford, P. (1958), 'Wordless Functional Analysis', *The Monthly Musical Record*, March–April.
Barnes, G. (1946a), 'The Aims of the Programme', *The Listener*, 26 September, supplement, pp. i–ii.
——— (1946b), 'For the Alert and Receptive Listener', *Radio Times*, 27 September, p. 5.
Beeson, R.A. (1971), 'Background and Model: A Concept in Musical Analysis', *The Music Review*, 32, pp. 349–59.
Bent, I. (1987), *Analysis*, Basingstoke: Macmillan.
Black, L. (1986), 'Hans Keller and the BBC', in programme to Hans Keller Memorial Concert, Wigmore Hall, 6 October.
——— (1990), 'Hans Keller (1919–1985)', *The Keller Column*, London: Lengnick.
Blom, E. (ed.) (1954), *Grove's Dictionary of Music and Musicians*, 5th edition, London: Macmillan, pp. xviii–xxiii.
——— (1956a) 'The New Approach', *The Observer*, 8 April, p. 10.
——— (1956b) 'Tethered Fancy', *The Observer*, 15 April, p. 14.
Blyth, A. (1981), *Remembering Britten*, London: Hutchinson.
Briggs, A. (1961), *The Birth of Broadcasting*, vol. 1 of *The History of Broadcasting in the United Kingdom*, London: Oxford University Press.

——— (1965), *The Golden Age of Wireless*, vol. 2 of *The History of Broadcasting in the United Kingdom*, London: Oxford University Press.

——— (1970), *The War of Words*, vol. 3 of *The History of Broadcasting in the United Kingdom*, London: Oxford University Press.

——— (1979a), *Sound and Vision*, vol. 4 of *The History of Broadcasting in the United Kingdom*, London: Oxford University Press.

——— (1979b), *Governing the BBC*, London: British Broadcasting Corporation.

——— (1995), *Competition*, vol. 5 of *The History of Broadcasting in the United Kingdom*, London: Oxford University Press.

British Broadcasting Corporation (1946–85), *BBC Yearbooks*.

——— (1946–85), *Radio Times*.

——— (1947), *The Third Programme: A Symposium of Opinions and Plans*, London.

——— (1969), *Broadcasting in the Seventies*, London.

——— (1971), *In the Public Interest: A six-part explanation of BBC policy*, London.

Campaign for Better Broadcasting (1969), *Crisis in Broadcasting*, London.

Cardew, C. (1974), *Stockhausen Serves Imperialism*, London: Latimer.

Carpenter, H. (1992), *Benjamin Britten: A Biography*, London: Faber and Faber.

——— (1996), *The Envy of the World: Fifty Years of the BBC Third Programme and Radio 3, 1946–1996*, London: Weidenfeld and Nicolson.

Cook, N. (1987), *Musical Analysis*, London: Dent.

Cooke, D. (1959a), 'In Defence of Functional Analysis', *The Musical Times*, 1399 (September), pp. 456–60.

——— (1959b), *The Language of Music*, London: Oxford University Press.

——— (1982), *Vindications: Essays on Romantic Music*, London: Faber and Faber.

Cooper, M. (1950), 'Educating the Musical Listener', *BBC Quarterly*, **5**/2 (Summer).

Cox, D. (1980), *The Henry Wood Proms*, London: British Broadcasting Corporation.

Curran, C. (1979), *A Seamless Robe*, London: Collins.

Doctor, J.R. (1999), *The BBC and Ultra-modern Music*, Cambridge: Cambridge University Press.

Donat, M. (1986), 'Hans Keller and Tonight's Music', in programme to Hans Keller Memorial Concert, Wigmore Hall, 6 October.

European Broadcasting Union (1977), *Rencontres de Tenerife 1976*, Madrid.

Flesch, C. (1990), *And Do You Also Play the Violin?*, London: Toccata Press.

Forster, E.M. (1951), 'Fifth Anniversary of the Third Programme', *The Listener*, 4 October, pp. 539–41.

Gillard, F. (1964), 'Sound Radio in a Television Age', BBC Lunchtime Lecture, 11 March.

Glock, W. (1963), 'The BBC's Music Policy', BBC Lunchtime Lecture, 10 April.
——— (1991), *Notes in Advance*, Oxford: Oxford University Press.
Goldie, G. W. (1940), 'BBC in Reverse', *The Listener*, **23**/531, 29 February, p. 441.
Haley, W. (1946a), 'Introduction to the Third Programme', *Radio Times*, 29 September, p. 1.
——— (1946b), 'Some Problems in Broadcasting Administration', *BBC Quarterly* (Spring), p. 5.
——— (1946c), 'A Third Choice', *The Listener*, 26 September, p. 400.
Hall, S. (1969), 'The Real BBC Crisis', *New Statesman*, 18 July, pp. 69–70.
Hearst, S. (1979), 'Has "Public Service Broadcasting" a Future?', *Encounter*, **52**/5 (May), pp. 10–19.
Higgens, G. (1983), *British Broadcasting 1922–1982: a selected and annotated bibliography*, London: British Broadcasting Corporation.
Hill, C. (1974), *Behind the Screen*, London: Sidgwick and Jackson.
Home Office (1951), Cmnd. 8117, *Report of the Broadcasting Committee 1949* [Beveridge Committee].
——— (1962), Cmnd. 1753, *Report of the Committee on Broadcasting, 1960* [Pilkington Committee].
——— (1977), Cmnd. 6753, *Report of the Committee on Broadcasting, 1974* [Annan Committee].
Kenyon, N. (1981), *The BBC Symphony Orchestra: The First Fifty Years 1930–1980*, London: British Broadcasting Corporation.
Laslett, P. (1957), *The Future of Sound Broadcasting*, Oxford: Blackwell.
——— (1958), 'Crisis in British Broadcasting', *Granta* **63**/1184, 18 October, pp. 17–20.
MacCabe, C. and Stewart, O. (eds) (1986), *The BBC and Public Service Broadcasting*, Manchester: Manchester University Press.
MacDonald, B. (1994), *Broadcasting in the United Kingdom: a guide to information sources* (revised 2nd edition), London: Mansell.
Mansell, G. (1969), 'Broadcasting in the Seventies', *Ariel*, 1 December, pp. 2–8.
——— (1982), *Let Truth be Told: Fifty Years of BBC External Broadcasting*, London: Weidenfeld & Nicolson.
Mason, C. (1957), 'Music Better than Words for Analysing Music', *Manchester Guardian*, 9 September, p. 4.
McIntyre, I. (1993), *The Expense of Glory: A Life of John Reith*, London: HarperCollins.
Mehta, V. (1963), 'Onward and Upward with the Arts: The Third', *The New Yorker*, 18 May, pp. 98–134.
Mitchell, D. (1986), 'Hans Keller (1919–1985)', *Tempo*, 156 (March).
——— (1987), 'Remembering Hans Keller', *London Review of Books*, 3 September.
——— (1995), *Cradles of the New*, London: Faber and Faber.

Morris, J. (ed.) (1956a), 'The Development of the Third Programme, its Influence on the Cultural Life of Great Britain and on International Cultural Exchange', *Unesco Reports and Papers on Mass Communications*, No. 23, December.

——— (1956b), *From the Third Programme: A Ten Years Anthology*, London: Nonesuch Press.

Murrill, H. (1950–51), 'Broadcast Music: The Listener's Duty', *BBC Quarterly*, **5**/4 (Winter), pp. 225–29.

Newby, P.H. (1965), 'The Third Programme', BBC Lunchtime Lecture, 20 October.

——— (1970), 'Views', *The Listener*, 3 December, pp. 770–71.

——— (1976), 'Radio, TV and the Arts', BBC Lunchtime Lecture, 15 January.

——— (1977), 'Broadcasting: A Professional View', *The Listener*, 24 February, p. 240–241.

Phillips, M. (1937), *The Education of the Emotions*, London: Allen & Unwin.

——— (1965), *Small Social Groups in England*, London: Methuen.

Reti, R. (1951), *The Thematic Process in Music*, New York: Macmillan.

Reich, W. (1971), *Schoenberg: a critical biography*, translated into English by Leo Black, Harlow: Longman.

Scannell, P. (1981), 'Music for the Multitude? The Dilemmas of the BBC's Music Policy 1923–1946', *Media, Culture and Society*, July, pp. 243–60.

Schafer, M. (1963), *British Composers in Interview*, London: Faber and Faber.

Schoenberg, A. (1964; 1st edn 1958), *Letters*, edited by E. Stein, translated by E. Wilkins and E. Kaiser, London: Faber and Faber, 1964.

——— (1967), *Fundamentals of Musical Composition*, London: Faber and Faber.

——— (1975), *Style and Idea*, edited by E. Stein, translated by L. Black, London: Faber and Faber.

Silvey, R. (1974), *Who's Listening? The Story of Audience Research*, London: Allen & Unwin.

Simpson, R. (1981), *The Proms and Natural Justice*, London: Toccata.

Sound Broadcasting Society (1957), *Unsound Broadcasting*, London: Faber and Faber.

Trethowan, I. (1970), *Radio in the Seventies*, London: British Broadcasting Corporation.

——— (1975), *The Development of Radio*, London: British Broadcasting Corporation.

——— (1977), *Broadcasting and Politics*, London: British Broadcasting Corporation.

——— (1981a), *The BBC and International Broadcasting*, London: British Broadcasting Corporation.

——— (1981b), *Broadcasting and Society*, London: British Broadcasting Corporation.

Trowell, B. (1972), 'Music and Broadcasting', *Music and Musicians*, June, pp. 34–43.

Walker, A. (1962), *A Study in Music Analysis*, London: Barrie & Rockliff.

——— (1966), *An Anatomy of Musical Criticism*, London: Barrie & Rockliff.

Weinberg, A. (1996a), 'Hans Keller: An Interview with Anton Weinberg', transcribed and edited by Mark Doran, *Tempo*, 195 (January), pp. 6–12.

——— (1996b), *The Keller Instinct*, Channel 4, February.

Wellesz, E. (1971), *Arnold Schoenberg*, translated into English by W.H. Kerridge, London: Galliard.

Wellington, L. (1957), 'The New Pattern of Sound Broadcasting', *Radio Times*, 27 September, p. 3.

Wheatcroft, G. (1989), *Absent Friends*, London: Hamish Hamilton.

Whitehead, K. (1989), *The Third Programme: A Literary History*, Oxford: Clarendon.

Whittall, A. (1980), 'Musicology in Great Britain since 1945: Analysis', *Acta Musicologica*, **52**/1 (January–June), pp. 57–62.

Williams, W.E. (1947), 'Listening to the Third Programme', *The Listener*, 2 October.

Wintle, C. (1983–84), 'Humpty Dumpty's Complaint', *Soundings*, 11 (Winter) pp. 14–45.

——— (ed.) (1986), 'Hans Keller: A Memorial Symposium', *Music Analysis*, **5**/2–3 (July/October), pp. 342–44.

——— (1994), 'The Quest for Keller', *The Musical Times*, **135**/1818 (August), pp. 487–493.

Index